Lewis Schwartz..Words Count: **84,473**

United States, Nashua, NH, 03063.............................Number of Pages: **335**

Documented Publishing LLC......................................Book Size: **5*8 Inches**

documented.publishing@gmail.com

Restoring <u>Mental</u> Health

How the Hidden Conversations Impact our Mood and Thinking.

Lewis Schwartz

As a huge thanks for landing on this page, you can enjoy these ***100% FREE Bonuses today!***

• <u>Bonus 1</u>

Join Our Exclusive Mastermind
"MEMBERS ONLY"
Group ***for FREE*** Where We Discuss
More About the Book, Share Our Opinions,
and Support Each Other.
Go to: https://bit.ly/Exclusive_Freebies

• <u>Bonus 2</u>

Love Audiobooks? Get Instant Access
to The ***Audio Version*** Once Available
For a Limited Time…
Secure Your FREE Copy
Here: bit.ly/Exclusive_Freebies

• <u>Bonus 3</u>

Get All Future Updates, Freebies and Offers
Directly with ***NO Extra Charges!***

Table of content

Introduction

Welcome to the world of mental health, a realm filled with complexities, challenges, and tremendous potential for growth and healing. In this book, we embark on a journey to explore the diverse landscape of mental health, shining a light on various topics that impact our well-being and offering insights, strategies, and support for individuals, caregivers, and professionals alike.

Through a collection of unique chapters, we delve into the multifaceted aspects of mental health, ranging from the mind-body connection and neurotransmitters to the role of genetics, childhood trauma, and the influence of culture and social media. Each chapter takes you on a deep dive into a specific theme, expanding your understanding, and providing you with practical tools and knowledge to navigate the challenges and promote mental well-being.

In our exploration, we recognize the importance of holistic approaches, understanding that mental health is not isolated from other aspects of our lives. We explore the intersectionality of mental health with areas such as workplace dynamics, relationships, spirituality, nutrition, exercise, and even the impact of technology and innovation. We embrace the notion that mental health is a complex tapestry interwoven with various factors, and by addressing these factors comprehensively, we can create a solid foundation for emotional well-being.

We aim to provide you with a warm and compassionate voice, guiding you through each chapter with empathy and understanding. Our intention is not to overwhelm, but to empower, offering practical insights, evidence-based strategies, and stories of resilience that inspire hope.

As you navigate these pages, you will discover the power of therapy modalities such as cognitive-behavioral therapy, dialectical behavior therapy, and trauma-focused therapy. You will explore the benefits of mindfulness, art therapy, animal-assisted therapy, and the integration of technology in mental health care. We shed light on the importance of self-care, resilience, and building healthy relationships. We address the unique needs of marginalized communities, veterans, students, older adults, and individuals with chronic illnesses.

In this book, we invite you to embark on a transformative journey—one that embraces the complexities of mental health while highlighting the possibilities for growth, healing, and empowerment. Our goal is to empower you with knowledge, equip you with practical tools, and instill a sense of hope and resilience as you navigate the challenges of your own mental well-being or support others on their journeys.

Remember, you are not alone. Whether you are seeking guidance for yourself or seeking to support a loved one, this book is designed to be a companion, providing you with insights and resources to light your path. Together, we can break down barriers, reduce stigma, and foster a world that prioritizes mental health and emotional well-being.

So, let us embark on this transformative journey together, as we dive into the depths of the human mind, explore the intricacies of mental health, and discover the strength and resilience within each and every one of us.

Chapter 1: Understanding the Mind-Body Connection in Mental Health

Have you ever wondered about the intricate relationship between your mind and body? It's fascinating how these two aspects of our being intertwine and influence each other, especially when it comes to mental health. In this chapter, we'll delve deeper into the mind-body connection and explore its significance in maintaining our mental well-being.

To truly grasp the mind-body connection, let's start by understanding that our bodies and minds are not separate entities but rather integral parts of a unified system. Our thoughts, emotions, and experiences have a profound impact on our physical health, just as our physical health can greatly influence our mental state. The mind and body are in constant communication, and this interaction can have both positive and negative effects on our mental well-being.

One of the key factors contributing to the mind-body connection is the intricate network of neurotransmitters in our brain. These chemical messengers play a crucial role in transmitting signals between brain cells, influencing our mood, emotions, and overall mental state. When the balance of neurotransmitters is disrupted, it can lead to mental health disorders such as depression, anxiety, or schizophrenia.

But how does our physical health affect our mental well-being? Well, let's consider the impact of exercise on our mood. Engaging in regular physical activity releases endorphins, often referred to as the "feel-good" hormones. These endorphins not only alleviate physical discomfort but also have a positive impact on our mental state, promoting feelings of happiness and well-being.

Furthermore, our lifestyle choices, such as nutrition and sleep patterns, can significantly affect our mental health. Research has shown that a diet rich in nutrients, such as omega-3 fatty acids and antioxidants, can support brain function and reduce the risk of mental health disorders. Similarly, adequate sleep is crucial for maintaining optimal cognitive functioning and emotional well-being.

Stress is another factor that highlights the mind-body connection. When we experience stress, our bodies respond by releasing stress hormones like cortisol. While short-term stress can be beneficial in certain situations, chronic stress can take a toll on our mental health. Prolonged exposure to high levels of cortisol can lead to anxiety, depression, and other mental health conditions.

On the flip side, our mental state can also influence our physical health. For instance, persistent feelings of sadness or anxiety can weaken our immune system, making us more susceptible to illnesses. Additionally, high levels of stress can manifest in physical symptoms such as headaches, muscle tension, and digestive issues.

Understanding the mind-body connection opens up a world of possibilities for promoting mental well-being. By nurturing both our physical and mental health, we can enhance our overall quality of life. Here are a few strategies you can incorporate into your daily routine:

Engage in regular exercise: Find an activity you enjoy, whether it's jogging, dancing, or practicing yoga. Regular physical activity not only benefits your physical health but also boosts your mood and reduces stress.

Prioritize self-care: Take time for yourself and engage in activities that bring you joy and relaxation. Whether it's reading a book, taking a bath, or pursuing a hobby, self-care activities can help reduce stress and improve your mental well-being.

Practice mindfulness and meditation: Cultivate a mindful approach to life by being fully present in the moment. Meditation and mindfulness exercises can help calm the mind, reduce anxiety, and enhance overall mental clarity.

Maintain a balanced diet: Incorporate nutrient-rich foods into your meals, including fruits, vegetables, whole grains, and lean proteins. A healthy diet provides the necessary building blocks for optimal brain function.

Foster social connections: Surround yourself with supportive and positive relationships. Connecting with others not only provides emotional support but also contributes to a sense of belonging and overall well-being.

Remember, the mind and body are intricately connected, and nurturing this relationship is vital for our mental health. By adopting a holistic approach that encompasses both physical and mental well-being, we can cultivate a balanced and fulfilling life.

In this chapter, we've explored the fascinating world of the mind-body connection and its significance in mental health. Understanding how our thoughts, emotions, and physical health intertwine opens up avenues for promoting mental well-being. By taking care of our bodies, nurturing our minds, and embracing a holistic approach to health, we can embark on a journey of optimal well-being and inner harmony.

Chapter 2: Unraveling the Complexities of Neurotransmitters and Mental Health

In this chapter, we will embark on a journey to unravel the complexities of these chemical messengers and gain a deeper understanding of their role in our mental well-being.

Imagine your brain as a bustling metropolis, with billions of neurons serving as the city's inhabitants. These neurons communicate with each other through chemical signals, and that's where neurotransmitters come into play. Think of neurotransmitters as messengers who deliver important information between neurons, allowing for smooth and efficient communication within the brain.

Neurotransmitters play a crucial role in regulating various aspects of our mental health, including mood, emotions, cognition, and behavior. They can be classified into different categories based on their functions and effects. Let's explore some of the key neurotransmitters and their impact on mental well-being:

Serotonin: Known as the "feel-good" neurotransmitter, serotonin is involved in regulating mood, sleep, appetite, and social behavior. Imbalances in serotonin levels have been linked to mood disorders such as depression and anxiety. Medications like selective serotonin reuptake inhibitors (SSRIs) work by increasing the availability of serotonin in the brain, helping to alleviate symptoms of these disorders.

Dopamine: Often associated with pleasure and reward, dopamine plays a vital role in motivation, focus, and movement. It contributes to feelings of pleasure and satisfaction, and imbalances in dopamine levels have been implicated in conditions like Parkinson's disease, schizophrenia, and addiction.

Noradrenaline (norepinephrine): This neurotransmitter is involved in the body's stress response, attention, and arousal. It helps regulate mood, energy levels, and focus. Dysregulation of noradrenaline has been associated with conditions such as depression, attention deficit hyperactivity disorder (ADHD), and post-traumatic stress disorder (PTSD).

GABA (gamma-aminobutyric acid): GABA is an inhibitory neurotransmitter that helps to calm and regulate brain activity. It plays a crucial role in reducing anxiety, promoting relaxation, and preventing excessive neuronal firing. Low levels of GABA have been linked to anxiety disorders and epilepsy.

Glutamate: As the most abundant excitatory neurotransmitter, glutamate is involved in promoting neuronal activity and facilitating learning and memory processes. However, excessive levels of glutamate can lead to overexcitation and neurotoxicity, potentially contributing to conditions like epilepsy, Alzheimer's disease, and schizophrenia.

These are just a few examples of the vast array of neurotransmitters present in our brains. It's important to note that mental health conditions are not solely caused by imbalances in a single neurotransmitter. Rather, it's a complex interplay of various factors, including genetic predispositions, environmental influences, and the intricate network of neurotransmitters.

Understanding neurotransmitters allows us to appreciate the significant role they play in mental health and opens up possibilities for targeted treatments. Medications, such as antidepressants or antipsychotics, can help restore balance to neurotransmitter levels and alleviate symptoms of certain mental health disorders. However, it's essential to recognize that these medications work in conjunction with therapy, lifestyle changes, and a holistic approach to mental well-being.

Apart from medications, there are other ways to support optimal neurotransmitter function and promote mental wellness:

Engage in regular exercise: Physical activity boosts the production of neurotransmitters like serotonin and dopamine, contributing to improved mood and overall mental well-being.

Prioritize a balanced diet: Consuming a nutrient-rich diet, including foods high in omega-3 fatty acids, B vitamins, and antioxidants, can support neurotransmitter synthesis and function.

Manage stress levels: Chronic stress can disrupt neurotransmitter balance. Engage in stress-reducing activities such as meditation, deep breathing exercises, or engaging hobbies to support mental well-being.

Foster positive social connections: Meaningful relationships and social support can positively impact neurotransmitter function and mental health. Surround yourself with supportive individuals who uplift and inspire you.

Get quality sleep: Sleep plays a vital role in neurotransmitter regulation. Establish a consistent sleep routine and create a conducive sleep environment to support optimal mental health.

Remember, the interplay between neurotransmitters and mental health is a complex and fascinating subject. While we've just scratched the surface of this vast field, understanding the role of neurotransmitters provides valuable insights into the mechanisms underlying mental health disorders. By nurturing neurotransmitter balance through lifestyle choices, therapy, and medication, when necessary, we can support our mental well-being and embark on a path towards a fulfilling and joyful life.

Chapter 3: The Role of Genetics in Mental Health Disorders

In this chapter, we will explore the fascinating interplay between our genes and mental well-being, shedding light on how genetics can contribute to the development of various mental health conditions.

Genetics, the study of genes and heredity, plays a significant role in shaping who we are. Our genes contain the instructions that determine our physical characteristics, such as eye color, height, and hair texture. However, genes also influence aspects of our mental health, including our susceptibility to certain mental health disorders.

It's important to note that genetics is just one piece of the puzzle when it comes to mental health. While genetic factors can contribute to the risk of developing a mental health disorder, they do not determine our fate. Environmental factors, life experiences, and lifestyle choices also play crucial roles in the development and progression of mental health conditions.

Research has shown that certain mental health disorders tend to run in families, suggesting a genetic component. For example, studies on mood disorders such as depression and bipolar disorder have revealed a higher likelihood of these conditions occurring in individuals with a family history of the disorder. Similarly, schizophrenia and autism spectrum disorders have been linked to genetic factors.

So, how do genes influence mental health? Our genes contain specific sequences of DNA that provide instructions for the production of proteins, which are essential for the structure and functioning of our cells. Variations or mutations in these genes can affect the production, function, or regulation of certain proteins, leading to changes in brain chemistry and neural pathways associated with mental health.

One example of a gene implicated in mental health disorders is the serotonin transporter gene. This gene codes for a protein that regulates the reuptake of serotonin, a neurotransmitter involved in mood regulation. Variations in this gene can influence serotonin levels in the brain, potentially impacting an individual's susceptibility to depression or anxiety.

Another gene of interest is the COMT gene, which codes for an enzyme that breaks down neurotransmitters like dopamine. Variations in this gene can affect dopamine levels in the brain, potentially influencing the risk of conditions such as schizophrenia or attention deficit hyperactivity disorder (ADHD).

However, it's crucial to understand that the relationship between genetics and mental health is complex. Most mental health disorders are polygenic, meaning they involve multiple genes, each contributing a small effect to the overall risk. Moreover, environmental factors, such as childhood experiences, trauma, and stress, can interact with genetic predispositions to trigger or exacerbate mental health conditions.

While we can't change our genetic makeup, understanding the genetic component of mental health disorders opens up possibilities for early detection, prevention, and personalized treatments. Genetic testing and advancements in genomic research provide valuable insights into an individual's risk profile, helping clinicians tailor treatment approaches and interventions.

It's important to recognize that genetics is not destiny. Having a genetic predisposition to a mental health disorder does not guarantee that an individual will develop the condition. Environmental factors and lifestyle choices can significantly influence whether or not genetic vulnerabilities manifest as a mental health disorder.

Promoting mental well-being in the context of genetics involves a multifaceted approach:

Awareness and education: Understanding the genetic component of mental health disorders reduces stigma and fosters empathy. Education empowers individuals to make informed decisions and seek appropriate support.

Early intervention: Identifying individuals at higher genetic risk can enable early intervention strategies, such as therapy, lifestyle modifications, or targeted treatments, to minimize the impact of genetic vulnerabilities.

Holistic approach: Recognizing that mental health is influenced by both genetic and environmental factors highlights the importance of addressing lifestyle choices, social support, and environmental stressors alongside genetic predispositions.

Personalized medicine: Advances in genetic research and personalized medicine allow for tailored treatments based on an individual's unique genetic profile, optimizing treatment outcomes, and minimizing side effects.

Support and community: Creating a supportive and inclusive environment for individuals with genetic predispositions to mental health disorders fosters resilience, acceptance, and understanding.

So, genetics plays a significant role in mental health, contributing to the risk and development of various mental health disorders. While genetic factors are important, they do not solely determine mental health outcomes. Environmental factors, lifestyle choices, and social support also influence mental well-being. By understanding the interplay between genetics and mental health, we can promote early intervention, personalized treatment approaches, and a compassionate society that embraces the complexities of mental health.

Chapter 4: Exploring the Impact of Childhood Trauma on Mental Health

In this chapter, we will explore the far-reaching effects of childhood trauma, understand the mechanisms involved, and shed light on the importance of healing and support.

Childhood should be a time of wonder, exploration, and growth. However, for many individuals, childhood experiences can be marked by various forms of trauma, such as physical or sexual abuse, neglect, domestic violence, or the loss of a loved one. These traumatic experiences can have long-lasting effects on mental health and well-being.

The effects of childhood trauma on mental health are vast and complex. Traumatic experiences can shape the way we perceive the world, ourselves, and others. They can disrupt the development of fundamental cognitive, emotional, and social skills, leading to a higher vulnerability to mental health disorders later in life.

One of the ways childhood trauma can impact mental health is through alterations in brain development. Trauma activates the body's stress response, flooding the brain with stress hormones such as cortisol. Prolonged exposure to high levels of stress hormones can disrupt the normal development of brain structures involved in emotional regulation, memory processing, and stress response modulation.

For example, the amygdala, a part of the brain responsible for processing emotions and fear responses, can become hypersensitive and overactive in individuals who have experienced trauma. This heightened reactivity can contribute to anxiety, hyperarousal, and difficulties in emotional regulation.

Another brain structure impacted by childhood trauma is the hippocampus, which plays a crucial role in memory consolidation and emotional regulation. Trauma-related stress can lead to a reduction in the size of the hippocampus, affecting memory functions and increasing the risk of developing conditions such as post-traumatic stress disorder (PTSD).

The effects of childhood trauma extend beyond brain structure. Trauma can also shape the way our genes are expressed, a phenomenon known as epigenetics. Traumatic experiences can modify gene expression patterns, influencing the body's stress response system and increasing the risk of mental health disorders. However, it's important to note that while these genetic modifications can increase vulnerability, they do not determine one's destiny. Resilience and protective factors can mitigate the impact of trauma on mental health.

Childhood trauma can manifest in a range of mental health conditions, including anxiety disorders, depression, substance abuse, eating disorders, self-harm, and borderline personality disorder. These conditions often arise as adaptive coping mechanisms in response to the overwhelming pain and distress experienced during childhood trauma.

Healing from childhood trauma requires compassion, support, and a comprehensive approach. Here are some strategies that can aid in the recovery process:

Seeking therapy: Professional therapy, such as trauma-focused cognitive-behavioral therapy (CBT) or eye movement desensitization and reprocessing (EMDR), can provide a safe space to process traumatic experiences, develop coping skills, and promote healing.

Building a support network: Connecting with empathetic and understanding individuals, whether through support groups, friends, or family, can offer validation, comfort, and a sense of belonging.

Practicing self-care: Engaging in self-care activities that promote relaxation, stress reduction, and emotional well-being, such as mindfulness, meditation, journaling, or engaging in hobbies, can nurture the healing process.

Creating safety and stability: Establishing a safe and stable environment is crucial for healing. This may involve setting healthy boundaries, seeking refuge in a supportive community, or creating a nurturing space for self-expression.

Cultivating resilience: Resilience is the ability to adapt and bounce back from adversity. Developing resilience involves fostering self-compassion, setting realistic goals, nurturing healthy coping mechanisms, and finding meaning and purpose in life.

It's essential to remember that healing from childhood trauma is a unique and deeply personal journey. Recovery takes time, and the path is not linear. It's okay to seek support, lean on others when needed, and prioritize self-care along the way.

By understanding the impact of childhood trauma on mental health and embracing a compassionate approach, we can foster a society that prioritizes the well-being and healing of those who have experienced trauma. Together, we can work towards creating safe spaces, reducing stigma, and providing the necessary support for individuals to embark on a journey of resilience, growth, and renewed hope.

Chapter 5: Navigating the Intersection of Culture and Mental Health

In this chapter, we will delve into how cultural factors influence our understanding, perception, and experiences of mental health, and how cultural competence plays a crucial role in providing effective and inclusive mental health care.

Culture is a dynamic and multifaceted aspect of our identity. It encompasses beliefs, values, traditions, language, customs, and social norms shared by a particular group of people. Our cultural background shapes our worldview, influences our behaviors, and deeply impacts our mental health.

Cultural factors influence how mental health is understood and perceived within a given community. Each culture has its unique beliefs and explanations for mental health issues. For instance, some cultures may attribute mental health challenges to spiritual or supernatural causes, while others may view them through a biomedical or psychological lens. Understanding these cultural perspectives is essential for providing appropriate and respectful mental health care.

Culture also plays a significant role in shaping the expression and presentation of mental health symptoms. Different cultures may have distinct ways of expressing distress or psychological symptoms. For example, some cultures may emphasize physical symptoms such as headaches or stomachaches, while others may focus on emotional or relational difficulties. Recognizing these cultural variations is crucial for accurate diagnosis and effective treatment.

Moreover, cultural factors influence help-seeking behaviors and attitudes towards mental health care. Stigma, discrimination, and lack of awareness can create significant barriers to accessing mental health support within certain cultural communities. Cultural norms around self-reliance, collectivism, or the importance of family cohesion can impact an individual's willingness to seek help. Addressing these cultural barriers requires culturally sensitive approaches and community engagement.

Cultural competence is a vital component of providing inclusive and effective mental health care. It involves developing an understanding of diverse cultural beliefs, values, and practices, and incorporating this knowledge into treatment approaches. Here are some key principles for navigating the intersection of culture and mental health:

Cultural humility: Approach individuals with cultural humility, recognizing that each person's experiences and beliefs are unique. Be open to learning from diverse cultural perspectives and avoid making assumptions.

Culturally informed assessment: Conduct assessments that consider cultural context, including the individual's cultural background, beliefs, and values. This helps ensure accurate diagnosis and treatment planning.

Collaborative decision-making: Engage in shared decision-making with individuals from diverse cultural backgrounds, respecting their autonomy and incorporating their cultural beliefs and preferences into the treatment process.

Culturally adapted interventions: Tailor interventions to align with cultural beliefs and practices. This may involve integrating traditional healing approaches, working with community leaders or cultural brokers, and considering the role of spirituality and faith in the healing process.

Addressing stigma and disparities: Actively work towards reducing mental health stigma within cultural communities, raising awareness, and providing culturally appropriate resources and support. Advocate for equitable access to mental health care for all individuals, regardless of cultural background.

Culturally competent mental health care requires ongoing learning and self-reflection. It involves developing cultural knowledge, engaging in cross-cultural dialogue, and cultivating respectful and empathetic communication skills. Mental health professionals must actively seek training and education to enhance their cultural competence and provide the best possible care for individuals from diverse backgrounds. Community engagement and collaboration are also critical in navigating the intersection of culture and mental health. Partnering with community organizations, leaders, and advocates can help develop culturally appropriate services, reduce stigma, and promote mental health awareness within cultural communities.

So, culture significantly influences our understanding, experiences, and perceptions of mental health. Recognizing the impact of culture is crucial for providing inclusive and effective mental health care. By embracing cultural competence, promoting cultural humility, and working towards reducing barriers and disparities, we can create a society that values and supports the diverse mental health needs of all individuals.

Chapter 6: The Influence of Social Media on Mental Health

In this chapter, we will explore the intricate relationship between our digital lives and mental well-being, examining both the positive and negative effects of social media.

Social media has revolutionized the way we connect, share information, and interact with the world. Platforms like Facebook, Instagram, Twitter, and TikTok have become integral parts of our daily lives, offering us opportunities to connect with friends, express ourselves, and explore a vast array of content. However, it's crucial to recognize that our online experiences can significantly impact our mental health.

Let's begin with the positive aspects of social media. These platforms provide spaces for self-expression, community building, and social support. They can be avenues for sharing experiences, advocating for causes, and finding like-minded individuals. For those who may feel isolated or marginalized, social media can offer a sense of belonging and empowerment.

Moreover, social media allows for the dissemination of valuable mental health information. It provides a platform for raising awareness, reducing stigma, and sharing resources. Online communities dedicated to mental health can be sources of support, offering a space for individuals to connect, share their stories, and seek advice.

However, it's important to balance the positive aspects with an awareness of the potential negative impacts of social media on mental health. Here are some key considerations:

Social comparison: Social media can create a breeding ground for social comparison. Seeing carefully curated posts and images of others' lives can lead to feelings of inadequacy, envy, and a distorted sense of reality. It's important to remember that what we see online is often a highlight reel and not a comprehensive representation of someone's life.

Fear of missing out (FOMO): The constant exposure to others' social activities and events on social media can exacerbate the fear of missing out. This fear can lead to anxiety, a sense of exclusion, and pressure to participate in activities to maintain a sense of belonging.

Cyberbullying and harassment: The anonymity and distance provided by social media can embolden individuals to engage in harmful behaviors such as cyberbullying or harassment. Such experiences can have severe psychological effects, including anxiety, depression, and decreased self-esteem.

Distorted self-image and body dissatisfaction: Social media can contribute to body image concerns and dissatisfaction. Exposure to idealized and unrealistic body standards can lead to negative self-comparisons, disordered eating behaviors, and a negative impact on self-esteem.

Information overload and mental clutter: The constant influx of information on social media can be overwhelming, leading to information overload and mental clutter. This can contribute to feelings of stress, anxiety, and a sense of being constantly "plugged in."
So, how can we navigate the influence of social media on our mental health in a healthy and balanced way? Here are some strategies:

Practice digital well-being: Set boundaries around social media usage. Create designated "tech-free" times or spaces to prioritize offline activities and self-care.

Curate your social media feed: Be intentional about who you follow and the content you engage with. Follow accounts that promote positivity, inspire you, or provide valuable information. Unfollow or mute accounts that make you feel negatively about yourself or trigger negative emotions.

Practice mindful consumption: Be mindful of how social media affects your emotions and mental well-being. Take breaks when needed, engage with content mindfully, and avoid excessive scrolling.

Foster in-person connections: While social media can be a valuable tool for connection, remember to cultivate meaningful relationships and connections offline. Prioritize face-to-face interactions and engage in activities that promote real-world connections.

Seek support when needed: If social media starts negatively impacting your mental health, don't hesitate to seek support from mental health professionals, friends, or support groups. They can provide guidance, validation, and resources to help you navigate the challenges.

Remember, the impact of social media on mental health is multifaceted and highly individual. It's essential to be self-aware, intentional, and mindful of your own well-being as you navigate the digital landscape. By finding a healthy balance, setting boundaries, and prioritizing your mental health, you can harness the positive aspects of social media while minimizing the potential negative effects.

So, social media has become an integral part of our lives, shaping the way we connect, communicate, and perceive the world. While it offers numerous opportunities for positive engagement and support, it's important to be aware of its potential impact on mental health. By adopting a mindful and balanced approach to social media usage, we can maximize its benefits and protect our mental well-being in the digital age.

Chapter 7: The Stigma Surrounding Mental Health and Its Consequences

In this chapter, we will delve into the complexities of mental health stigma, examine its far-reaching consequences, and explore strategies for combating it.

Stigma, simply put, is a mark of disgrace or shame associated with a particular attribute or characteristic. When it comes to mental health, stigma refers to the negative beliefs, attitudes, and stereotypes surrounding individuals with mental health conditions. It manifests in various ways, such as discrimination, prejudice, and social exclusion.

Mental health stigma is deeply rooted in society, often fueled by misconceptions, fear, and a lack of understanding. People with mental health conditions are often unfairly labeled as "crazy," "unstable," or "weak," perpetuating harmful stereotypes and misconceptions. This stigma can be internalized by those who experience mental health challenges, leading to self-stigma and a reluctance to seek help or disclose their struggles.

The consequences of mental health stigma are far-reaching and can significantly impact individuals and communities:

Barriers to seeking help: Stigma acts as a major barrier to seeking mental health support. Many individuals fear judgment, rejection, or the potential impact on their personal and professional lives. This reluctance to seek help can delay diagnosis, treatment, and recovery, leading to further distress and potentially worsening mental health outcomes.

Social isolation and loneliness: Stigma often results in social exclusion and isolation. Individuals with mental health conditions may face discrimination, strained relationships, and reduced opportunities for social connection. This isolation can exacerbate feelings of loneliness, leading to a vicious cycle of deteriorating mental health.

Impact on self-esteem and self-worth: Stigma can erode an individual's sense of self-worth and self-esteem. Internalized stigma can lead to feelings of shame, self-blame, and diminished self-confidence.

This can hinder personal growth, limit opportunities, and impact overall well-being.

Employment and educational challenges: Stigma can have a significant impact on an individual's educational and employment opportunities. Prejudice and discrimination may lead to reduced job prospects, workplace harassment, and limited access to educational resources. This not only affects financial stability but also contributes to feelings of marginalization and inequality.

Lack of access to quality care: Stigma can perpetuate systemic barriers to mental health care. Limited resources, inadequate funding, and a lack of specialized services can further marginalize individuals with mental health conditions. Stigma also deters healthcare professionals from entering the field, exacerbating the scarcity of mental health providers.

Combatting mental health stigma requires collective effort and a multifaceted approach. Here are some strategies for creating a stigma-free society:

Education and awareness: Promote mental health literacy and dispel myths and misconceptions. By increasing knowledge and understanding, we can challenge stigma and foster empathy and compassion.

Language matters: Promote the use of person-first language, emphasizing the person rather than the condition. Avoid using derogatory terms or language that perpetuates stereotypes. Encourage respectful and inclusive language that recognizes the individual's unique experiences.

Share personal stories: Encourage individuals with lived experiences to share their stories, highlighting the diversity of mental health journeys and fostering empathy. Personal narratives humanize mental health conditions and challenge stereotypes.

Supportive environments: Create safe and supportive environments in schools, workplaces, and communities. Foster a culture that values and prioritizes mental health, promoting open conversations and providing resources for support.

Advocate for policy change: Advocate for policies that prioritize mental health, including increased funding for mental health services, legislation against mental health discrimination, and the inclusion of mental health education in school curricula.

Lead by example: Challenge your own biases and attitudes towards mental health. Treat individuals with mental health conditions with respect, empathy, and kindness. By modeling inclusive behavior, we can create a ripple effect of change.

Remember, combating mental health stigma is an ongoing process that requires a collective effort. Every action, no matter how small, contributes to a stigma-free society. By fostering understanding, empathy, and support, we can create an environment where individuals with mental health conditions feel accepted, valued, and empowered.

So, mental health stigma poses significant barriers to the well-being and recovery of individuals with mental health conditions. Its consequences are far-reaching, impacting personal lives, relationships, opportunities, and overall societal well-being. By challenging stigma, promoting education, and fostering inclusive environments, we can dismantle the walls of stigma and build a society that embraces and supports mental health for all.

Chapter 8: Promoting Mental Health in the Workplace

In this chapter, we will delve into the importance of fostering a mentally healthy work environment, examine the challenges faced by employees, and explore strategies for promoting mental well-being.

The workplace is a significant part of our lives, where we spend a substantial amount of time and energy. As such, it plays a crucial role in our overall well-being, including our mental health. A mentally healthy workplace is one that prioritizes the emotional well-being of its employees, promotes a supportive culture, and creates an environment where individuals can thrive.

Unfortunately, many employees face various challenges that can impact their mental health. Factors such as high workloads, excessive pressure, long hours, lack of work-life balance, limited autonomy, and poor interpersonal relationships can contribute to stress, burnout, and a decline in mental well-being.

Promoting mental health in the workplace is not only the right thing to do, but it also makes good business sense. When employees feel supported, valued, and empowered, they are more engaged, productive, and resilient. Here are some strategies for creating a mentally healthy work environment:

Foster a supportive culture: Cultivate a culture of support, empathy, and open communication. Encourage managers and leaders to actively listen to employees, provide feedback and recognition, and create a safe space for discussing mental health concerns without fear of stigma or reprisal.

Promote work-life balance: Encourage a healthy balance between work and personal life. Offer flexible work arrangements, promote boundaries around work hours, and discourage the expectation of constant availability outside of work. Encouraging employees to take breaks, utilize vacation time, and prioritize self-care helps prevent burnout and supports mental well-being.

Provide mental health resources and support: Offer access to mental health resources, such as employee assistance programs (EAPs), counseling services, or educational materials. Communicate these resources effectively and ensure confidentiality, so employees feel comfortable seeking help when needed.

Reduce stigma and increase awareness: Educate employees about mental health, reduce stigma, and foster a culture of understanding. Conduct mental health awareness campaigns, provide training on mental health topics, and encourage open conversations about mental well-being.

Encourage self-care and stress management: Promote activities and initiatives that support self-care and stress management. Offer wellness programs, organize mindfulness or meditation sessions, provide access to exercise facilities or classes, and encourage breaks throughout the workday.

Build supportive networks: Encourage the formation of supportive networks within the workplace, such as employee resource groups or peer support programs. These networks can provide a sense of community, reduce isolation, and offer opportunities for sharing experiences and coping strategies.

Train managers and leaders: Provide training to managers and leaders on recognizing signs of mental health challenges, offering support, and effectively managing workloads. Equipping leaders with the tools and knowledge to create a mentally healthy work environment is vital for fostering employee well-being.

Regularly assess and address workload and expectations: Regularly review workloads, set realistic expectations, and provide resources and support to help employees manage their responsibilities effectively. Addressing excessive workload and creating a sense of control and autonomy can reduce stress and promote mental well-being. Remember, promoting mental health in the workplace is an ongoing effort that requires commitment, collaboration, and continuous evaluation. Regularly seeking feedback from employees, conducting surveys, and assessing the impact of implemented strategies are essential for creating a work environment that supports mental well-being.

So, prioritizing mental health in the workplace is crucial for both employees and employers. A mentally healthy work environment enhances well-being, engagement, and productivity. By fostering a supportive culture, promoting work-life balance, providing resources and support, and reducing stigma, organizations can create a space where employees can thrive and flourish. Together, let's strive for mentally healthy workplaces that prioritize the well-being of every individual.

Chapter 9: Strategies for Building Resilience and Mental Well-being

In this chapter, we will dive into practical and actionable steps that can help you navigate life's challenges, cultivate resilience, and prioritize your mental health.

Life is full of ups and downs, and building resilience is an essential skill that can help you effectively cope with adversity, bounce back from setbacks, and maintain your mental well-being. Resilience is not about being invincible or immune to stress; it's about developing the tools and mindset to adapt, grow, and thrive in the face of challenges. Here are some strategies to help you build resilience and nurture your mental well-being:

Develop self-awareness: Self-awareness is the foundation of resilience. Take the time to understand your emotions, thoughts, and reactions. Reflect on your strengths, values, and areas for growth. Cultivating self-awareness allows you to identify triggers, manage stress, and make intentional choices aligned with your well-being.

Cultivate a positive mindset: Adopting a positive mindset does not mean ignoring or denying negative emotions. It's about finding silver linings, reframing challenges as opportunities for growth, and nurturing a sense of optimism. Practice gratitude, focus on your strengths, and engage in positive self-talk. Embracing positivity can help you navigate difficulties with resilience and hope.

Build a support network: Surround yourself with a supportive network of friends, family, or mentors. Cultivate relationships that provide empathy, understanding, and encouragement. Reach out for support when needed, and be willing to offer support to others as well. Having a strong support system can enhance resilience and provide a sense of belonging.

Practice self-care: Prioritize self-care activities that nourish your body, mind, and spirit. Engage in activities that bring you joy, relaxation, and rejuvenation. This may include exercise, practicing mindfulness or meditation, spending time in nature, pursuing hobbies, or enjoying quality time with loved ones. Self-care replenishes your energy and equips you to face challenges with resilience.

Develop problem-solving skills: Enhance your problem-solving skills to effectively address challenges. Break problems down into manageable steps, seek alternative perspectives, and explore creative solutions. Developing problem-solving skills builds confidence, reduces feelings of helplessness, and empowers you to take control of difficult situations.

Cultivate flexibility and adaptability: Life is unpredictable, and being adaptable is a key aspect of resilience. Embrace change, practice flexibility in your thinking, and adjust your approach when necessary. Adapting to new circumstances with an open mind helps you navigate transitions and challenges more effectively.

Practice stress management techniques: Chronic stress can take a toll on your mental well-being. Explore stress management techniques such as deep breathing exercises, progressive muscle relaxation, or engaging in activities that help you unwind and recharge. Prioritizing stress management supports resilience and prevents burnout.

Set realistic goals and take action: Set realistic, achievable goals that align with your values and aspirations. Break larger goals into smaller, actionable steps. Taking consistent action towards your goals boosts self-confidence, provides a sense of accomplishment, and fosters resilience in the face of obstacles.

Seek professional support when needed: Recognize that seeking professional support is a sign of strength, not weakness. If you're facing persistent challenges or struggling with your mental well-being, reach out to mental health professionals. They can provide guidance, support, and therapeutic interventions tailored to your needs.

Practice self-compassion: Treat yourself with kindness and compassion, especially during difficult times. Acknowledge that setbacks and mistakes are part of the human experience. Practice self-compassion by offering yourself understanding, forgiveness, and encouragement. Embracing self-compassion enhances resilience and fosters a positive relationship with yourself.

Remember, building resilience and nurturing your mental well-being is a lifelong journey. It requires commitment, practice, and self-reflection.

Embrace challenges as opportunities for growth, celebrate your progress, and be patient with yourself along the way.

By implementing these strategies and prioritizing your mental well-being, you can cultivate resilience, navigate life's challenges with grace, and foster a sense of inner strength and peace. Embrace the power within you to thrive and create a life that is grounded in resilience and well-being.

Chapter 10: Addressing the Mental Health Needs of LGBTQ+ Individuals

In this chapter, we will delve into the unique challenges faced by the LGBTQ+ community, examine the impact on mental well-being, and discuss strategies for providing support.

The LGBTQ+ community encompasses individuals who identify as lesbian, gay, bisexual, transgender, queer, or other diverse sexual orientations and gender identities. While society has made significant progress in recognizing and accepting LGBTQ+ individuals, they still face unique challenges that can impact their mental health and overall well-being.

One of the primary challenges faced by LGBTQ+ individuals is societal stigma and discrimination. Homophobia, transphobia, and prejudice can lead to social exclusion, rejection from family or friends, and workplace discrimination. These experiences can contribute to increased stress, anxiety, depression, and a higher risk of mental health disorders.

Internalized stigma, or self-stigma, is another significant concern within the LGBTQ+ community. This occurs when individuals internalize negative beliefs and stereotypes about their own sexual orientation or gender identity. It can lead to feelings of shame, guilt, and a negative impact on self-esteem and mental well-being.

The process of coming out, or revealing one's sexual orientation or gender identity, can also be a significant source of stress for LGBTQ+ individuals. Fear of rejection, isolation, or discrimination can create immense emotional turmoil. The support or lack thereof during the coming-out process can have a profound impact on an individual's mental health.

Transgender individuals face unique challenges related to gender dysphoria, the distress experienced when one's gender identity does not align with their assigned sex at birth. Access to gender-affirming healthcare, acceptance within society, and legal recognition can greatly impact mental well-being.

Creating inclusive and affirming spaces for LGBTQ+ individuals is crucial for supporting their mental health. Here are some strategies to consider:

Education and awareness: Foster education and awareness about LGBTQ+ identities, experiences, and mental health disparities. Provide training to staff and community members to promote understanding, empathy, and cultural competence.

Safe and inclusive environments: Create safe and inclusive spaces where LGBTQ+ individuals feel respected, valued, and affirmed. Implement non-discrimination policies and codes of conduct that explicitly protect LGBTQ+ individuals. Display visible signs of support, such as inclusive signage or LGBTQ+ pride symbols.

Cultivate supportive networks: Establish support groups or organizations specifically for LGBTQ+ individuals. These spaces can provide community, validation, and resources for mental health support. Encourage peer support and mentoring programs within the LGBTQ+ community.

Provide LGBTQ+-affirming mental health services: Ensure mental health services are accessible, inclusive, and culturally sensitive to the needs of LGBTQ+ individuals. Train mental health professionals on LGBTQ+ issues, foster an accepting therapeutic environment, and provide resources for gender-affirming care.

Advocacy and policy change: Advocate for LGBTQ+ rights and policy changes that protect against discrimination in areas such as healthcare, employment, and housing. Support legislation that promotes equality, social acceptance, and mental well-being for LGBTQ+ individuals.

Celebrate diversity and representation: Embrace diversity within the LGBTQ+ community and celebrate different identities and experiences. Highlight positive role models and LGBTQ+ representation in media, literature, and public spaces to foster a sense of belonging and empowerment.

Collaborate with LGBTQ+ organizations: Partner with LGBTQ+ organizations and community leaders to develop comprehensive programs, outreach initiatives, and support networks.

Engage in ongoing collaboration to address the evolving needs of the LGBTQ+ community.

It's important to remember that LGBTQ+ individuals are not defined solely by their sexual orientation or gender identity. They are individuals with diverse backgrounds, experiences, strengths, and challenges. Supporting mental health within the LGBTQ+ community requires an intersectional approach that acknowledges the multiple identities and experiences of individuals.

So, addressing the mental health needs of LGBTQ+ individuals is crucial for fostering inclusivity, well-being, and equality. By creating affirming spaces, advocating for LGBTQ+ rights, and providing culturally competent mental health support, we can help mitigate the challenges faced by this community. Together, let's strive for a world where all LGBTQ+ individuals feel embraced, validated, and supported in their mental health journey.

Chapter 11: Managing Anxiety and Stress in a Fast-Paced World

In this chapter, we will delve into the impacts of a hectic lifestyle on mental well-being, examine the causes and symptoms of anxiety and stress, and discuss practical techniques for finding balance and promoting calm.

In our modern society, it's common to experience a constant rush and pressure to keep up with the demands of work, relationships, and personal responsibilities. This fast-paced lifestyle can take a toll on our mental health, leading to increased anxiety and stress levels. However, with awareness and effective coping strategies, we can navigate these challenges and find a sense of calm amidst the chaos.

Anxiety is a natural response to perceived threats or challenges, but when it becomes persistent and overwhelming, it can interfere with our daily lives. Stress, on the other hand, is the body's response to demands or pressures. While some stress can be motivating and beneficial, chronic stress can have detrimental effects on our mental and physical well-being.

Here are some strategies to help manage anxiety and stress in today's fast-paced world:

Prioritize self-care: Self-care is not a luxury; it is a necessity for maintaining mental well-being. Make time for activities that promote relaxation, self-reflection, and self-nurturing. Engage in activities such as exercise, mindfulness or meditation, spending time in nature, practicing hobbies, or enjoying quality time with loved ones. Prioritizing self-care replenishes your energy and helps you cope with stress.

Practice stress management techniques: Explore stress management techniques that work for you. Deep breathing exercises, progressive muscle relaxation, or engaging in activities that help you unwind can help reduce stress levels. Experiment with different techniques and find what resonates with you. Regularly incorporating these practices into your routine can help you manage stress more effectively.

Set realistic expectations: Be realistic about what you can accomplish within a given time frame. Set achievable goals and break them down into smaller, manageable tasks. Avoid overcommitting or trying to do everything at once. Setting realistic expectations helps reduce the pressure and stress associated with high expectations.

Establish healthy boundaries: Learn to set boundaries to protect your time, energy, and mental well-being. Say no when necessary and prioritize your needs. Establish boundaries around work hours, personal time, and commitments. Communicate your limits clearly to others, and don't be afraid to ask for support or delegate tasks when needed.

Practice time management: Effectively managing your time can help alleviate stress. Prioritize tasks, create a schedule, and allocate time for important activities. Break tasks into smaller, more manageable chunks, and tackle them one at a time. Avoid multitasking, as it can increase stress levels and decrease productivity.

Nurture a supportive network: Surround yourself with supportive individuals who uplift and encourage you. Foster relationships that provide empathy, understanding, and a safe space for expressing your feelings. Seek support from friends, family, or support groups when you are feeling overwhelmed. Connecting with others can help reduce anxiety and provide a sense of belonging.

Challenge negative thinking: Anxiety and stress often go hand in hand with negative thinking patterns. Become aware of your negative thoughts and challenge them with more realistic and positive perspectives. Practice reframing negative situations and focusing on solutions rather than dwelling on problems. Cultivating a positive mindset can help reduce anxiety and improve overall well-being.

Seek professional support: If anxiety or stress becomes overwhelming and interferes with your daily life, don't hesitate to seek professional help. Mental health professionals can provide guidance, support, and evidence-based interventions tailored to your needs. Therapy, counseling, or other forms of treatment can be effective in managing anxiety and stress.

Engage in activities that bring joy: Make time for activities that bring you joy and allow you to relax and unwind. Engaging in hobbies, pursuing creative outlets, or participating in activities that you enjoy can help reduce anxiety and stress levels. Find activities that resonate with you and incorporate them into your routine.

Practice self-compassion: Be kind and compassionate towards yourself. Acknowledge that it's okay to feel stressed or anxious at times. Treat yourself with understanding and offer self-compassion during challenging moments. Practice self-care, self-acceptance, and self-encouragement. Embracing self-compassion can help you navigate anxiety and stress with greater resilience.

Remember, managing anxiety and stress is a journey that requires ongoing effort and self-reflection. It's important to be patient with yourself as you implement these strategies and find what works best for you. By incorporating these practices into your daily life, you can create a foundation of calm and resilience, even in the midst of a fast-paced world.

So, the fast-paced nature of today's world can contribute to increased anxiety and stress levels. However, by prioritizing self-care, practicing stress management techniques, setting realistic expectations, nurturing supportive relationships, challenging negative thinking, and seeking professional support when needed, you can effectively manage anxiety and stress. Embrace these strategies, and cultivate a sense of balance, calm, and well-being in your life.

Chapter 12: Understanding and Coping with Depression

In this chapter, we will delve into the various aspects of depression, its impact on daily life, and discuss effective coping mechanisms.

Depression is a common mental health disorder that affects millions of people worldwide. It goes beyond feeling sad or experiencing temporary low moods. Depression is characterized by persistent feelings of sadness, loss of interest or pleasure in activities, changes in appetite and sleep patterns, low energy levels, difficulty concentrating, and a sense of hopelessness. It can significantly impact all aspects of life, including relationships, work, and overall well-being.

Understanding depression is crucial for effectively managing and seeking support. Here are some key points to consider:

Recognizing the signs: Depression can manifest differently in individuals, but common signs and symptoms include a persistent low mood, loss of interest or pleasure, changes in appetite or weight, disrupted sleep patterns, fatigue or lack of energy, difficulty concentrating, feelings of worthlessness or guilt, and thoughts of death or suicide. It's important to note that not everyone experiences depression in the same way, and symptoms may vary.

Causes and risk factors: Depression is a complex condition influenced by a combination of genetic, biological, environmental, and psychological factors. Some common risk factors include a family history of depression, certain medical conditions, major life changes or trauma, chronic stress, and a history of substance abuse. However, it's essential to remember that depression can affect anyone, regardless of their background or circumstances.

Seeking professional help: If you suspect you or someone you know may be experiencing depression, it is crucial to seek professional help. Mental health professionals, such as therapists, psychologists, or psychiatrists, are trained to assess, diagnose, and provide evidence-based treatments for depression. They can guide you through the process of understanding and managing your symptoms.

Coping with depression requires a holistic approach that encompasses various aspects of well-being. Here are some strategies to help cope with depression:

Building a support network: Reach out to trusted friends, family members, or support groups who can provide emotional support and understanding. Sharing your thoughts and feelings with others can help alleviate feelings of isolation and provide a sense of belonging. Remember, you don't have to face depression alone.

Seeking therapy: Engaging in therapy can be highly beneficial for individuals with depression. Different therapeutic approaches, such as cognitive-behavioral therapy (CBT), interpersonal therapy (IPT), or psychodynamic therapy, can help address underlying issues, develop coping skills, and promote emotional well-being. Working with a therapist provides a safe space to explore and process emotions, thoughts, and behaviors related to depression.

Practicing self-care: Self-care plays a crucial role in managing depression. Focus on activities that nourish your physical, mental, and emotional well-being. This may include engaging in regular exercise, maintaining a balanced diet, getting enough sleep, spending time in nature, practicing relaxation techniques, or pursuing hobbies and interests that bring you joy. Prioritizing self-care supports overall well-being and can alleviate symptoms of depression.

Establishing a routine: Creating a daily routine can provide structure and stability, which is often lacking in the midst of depression. Set small, achievable goals and establish a schedule that incorporates self-care activities, work or study commitments, and social interactions. Having a routine can give you a sense of purpose and help anchor you during difficult times.

Engaging in pleasurable activities: Even if you may not initially feel motivated, try engaging in activities that you once enjoyed or activities that you find pleasurable. It could be as simple as listening to music, reading a book, watching a movie, or spending time with loved ones. Engaging in activities that bring you pleasure can provide temporary relief from depressive symptoms and increase feelings of positivity.

Practicing mindfulness and relaxation techniques: Mindfulness and relaxation techniques, such as meditation, deep breathing exercises, or yoga, can help manage stress and promote a sense of calm. These practices cultivate awareness of the present moment, reduce rumination, and help build resilience to negative thoughts and emotions.

Setting realistic goals: Set small, achievable goals that align with your current capabilities and energy levels. Break larger tasks into smaller, manageable steps. Celebrate even the smallest accomplishments, as they contribute to your progress and well-being. Setting realistic goals fosters a sense of achievement and improves self-esteem.

Managing stress and seeking balance: Identify and manage stressors in your life as much as possible. This may involve setting boundaries, learning to say no when necessary, and prioritizing self-care. Strive to achieve a balance between work, personal life, and self-care activities. Prioritizing stress management supports overall mental well-being and reduces the risk of depressive episodes.

Remember, coping with depression is a journey that varies from person to person. It's important to be patient and compassionate with yourself as you navigate through the ups and downs. Celebrate your progress, seek support when needed, and remember that there is hope for recovery.

So, depression is a complex mental health condition that requires understanding, compassion, and effective coping strategies. By building a support network, seeking professional help, practicing self-care, establishing routines, engaging in pleasurable activities, practicing mindfulness, setting realistic goals, and managing stress, you can effectively manage and cope with depression. Together, let's strive for a future where mental health is prioritized, stigma is diminished, and support is readily available to all who need it.

Chapter 13: Breaking Down Bipolar Disorder: Symptoms and Treatments

In this chapter, we will delve into the symptoms and subtypes of bipolar disorder, explore its impact on daily life, and discuss available treatments.

Bipolar disorder is a chronic condition that affects millions of people worldwide. It is characterized by episodes of extreme mood swings that range from elevated, manic states to depressive episodes. These mood shifts can significantly impact a person's thoughts, emotions, behaviors, and overall functioning.

To better understand bipolar disorder, let's explore its key features:

Bipolar I disorder: This is the most severe form of bipolar disorder, characterized by manic episodes that typically last for at least one week. During manic episodes, individuals may experience elevated mood, increased energy levels, impulsive behavior, reduced need for sleep, racing thoughts, and grandiose beliefs. Manic episodes can be accompanied by depressive episodes, where individuals may feel sad, hopeless, experience changes in appetite and sleep patterns, and have a loss of interest in activities they once enjoyed.

Bipolar II disorder: In bipolar II disorder, individuals experience depressive episodes and hypomanic episodes, which are less severe than full-blown manic episodes. Hypomanic episodes involve similar symptoms as manic episodes but to a lesser intensity. Individuals with bipolar II disorder often spend more time in depressive states.

Cyclothymic disorder: Cyclothymic disorder is characterized by chronic fluctuations between periods of hypomanic symptoms and depressive symptoms that do not meet the full criteria for a major depressive or manic episode. These fluctuations may persist for at least two years in adults (one year in children and adolescents).

Now that we have a general understanding of bipolar disorder and its subtypes, let's explore the impact it can have on daily life and the available treatments:

Impact on daily life: Bipolar disorder can disrupt various aspects of life, including work, relationships, and overall functioning.

During manic episodes, individuals may engage in impulsive or risky behaviors, experience difficulty concentrating, and have strained relationships due to irritability or aggressive behavior. Depressive episodes can lead to decreased energy levels, feelings of worthlessness, difficulties with decision-making, and social withdrawal. It is important to remember that the severity and duration of episodes can vary from person to person.

Medication: Medication plays a key role in managing bipolar disorder. Mood stabilizers, such as lithium or certain anticonvulsant medications, are commonly prescribed to help stabilize mood and prevent episodes. Antidepressants may be prescribed during depressive episodes, but caution is exercised to avoid triggering manic episodes. It is essential to work closely with a healthcare professional to find the most effective medication and dosage for each individual's needs.

Psychotherapy: Psychotherapy, such as cognitive-behavioral therapy (CBT) or psychoeducation, can be beneficial in managing bipolar disorder. These therapeutic approaches help individuals identify and change negative thought patterns, develop coping strategies, and improve communication and problem-solving skills. Psychotherapy also provides a safe space to explore the impact of bipolar disorder on relationships and overall well-being.

Lifestyle adjustments: Making lifestyle adjustments can play a significant role in managing bipolar disorder. Maintaining a consistent sleep schedule, engaging in regular exercise, and practicing stress reduction techniques can help stabilize mood and reduce the risk of triggering episodes. It is important to establish a supportive routine that includes self-care activities and healthy habits.

Support network: Building a strong support network is crucial for individuals living with bipolar disorder. Surround yourself with understanding family members, friends, or support groups who can provide emotional support, encouragement, and practical assistance when needed. Engaging in peer support groups can help individuals connect with others who share similar experiences and foster a sense of belonging.

Self-monitoring: Keeping track of mood fluctuations and early warning signs can help individuals with bipolar disorder identify triggers and take preventive measures. Self-monitoring tools, such as mood charts or journaling, can provide insights into mood patterns and help individuals communicate effectively with healthcare professionals.

Ongoing treatment and management: Bipolar disorder requires ongoing treatment and management to reduce the risk of relapse and optimize well-being. Regular check-ins with healthcare professionals, medication adjustments when necessary, and consistent engagement in therapy or counseling are vital components of long-term management. It is important to recognize that bipolar disorder affects individuals in unique ways, and treatment plans should be tailored to each person's needs. Finding the right combination of medication, therapy, and lifestyle adjustments may take time, and it's essential to be patient and work closely with healthcare professionals to achieve the best possible outcomes.

If you or someone you know is struggling with bipolar disorder, remember that help is available. Reach out to mental health professionals who specialize in bipolar disorder to receive an accurate diagnosis and develop an individualized treatment plan. With proper support, treatment, and self-care, individuals with bipolar disorder can lead fulfilling lives and effectively manage their condition.

So, bipolar disorder is a complex mental health condition characterized by extreme mood swings. It impacts various aspects of life and requires a multifaceted approach to treatment and management. By understanding the symptoms, seeking appropriate treatments, making lifestyle adjustments, building a support network, and consistently engaging in self-care, individuals with bipolar disorder can effectively navigate their condition and work towards achieving stability and well-being.

Chapter 14: Overcoming Obsessive-Compulsive Disorder (OCD)

In this chapter, we will delve into the intricacies of OCD, explore its impact on daily life, discuss available treatments, and provide practical strategies for managing and overcoming this challenging mental health condition.

Obsessive-compulsive disorder (OCD) is a chronic mental health condition that affects millions of people worldwide. It is characterized by intrusive, unwanted thoughts (obsessions) and repetitive behaviors or mental acts (compulsions) performed to alleviate anxiety or distress. OCD can significantly impact a person's thoughts, emotions, behaviors, and overall functioning.

To better understand OCD, let's explore its key features:

Obsessions: Obsessions are intrusive and distressing thoughts, images, or urges that repeatedly enter a person's mind. Common obsessions include fears of contamination, doubts about safety, a need for symmetry or order, or taboo thoughts related to morality or aggression. These obsessions are often accompanied by intense anxiety or fear.

Compulsions: Compulsions are repetitive behaviors or mental acts that individuals with OCD engage in to reduce the distress caused by their obsessions. Compulsions can be physical actions (such as excessive handwashing or checking) or mental rituals (such as counting or repeating phrases). While these behaviors may provide temporary relief, they are time-consuming and can interfere with daily life.

Now that we have a general understanding of OCD, let's explore its impact on daily life and the available treatments:

Impact on daily life: OCD can significantly impact various aspects of life, including work, relationships, and overall well-being. Individuals with OCD often spend a significant amount of time and energy engaging in rituals or attempting to suppress intrusive thoughts. This can lead to impaired concentration, reduced productivity, strained relationships, and a decreased quality of life.

Cognitive-behavioral therapy (CBT): CBT is the gold standard treatment for OCD. Specifically, a type of CBT called exposure and response prevention (ERP) is highly effective. ERP involves gradually exposing individuals to their feared situations or thoughts and preventing the accompanying compulsive behaviors. Over time, this helps individuals learn that their anxiety decreases without engaging in the compulsions, leading to a reduction in OCD symptoms.

Medication: Medication can be prescribed to help manage OCD symptoms, especially in combination with therapy. Selective serotonin reuptake inhibitors (SSRIs) are commonly used to regulate serotonin levels in the brain, which can help reduce anxiety and obsessions. It is essential to work closely with a healthcare professional to find the most suitable medication and dosage for each individual.

Mindfulness and acceptance-based approaches: Mindfulness techniques, such as meditation or mindful awareness of OCD symptoms, can help individuals develop a non-judgmental and accepting attitude towards their obsessions and discomfort. Acceptance and commitment therapy (ACT) can also be beneficial by helping individuals identify their values and commit to actions aligned with those values, even in the presence of OCD-related distress.

Support network: Building a strong support network is crucial for individuals living with OCD. Share your experience with trusted friends, family members, or support groups who can provide empathy, understanding, and practical assistance. Engaging in peer support groups can help individuals connect with others who share similar experiences and provide a sense of validation and support.

Self-care and stress management: Engaging in self-care activities and stress management techniques can help individuals cope with OCD. Regular exercise, proper sleep, a balanced diet, and stress reduction techniques such as deep breathing exercises or engaging in hobbies can contribute to overall well-being and reduce OCD-related distress.

Psychoeducation: Educating yourself and loved ones about OCD can foster understanding and empathy. Learn about the condition, its causes, and available treatments. Understanding that OCD is a medical condition and not a reflection of one's character or intelligence can help reduce self-blame and stigma.

Gradual exposure and self-directed therapy: In addition to therapy with a mental health professional, individuals with OCD can practice gradual exposure to feared situations or thoughts on their own. Start with manageable challenges and gradually increase the difficulty over time. This can help build resilience, reduce anxiety, and strengthen one's ability to resist compulsions.

It's important to recognize that overcoming OCD is a journey that varies from person to person. With time, patience, and consistent effort, individuals can experience significant improvements in their symptoms and overall well-being.

If you or someone you know is struggling with OCD, remember that help is available. Seek support from mental health professionals specializing in OCD to receive an accurate diagnosis and develop an individualized treatment plan. By incorporating therapeutic techniques, building a support network, practicing self-care, and engaging in gradual exposure, individuals with OCD can effectively manage their symptoms and work towards reclaiming their lives.

So, OCD is a challenging mental health condition characterized by intrusive thoughts and compulsive behaviors. Through cognitive-behavioral therapy, medication, mindfulness, self-care, and the support of a network of understanding individuals, individuals with OCD can manage and overcome their symptoms. By embracing strategies for coping and seeking appropriate treatment, individuals with OCD can experience a greater sense of control and lead fulfilling lives.

Chapter 15: Examining the Link Between Substance Abuse and Mental Health

In this chapter, we will delve into the link between these two conditions, examine the impact they have on each other, and discuss strategies for addressing and managing this complex co-occurrence.

Substance abuse and mental health disorders often coexist, creating a challenging cycle that can have profound effects on individuals' well-being. The relationship between substance abuse and mental health is bidirectional, meaning that one can contribute to the development or exacerbation of the other. Let's explore this link more closely:

Self-medication hypothesis: Many individuals with mental health disorders turn to substances as a way to self-medicate and alleviate their symptoms temporarily. For example, someone experiencing depression may use .... or drugs to numb their emotional pain, while someone with anxiety may rely on substances to reduce their feelings of restlessness or worry. However, while substances may provide temporary relief, they ultimately exacerbate mental health symptoms and can lead to addiction.

Vulnerability hypothesis: On the other hand, substance abuse can increase the risk of developing mental health disorders. Prolonged substance use disrupts the brain's chemistry and can lead to imbalances in neurotransmitters, which play a crucial role in regulating mood, emotions, and overall mental health. Substance abuse can trigger or worsen mental health symptoms, leading to conditions such as depression, anxiety, or psychosis.

Now that we understand the link between substance abuse and mental health, let's explore the impact they have on each other and discuss strategies for addressing this complex co-occurrence:

Integrated treatment: It is essential to address both substance abuse and mental health disorders simultaneously through integrated treatment approaches. Integrated treatment combines therapies for substance use disorders and mental health conditions to address the interconnected nature of these conditions. This holistic approach helps individuals develop coping skills, manage cravings, and address the underlying causes of their substance abuse and mental health symptoms.

Psychotherapy: Psychotherapy, such as cognitive-behavioral therapy (CBT), dialectical behavior therapy (DBT), or motivational interviewing, is effective in treating both substance abuse and mental health disorders. These therapeutic approaches help individuals identify and change negative thought patterns, develop healthier coping mechanisms, improve emotional regulation, and strengthen motivation for change.

Medication management: In some cases, medication may be necessary to address underlying mental health disorders. Antidepressants, anti-anxiety medications, or mood stabilizers may be prescribed to alleviate symptoms and support recovery. Medication management should be conducted under the guidance of a healthcare professional who can monitor effectiveness and adjust dosages when needed.

Dual diagnosis support groups: Engaging in support groups specifically tailored for individuals with dual diagnoses can provide a sense of validation, support, and shared experiences. These groups offer a safe space for individuals to discuss their challenges, gain insights from others, and develop a sense of belonging.

Building a strong support network: Surround yourself with a supportive network of friends, family, or mentors who understand your journey and can provide empathy, understanding, and encouragement. Engage in activities that promote a sense of connection and support, such as joining recovery groups, attending community events, or participating in hobbies and interests that bring you joy.

Stress management and self-care: Developing healthy coping mechanisms and engaging in self-care activities are crucial for managing both substance abuse and mental health symptoms. Practice stress reduction techniques such as mindfulness, deep breathing exercises, or engaging in activities that promote relaxation and rejuvenation. Prioritize self-care activities that nourish your physical, mental, and emotional well-being.

Healthy lifestyle changes: Adopting a healthy lifestyle can positively impact both substance abuse and mental health. This includes getting regular exercise, maintaining a balanced diet, prioritizing sleep, and avoiding triggers or environments that may encourage substance abuse. Incorporate activities that promote physical and mental well-being into your daily routine.

Seek professional help: It is essential to seek professional help from healthcare providers specializing in both substance abuse and mental health. They can conduct comprehensive assessments, provide evidence-based treatments, and guide you towards recovery. Remember, seeking help is a sign of strength and taking the first step towards reclaiming your well-being.

It's important to recognize that overcoming the co-occurrence of substance abuse and mental health disorders is a journey that requires dedication, patience, and support. Recovery is possible, and with the right treatment and strategies, individuals can find a path towards healing and well-being.

If you or someone you know is struggling with substance abuse and mental health concerns, reach out to healthcare professionals or addiction specialists to receive an accurate diagnosis and develop an individualized treatment plan. By addressing both substance abuse and mental health disorders simultaneously, individuals can break free from the cycle of addiction and improve their overall mental well-being.

So, the link between substance abuse and mental health is complex and bidirectional. By understanding this relationship and addressing both conditions through integrated treatment, psychotherapy, medication management, support networks, stress management, and healthy lifestyle changes, individuals can effectively manage and overcome this co-occurrence. Embrace the support available to you, believe in your resilience, and work towards a future where recovery and mental well-being are within reach.

Chapter 16: The Impact of Sleep on Mental Health and Well-being

In this chapter, we will delve into the importance of quality sleep, examine the link between sleep and mental health, and discuss practical strategies for improving sleep.

Sleep plays a vital role in our physical and mental health. It is during sleep that our bodies and minds undergo essential restorative processes. Getting enough high-quality sleep is crucial for optimal functioning and overall well-being.

Let's explore the connection between sleep and mental health more closely:

Sleep and mood: The quality and quantity of sleep can significantly influence our mood and emotional well-being. When we don't get enough sleep or experience disrupted sleep patterns, we may be more prone to irritability, mood swings, and difficulty managing stress. Lack of sleep can contribute to an increased risk of developing mental health disorders, such as depression and anxiety.

Sleep and cognitive function: Sleep plays a crucial role in cognitive processes, such as attention, concentration, memory, and decision-making. When we are sleep-deprived, our cognitive abilities suffer, leading to difficulties in processing information, problem-solving, and retaining new knowledge. Chronic sleep deprivation can impair overall cognitive function and negatively impact daily performance and productivity.

Sleep and emotional regulation: Sufficient sleep is essential for regulating our emotions effectively. During sleep, our brains process and consolidate emotional experiences, helping us navigate and cope with our emotions in a balanced way. When sleep is compromised, we may experience heightened emotional reactivity, increased vulnerability to stressors, and challenges in managing emotional responses.

Now that we understand the impact of sleep on mental health, let's discuss strategies for improving sleep quality and promoting overall well-being:

Establish a consistent sleep routine: Going to bed and waking up at the same time every day, even on weekends, helps regulate your body's internal clock and promote better sleep. Establish a relaxing pre-sleep routine that signals to your body that it's time to wind down. This may include activities such as reading, taking a warm bath, practicing relaxation techniques, or listening to calming music.

Create a sleep-friendly environment: Ensure your sleep environment is conducive to quality sleep. Keep your bedroom cool, dark, and quiet. Invest in a comfortable mattress and pillow that support your body. Consider using blackout curtains, earplugs, or white noise machines to minimize disturbances that can disrupt your sleep.

Limit exposure to electronic devices before bed: The blue light emitted by electronic devices can interfere with your body's natural sleep-wake cycle. Limit exposure to screens, such as smartphones, tablets, or computers, at least one hour before bedtime. Instead, engage in relaxing activities that promote winding down, such as reading a book, practicing gentle stretching, or journaling.

Manage stress and practice relaxation techniques: Stress and anxiety can significantly impact sleep quality. Prioritize stress management techniques such as deep breathing exercises, meditation, or mindfulness practices to promote relaxation and reduce racing thoughts before bed. Engaging in calming activities can help shift your focus away from daily stressors and prepare your mind for restful sleep.

Limit caffeine and .... intake: Caffeine is a stimulant that can interfere with sleep. Limit your consumption of caffeinated beverages, such as coffee or energy drinks, especially in the afternoon and evening. While .... may initially make you feel drowsy, it can disrupt the quality of your sleep and lead to frequent awakenings during the night. It's best to avoid .... close to bedtime.

Regular exercise: Engaging in regular physical activity can promote better sleep quality. Aim for at least 30 minutes of moderate intensity exercise most days of the week. However, avoid exercising too close to bedtime, as it can be stimulating and interfere with falling asleep. Find the exercise routine that works best for you, whether it's walking, jogging, yoga, or dancing.

Create a comfortable wind-down routine: As bedtime approaches, engage in activities that promote relaxation and prepare your mind and body for sleep. This may include gentle stretching, reading a book, practicing gratitude or mindfulness exercises, or listening to calming music. Avoid stimulating activities or engaging in intense discussions close to bedtime.

Seek professional help if needed: If you continue to struggle with sleep issues despite implementing these strategies, it may be beneficial to seek professional help. Consult with a healthcare professional who specializes in sleep medicine or a mental health professional who can assess your sleep patterns and provide tailored recommendations or interventions.

Remember, improving sleep quality is a process that requires patience and consistency. Implementing these strategies and making sleep a priority can positively impact your mental health, cognitive function, and overall well-being.

So, sleep plays a crucial role in our mental health and overall well-being. By understanding the link between sleep and mental health, and implementing strategies such as establishing a consistent sleep routine, creating a sleep-friendly environment, managing stress, limiting caffeine and .... intake, engaging in regular exercise, and seeking professional help when needed, you can promote quality sleep and enhance your overall mental well-being. Embrace the power of sleep as a foundation for optimal health and thrive in all areas of your life.

Chapter 17: Body Dysmorphic Disorder: A Look into Perceived Flaws

In this chapter, we will delve into the intricacies of BDD, explore its impact on individuals' lives, and discuss strategies for managing and overcoming this challenging disorder.

Body dysmorphic disorder is more than just feeling self-conscious or dissatisfied with one's appearance. It involves an obsessive focus on specific body parts or features, believing that they are flawed, despite little or no evidence to support these beliefs. Individuals with BDD may spend hours each day checking their appearance, seeking reassurance, and engaging in repetitive behaviors to manage their perceived flaws.

Let's explore body dysmorphic disorder in more detail:

Preoccupation with perceived flaws: Individuals with BDD have a relentless preoccupation with specific aspects of their appearance that they perceive as flawed. These perceived flaws may relate to any part of the body, but common areas of concern include the skin, nose, hair, weight, or body shape. The perceived flaws may be minor or non-existent to others, but they cause significant distress and can interfere with daily life.

Negative self-image: Individuals with BDD often have a distorted self-image, seeing themselves as unattractive or deformed due to their perceived flaws. This negative self-perception can have a profound impact on self-esteem, causing feelings of shame, embarrassment, and social isolation.

Compulsive behaviors and avoidance: BDD is often accompanied by compulsive behaviors and avoidance strategies. Individuals may engage in excessive grooming, mirror checking, comparing themselves to others, seeking reassurance, or seeking cosmetic procedures to address their perceived flaws. They may also avoid social situations, intimate relationships, or activities that they believe draw attention to their flaws.

Now that we understand the basics of BDD, let's discuss strategies for managing and overcoming this challenging disorder:

Seek professional help: If you suspect you may have BDD, it is essential to seek professional help. Mental health professionals, such as therapists or psychiatrists specializing in body dysmorphic disorder, can provide a proper diagnosis and develop an individualized treatment plan. They can help you challenge negative beliefs, learn coping strategies, and explore underlying factors contributing to BDD.

Cognitive-behavioral therapy (CBT): CBT is the most effective treatment for BDD. CBT focuses on identifying and challenging negative thought patterns, developing more realistic and positive beliefs about one's appearance, and learning healthier ways to cope with distress. Through CBT, individuals can gain a better understanding of the role their thoughts play in perpetuating their preoccupation with perceived flaws.

Medication: In some cases, medication may be prescribed to manage symptoms of BDD. Selective serotonin reuptake inhibitors (SSRIs) are commonly used to reduce obsessive thoughts, compulsive behaviors, and depressive symptoms associated with BDD. Medication should be prescribed and monitored by a healthcare professional experienced in treating BDD.

Support network: Building a strong support network of trusted family members, friends, or support groups can provide invaluable emotional support and understanding. Sharing your experiences with others who have similar struggles can help reduce feelings of isolation and provide a sense of belonging. Online communities and local support groups dedicated to BDD can be valuable resources.

Self-compassion and self-care: Practicing self-compassion is crucial for individuals with BDD. Be gentle and kind to yourself, acknowledging that BDD is a challenging disorder that does not define your worth. Engage in self-care activities that promote overall well-being, such as regular exercise, getting enough restful sleep, pursuing hobbies, or engaging in relaxation techniques. Prioritize activities that nurture your physical, mental, and emotional health.

Challenge negative beliefs: Work on challenging and reframing negative beliefs about your appearance. Notice when negative thoughts arise and question their validity. Practice replacing negative self-talk with more realistic and compassionate statements. Remind yourself that everyone has perceived flaws and that true beauty comes from within.

Limit mirror checking and seeking reassurance: Reduce the time spent checking your appearance in mirrors or seeking reassurance from others about your perceived flaws. Set limits on mirror use and gradually decrease the frequency of seeking reassurance. This may feel challenging at first, but it can help break the cycle of preoccupation and compulsive behaviors associated with BDD.

Practice self-acceptance: Cultivate a mindset of self-acceptance and focus on your positive qualities, talents, and achievements. Celebrate your uniqueness and appreciate the diverse range of beauty in the world. Surround yourself with positive influences and reminders of self-acceptance, such as affirmations or inspiring quotes.

It's important to recognize that overcoming body dysmorphic disorder is a journey that varies from person to person. Be patient with yourself, celebrate small victories, and acknowledge that recovery takes time. Surround yourself with supportive individuals, seek professional help, and engage in self-care practices to support your journey towards healing and self-acceptance.

So, body dysmorphic disorder is a complex mental health condition characterized by a preoccupation with perceived flaws in one's appearance. By seeking professional help, engaging in cognitive-behavioral therapy, building a support network, practicing self-compassion, challenging negative beliefs, limiting compulsive behaviors, and cultivating self-acceptance, individuals with BDD can manage and overcome this challenging disorder. Embrace the journey of self-discovery, focus on inner beauty, and work towards a future where self-acceptance and well-being thrive.

Chapter 18: Exploring Eating Disorders and Their Psychological Underpinnings

In this chapter, we will delve into the intricacies of eating disorders, explore their psychological underpinnings, and discuss strategies for addressing and managing these challenging disorders.

Eating disorders are much more than just a matter of food or body weight. They are complex illnesses that affect individuals physically, emotionally, and mentally. They often stem from a combination of genetic, environmental, and psychological factors, making them challenging to navigate and overcome.

Let's explore eating disorders and their psychological underpinnings more closely:

Anorexia nervosa: Anorexia nervosa is characterized by an intense fear of gaining weight and a distorted body image. Individuals with anorexia may restrict food intake, engage in excessive exercise, and have an excessive preoccupation with weight, body shape, and food. Psychological factors that contribute to anorexia include perfectionism, low self-esteem, feelings of inadequacy, and a desire for control.

Bulimia nervosa: Bulimia nervosa involves a cycle of binge eating followed by compensatory behaviors, such as self-induced vomiting, excessive exercise, or the misuse of laxatives or diuretics. Individuals with bulimia often have a negative body image, low self-esteem, and feelings of guilt and shame. Psychological factors that contribute to bulimia include low self-worth, impulsivity, and difficulties in managing emotions.

Binge eating disorder: Binge eating disorder involves recurrent episodes of consuming large quantities of food within a short period, accompanied by a sense of loss of control. Unlike bulimia, individuals with binge eating disorder do not engage in compensatory behaviors. Psychological factors that contribute to binge eating disorder include emotional distress, low self-esteem, and using food as a way to cope with difficult emotions.

Other specified feeding or eating disorders (OSFED): OSFED encompasses a range of eating disorders that do not meet the full criteria for anorexia nervosa, bulimia nervosa, or binge eating disorder. Psychological factors that contribute to OSFED may vary depending on the specific subtype but often include body dissatisfaction, negative body image, and difficulties with emotional regulation.

Now that we understand the basics of eating disorders and their psychological underpinnings, let's discuss strategies for addressing and managing these complex disorders:

Seek professional help: If you suspect you may have an eating disorder, it is crucial to seek professional help. Mental health professionals specializing in eating disorders can provide a proper diagnosis, assess your unique needs, and develop an individualized treatment plan. They can help you address the underlying psychological factors contributing to the disorder and guide you towards recovery.

Therapy and counseling: Psychotherapy, such as cognitive-behavioral therapy (CBT), is an effective treatment for eating disorders. Therapy can help individuals challenge distorted thoughts and beliefs about their bodies, develop healthy coping mechanisms, improve self-esteem, and address underlying psychological issues. Family-based therapy or interpersonal therapy may also be beneficial, depending on the specific eating disorder and individual needs.

Nutritional counseling: Working with a registered dietitian experienced in eating disorders can be beneficial in establishing a balanced and healthy relationship with food. Nutritional counseling can help individuals develop a meal plan that meets their nutritional needs, addresses specific concerns related to their eating disorder, and promotes overall well-being.

Support network: Building a strong support network is crucial for individuals recovering from eating disorders. Surround yourself with understanding family members, friends, or support groups who can provide empathy, encouragement, and practical assistance. Engaging in support groups can help individuals connect with others who share similar experiences and provide a sense of validation and understanding.

Body acceptance and self-compassion: Cultivating body acceptance and self-compassion is essential for individuals recovering from eating disorders. Embrace the concept of body diversity and challenge societal beauty ideals. Focus on the unique qualities that make you who you are, rather than solely on external appearance. Practice self-compassion and treat yourself with kindness and understanding throughout your recovery journey.

Address underlying psychological factors: Eating disorders are often intertwined with underlying psychological factors, such as low self-esteem, perfectionism, anxiety, or trauma. It is important to work with mental health professionals to address these factors through individual therapy, group therapy, or specialized trauma therapies, as needed.

Develop healthy coping mechanisms: Eating disorders often serve as coping mechanisms for underlying emotional distress. Identify and develop healthier coping mechanisms that do not involve disordered eating behaviors. This may include engaging in creative outlets, practicing mindfulness, seeking social support, journaling, or engaging in physical activities that bring you joy.

Set realistic goals: Recovery from an eating disorder is a gradual process. Set realistic goals and celebrate each small step towards progress. Focus on improving your overall well-being and developing a healthier relationship with your body and food, rather than solely on weight or appearance-related goals.

It's important to recognize that overcoming an eating disorder takes time, patience, and support. Surround yourself with compassionate professionals and loved ones who can guide you on your journey towards recovery. Remember, your worth is not defined by your appearance or the number on the scale. You deserve to live a life free from the grips of an eating disorder and to embrace your true self.

So, eating disorders are complex mental health conditions with psychological underpinnings. By seeking professional help, engaging in therapy, building a support network, cultivating body acceptance and self-compassion, addressing underlying psychological factors, developing healthy coping mechanisms, and setting realistic goals, individuals can address and manage eating disorders. Embrace the journey of self-discovery, focus on inner strength and resilience, and work towards a future where self-acceptance and well-being thrive.

Chapter 19: Understanding Dissociative Disorders: From Identity Crisis to Integration

In this chapter, we will delve into the intricacies of dissociative disorders, explore their various forms, and discuss strategies for understanding, managing, and integrating the different aspects of self.

Dissociative disorders are characterized by a disruption or detachment from one's thoughts, memories, feelings, or sense of identity. They often develop as a response to traumatic experiences and serve as a way for the mind to cope with overwhelming emotions or distress. Dissociative disorders manifest in various forms, including dissociative identity disorder (DID), dissociative amnesia, and depersonalization/derealization disorder.

Let's explore dissociative disorders and their manifestations more closely:

Dissociative identity disorder (DID): DID, previously known as multiple personality disorder, is characterized by the presence of two or more distinct personality states or identities within an individual. These identities may have their own unique traits, memories, and ways of relating to the world. Individuals with DID often experience gaps in memory or time, experience significant distress, and may struggle with identity integration.

Dissociative amnesia: Dissociative amnesia involves a significant memory loss that goes beyond ordinary forgetfulness. It may encompass specific events or a period of time related to a traumatic experience. Individuals with dissociative amnesia may have difficulty recalling personal information, important events, or even their own identity. Memory gaps are typically a result of psychological distress rather than organic brain damage.

Depersonalization/derealization disorder: Depersonalization/derealization disorder is characterized by persistent or recurrent experiences of feeling detached from oneself (depersonalization) or the external world (derealization). Individuals may feel as if they are observing themselves from outside their bodies or that their surroundings are unreal or distorted. These experiences can be distressing and interfere with daily functioning.

Now that we understand the basics of dissociative disorders, let's discuss strategies for understanding, managing, and integrating the different aspects of self:

Seek professional help: If you suspect you may have a dissociative disorder, it is crucial to seek professional help. Mental health professionals specializing in dissociative disorders can provide a proper diagnosis, assess your unique needs, and develop an individualized treatment plan. They can help you navigate the complexities of the disorder and guide you towards integration and healing.

Psychotherapy: Psychotherapy, particularly specialized approaches such as trauma-focused therapy and dialectical behavior therapy, is the primary treatment for dissociative disorders. Therapy aims to help individuals gain insight into their dissociative experiences, process traumatic memories, improve emotion regulation skills, and foster integration of different aspects of self. The therapeutic relationship provides a safe space to explore and understand the underlying causes of dissociation.

Grounding techniques: Grounding techniques can help individuals experiencing dissociation reconnect with the present moment and their physical surroundings. These techniques may involve focusing on the senses, such as deep breathing exercises, holding a comforting object, or observing and describing the immediate environment. Grounding techniques can provide a sense of stability and help manage distress during dissociative episodes.

Self-care and self-compassion: Engaging in self-care activities and cultivating self-compassion are crucial for individuals with dissociative disorders. Practice self-care routines that promote overall well-being, such as engaging in relaxation exercises, pursuing creative outlets, connecting with nature, or participating in activities that bring joy and a sense of grounding. Treat yourself with kindness and understanding as you navigate the complexities of the disorder.

Journaling and creative expression: Expressing thoughts, emotions, and experiences through journaling, art, or other creative outlets can be therapeutic for individuals with dissociative disorders. It provides a safe and private space to explore and make sense of different aspects of self. Through creative expression, individuals can enhance self-awareness, foster communication between different identities, and facilitate integration.

Support network: Building a strong support network is essential for individuals with dissociative disorders. Surround yourself with understanding family members, friends, or support groups who can provide empathy, validation, and a safe space to share your experiences. Engaging in support groups or online communities specific to dissociative disorders can offer a sense of belonging and connection with others who understand your journey.

Gradual integration and communication: Integration of different aspects of self in dissociative disorders is a complex process that occurs gradually and with the guidance of a mental health professional. Foster open communication and collaboration among identities, respecting their unique experiences and contributions. Gradual integration aims to establish a cohesive sense of self and enhance functioning.

Patience and self-acceptance: Recovery from dissociative disorders takes time, patience, and self-acceptance. Be gentle with yourself as you navigate the challenges and progress towards integration. Recognize that healing is a nonlinear journey, and setbacks may occur along the way. Celebrate each step forward and practice self-compassion throughout your recovery process.

So, dissociative disorders involve disruptions in identity, memory, and perception of reality. By seeking professional help, engaging in therapy, practicing grounding techniques, cultivating self-care and self-compassion, building a support network, fostering gradual integration, and embracing patience and self-acceptance, individuals with dissociative disorders can understand, manage, and integrate the different aspects of self. Embrace the journey of self-discovery and healing, focus on inner strength, and work towards a future where integration and well-being thrive.

Chapter 20: Post-Traumatic Stress Disorder (PTSD) and Effective Therapies

In this chapter, we will delve into the intricacies of PTSD, examine its impact on individuals' lives, and discuss strategies for healing and recovery.

Post-traumatic stress disorder is a mental health condition that can develop after experiencing or witnessing a traumatic event. Traumatic events may include natural disasters, accidents, physical or sexual assault, military combat, or other life-threatening situations. PTSD is characterized by a range of symptoms that can persist long after the traumatic event has occurred.

Let's explore PTSD and its impact on individuals' lives more closely:

Re-experiencing symptoms: Individuals with PTSD often experience distressing and intrusive memories of the traumatic event. These memories may manifest as vivid nightmares, flashbacks, or distressing thoughts or images. Re-experiencing symptoms can be triggered by reminders of the traumatic event and can cause intense emotional and physical reactions.

Avoidance and numbing: Avoidance is a common coping mechanism in PTSD. Individuals may avoid places, activities, or people that remind them of the traumatic event. They may also experience a sense of emotional numbing, feeling disconnected from others and losing interest in previously enjoyed activities. Avoidance and numbing serve as attempts to protect oneself from further distress.

Hyperarousal and hypervigilance: Hyperarousal refers to a state of heightened alertness and constant vigilance. Individuals with PTSD may have difficulty sleeping, experience irritability or anger outbursts, and have an exaggerated startle response. They may feel constantly on edge, as if danger is always present, and struggle to relax or feel a sense of safety.

Now that we understand the basics of PTSD, let's discuss effective therapies for managing its symptoms:

Trauma-focused therapy: Trauma-focused therapy, such as cognitive processing therapy (CPT) and eye movement desensitization and reprocessing (EMDR), is considered highly effective in treating PTSD. These therapies focus on helping individuals process and reframe traumatic memories, challenge negative beliefs about themselves and the world, and develop healthier coping mechanisms. They provide a safe space for individuals to explore their experiences, regulate emotions, and gradually reduce the impact of the traumatic event on their lives.

Cognitive-behavioral therapy (CBT): CBT is a widely used therapeutic approach for PTSD. It helps individuals identify and change unhelpful thought patterns and behaviors that contribute to distress. CBT aims to develop coping strategies, enhance problem-solving skills, and provide tools for managing symptoms. By challenging negative beliefs and developing more adaptive responses, individuals can regain a sense of control and reduce the impact of PTSD on their daily lives.

Group therapy: Group therapy offers a supportive and empathetic environment for individuals with PTSD to connect with others who have similar experiences. Sharing experiences, gaining insights from others, and receiving support can be invaluable in the recovery process. Group therapy provides a sense of validation, reduces feelings of isolation, and fosters a sense of belonging.

Medication: In some cases, medication may be prescribed to manage symptoms of PTSD. Selective serotonin reuptake inhibitors (SSRIs) are commonly used to reduce anxiety, depression, and hyperarousal symptoms. Medication should be prescribed and monitored by a healthcare professional experienced in treating PTSD, as it is not a standalone treatment and is often used in conjunction with therapy.

Self-care and stress management: Engaging in self-care activities and practicing stress management techniques are crucial for individuals with PTSD. Regular exercise, adequate sleep, balanced nutrition, and relaxation techniques such as deep breathing exercises or mindfulness practices can help regulate emotions, reduce hyperarousal, and promote overall well-being. Prioritizing self-care activities that bring joy and relaxation is essential in managing PTSD symptoms.

Social support and connection: Building a strong support network is vital for individuals with PTSD. Surround yourself with understanding family members, friends, or support groups who can provide empathy, validation, and practical assistance. Engaging in activities that foster social connection and support, such as joining support groups, participating in community events, or seeking out trusted individuals to share your experiences with, can significantly aid the healing process.

Gradual exposure: Gradual exposure therapy involves facing the triggers and reminders of the traumatic event in a controlled and safe environment. Under the guidance of a therapist, individuals gradually confront the thoughts, feelings, and situations associated with the trauma. Over time, exposure therapy can help reduce avoidance behaviors and decrease the distressing impact of triggers.

Mind-body techniques: Mind-body techniques such as yoga, meditation, and mindfulness can complement traditional therapies for PTSD. These practices help individuals cultivate a sense of calm, regulate their emotions, and develop greater self-awareness. Mind-body techniques can enhance relaxation, improve sleep quality, and foster a sense of empowerment and self-compassion.

Recovering from PTSD is a unique and individual journey. It requires patience, self-compassion, and support. By seeking professional help, engaging in trauma-focused therapy, practicing self-care, cultivating social support, and exploring complementary techniques, individuals can effectively manage PTSD symptoms and work towards healing and recovery.

So, post-traumatic stress disorder is a complex mental health condition that can have a profound impact on individuals' lives. By understanding the symptoms of PTSD and exploring effective therapies such as trauma-focused therapy, cognitive-behavioral therapy, group therapy, medication, self-care, social support, gradual exposure, and mind-body techniques, individuals can regain control over their lives and embark on a path of healing and recovery. Embrace the journey of resilience, focus on self-care and self-compassion, and work towards a future where healing and well-being thrive.

Chapter 21: Breaking the Cycle of Self-Harm and Understanding Its Root Causes

In this chapter, we will delve into the intricacies of self-harm, explore its root causes, and discuss strategies for breaking the cycle and fostering healing and recovery.

Self-harm is a coping mechanism that individuals may use to deal with overwhelming emotional pain or distress. It involves deliberately causing harm to oneself, typically through methods such as cutting, burning, scratching, or hitting. Self-harm is often a sign of underlying emotional turmoil, and it is important to approach this topic with empathy, understanding, and non-judgment.

Let's explore self-harm and its root causes more closely:

Emotional pain and distress: Self-harm is often a response to intense emotional pain or distress that an individual may find overwhelming or difficult to express in words. It can serve as a way to release or distract from emotional pain, provide a sense of control, or temporarily alleviate emotional numbness.

Coping mechanism: For some individuals, self-harm may serve as a coping mechanism to deal with overwhelming emotions or difficult life circumstances. It can provide a temporary sense of relief or serve as a means of self-punishment, expressing feelings of guilt or shame.

Communication and expression: In some cases, self-harm may be a way for individuals to communicate their inner pain or distress when they struggle to verbalize their emotions or seek help. It can serve as a visible manifestation of an internal struggle, a cry for help, or an attempt to express something deeply personal that is difficult to put into words.

Now that we understand the basics of self-harm and its root causes, let's discuss strategies for breaking the cycle and fostering healing and recovery:

Seek professional help: If you or someone you know is engaging in self-harm, it is crucial to seek professional help. Mental health professionals experienced in working with self-harm can provide a safe and non-judgmental space to explore the underlying causes and develop strategies for healing and recovery. Therapy, such as dialectical behavior therapy (DBT) or cognitive-behavioral therapy (CBT), can be effective in addressing self-harm behaviors and the root causes behind them.

Develop alternative coping mechanisms: Finding healthier and more constructive ways to cope with emotional distress is essential in breaking the cycle of self-harm. This may involve learning and practicing relaxation techniques, engaging in creative outlets such as art or writing, participating in physical activities that promote emotional release, or seeking support from trusted individuals.

Build a support network: Surround yourself with understanding and supportive individuals who can provide empathy, validation, and practical assistance. Reach out to friends, family, or support groups dedicated to self-harm recovery. Building a strong support network can help combat feelings of isolation, offer a sense of belonging, and provide resources for managing emotional distress.

Develop a safety plan: Creating a safety plan can provide structure and guidance in moments of crisis or when self-harm urges arise. A safety plan includes strategies for managing distress, identifying triggers, contacting support networks, and seeking professional help. Having a plan in place can increase feelings of safety and empower individuals to navigate challenging moments more effectively.

Address underlying emotional issues: It is crucial to address the underlying emotional issues that contribute to self-harm. This may involve exploring and processing traumatic experiences, working through feelings of guilt or shame, and developing healthier ways to express emotions and seek support. Therapy can provide a safe and supportive environment to explore these underlying issues.

Practice self-compassion and self-care: Cultivating self-compassion and prioritizing self-care are vital in the journey of healing and recovery. Be gentle with yourself and acknowledge that self-harm is a coping mechanism that developed in response to pain. Engage in activities that promote your well-being, such as getting enough restful sleep, practicing relaxation techniques, pursuing hobbies or interests, and nurturing supportive relationships.

Replace self-harm with self-soothing techniques: Develop a toolkit of self-soothing techniques to use when self-harm urges arise. This can include deep breathing exercises, listening to calming music, taking a warm bath, writing in a journal, using grounding techniques, or engaging in physical activities that promote relaxation and emotional release. Experiment with different techniques to find what works best for you.

Set realistic goals and celebrate progress: Breaking the cycle of self-harm is a journey that takes time and effort. Set realistic goals and celebrate each step forward, no matter how small. Recovery is not linear, and setbacks may occur along the way. Remember that progress is a personal journey, and healing and recovery are possible with time, support, and dedication.

It is important to remember that overcoming self-harm is a process that requires patience, understanding, and support. By seeking professional help, developing alternative coping mechanisms, building a support network, addressing underlying emotional issues, practicing self-compassion and self-care, replacing self-harm with self-soothing techniques, setting realistic goals, and celebrating progress, individuals can break the cycle of self-harm and foster healing and recovery.

So, self-harm is a complex behavior that individuals may engage in as a coping mechanism for emotional distress. By understanding the root causes of self-harm and implementing strategies for breaking the cycle, individuals can foster healing, develop healthier coping mechanisms, and work towards a future where emotional well-being thrives. Embrace the journey of self-discovery and recovery, surround yourself with support, and remember that there is hope for healing and growth.

Chapter 22: Exploring Borderline Personality Disorder and Emotional Instability

In this chapter, we will delve into the intricacies of BPD, explore its impact on individuals' lives, and discuss strategies for managing emotions and fostering stability.

Borderline personality disorder is a complex mental health condition characterized by intense emotional experiences, difficulty regulating emotions, unstable relationships, and a distorted sense of self. Individuals with BPD often experience intense fear of abandonment, have a fragile self-image, and struggle with impulsivity. While living with BPD can be challenging, it is important to approach this topic with empathy, understanding, and non-judgment.

Let's explore borderline personality disorder and emotional instability more closely:

Emotional dysregulation: Emotional dysregulation is a core feature of BPD. Individuals with BPD may experience emotions more intensely and have difficulty managing or recovering from emotional upsets. They may have rapid and intense mood swings, experience feelings of emptiness or chronic boredom, and struggle with emotional reactivity. Emotions can fluctuate quickly, causing distress and impacting relationships and daily functioning.

Fear of abandonment: Individuals with BPD often have an intense fear of abandonment. They may go to great lengths to avoid real or perceived abandonment, such as becoming overly dependent on others, engaging in impulsive behaviors, or experiencing intense anger or anxiety when they anticipate separation. This fear can strain relationships and contribute to a cycle of emotional instability.

Unstable relationships: BPD is often associated with unstable and intense relationships. Individuals with BPD may have difficulty maintaining consistent and healthy relationships. They may idealize others initially, but quickly switch to devaluing them, leading to frequent conflicts and emotional turmoil. This pattern can make it challenging to develop and sustain stable connections with others.

Now that we understand the basics of BPD and emotional instability, let's discuss strategies for managing emotions and fostering stability:

Seek professional help: If you suspect you may have BPD, it is crucial to seek professional help. Mental health professionals experienced in working with BPD can provide a proper diagnosis, assess your unique needs, and develop an individualized treatment plan. Therapy, such as dialectical behavior therapy (DBT), is considered the gold standard for BPD treatment and focuses on building skills for emotion regulation, distress tolerance, and interpersonal effectiveness.

Develop emotion regulation skills: Learning effective strategies for managing and regulating emotions is key for individuals with BPD. This may involve identifying triggers and warning signs, practicing mindfulness techniques to increase self-awareness, and learning healthy coping mechanisms such as deep breathing exercises, grounding techniques, or engaging in activities that promote relaxation and self-soothing.

Build a support network: Surround yourself with understanding and supportive individuals who can provide empathy, validation, and practical assistance. Engage in therapy groups specifically designed for BPD, such as DBT skills groups, to connect with others who share similar experiences. Building a strong support network can help combat feelings of isolation, offer a sense of belonging, and provide resources for managing emotional instability.

Practice self-care: Prioritize self-care activities that promote your overall well-being. Engage in activities that bring you joy, relaxation, and a sense of fulfillment. This may include pursuing hobbies, spending time in nature, practicing self-compassion, getting enough restful sleep, and maintaining a balanced lifestyle. Taking care of your physical, mental, and emotional health can contribute to greater stability and well-being.

Develop healthy coping mechanisms: Focus on developing healthy coping mechanisms to manage stress and emotional triggers. This may involve engaging in regular exercise, practicing relaxation techniques such as yoga or meditation, journaling, seeking creative outlets, or participating in support groups. Healthy coping mechanisms can provide a sense of control, promote emotional regulation, and foster stability.

Set boundaries: Establishing clear boundaries in relationships is essential for individuals with BPD. Communicate your needs, preferences, and limits with others. Learning to say no, expressing your emotions assertively, and maintaining a balance between independence and interdependence can help create healthier and more stable connections with others.

Develop a crisis plan: Creating a crisis plan can provide structure and guidance during moments of intense emotional distress. A crisis plan includes strategies for managing emotional crises, identifying emergency contacts, and utilizing professional resources. Having a plan in place can increase feelings of safety, promote stability, and empower individuals to seek appropriate support when needed.

Celebrate progress and practice self-acceptance: Recognize and celebrate your progress, no matter how small. Recovery from BPD is a journey that takes time and effort. Embrace self-acceptance, acknowledging that you are worthy of love and understanding. Practice self-compassion and be patient with yourself as you navigate the ups and downs of emotional instability. Remember that healing and growth are possible with dedication and support.

So, borderline personality disorder is a complex mental health condition characterized by emotional dysregulation, fear of abandonment, and unstable relationships. By seeking professional help, developing emotion regulation skills, building a support network, practicing self-care, developing healthy coping mechanisms, setting boundaries, creating a crisis plan, and embracing self-acceptance, individuals with BPD can manage their emotions, foster stability, and work towards a future where emotional well-being thrives. Embrace the journey of self-discovery and healing, focus on self-care and self-compassion, and remember that there is hope for stability and growth.

Chapter 23: The Challenges of Schizophrenia and Approaches to Treatment

In this chapter, we will delve into the intricacies of schizophrenia, explore its impact on individuals' lives, and discuss approaches to treatment and management.

Schizophrenia is a chronic mental health disorder that affects a person's perception of reality, thinking patterns, emotions, and behavior. It is characterized by a range of symptoms, including hallucinations, delusions, disorganized thinking, disorganized speech, and diminished emotional expression. While living with schizophrenia can be challenging, it is important to approach this topic with empathy, understanding, and non-judgment.

Let's explore the challenges of schizophrenia and the approaches to treatment and management more closely:

Hallucinations and delusions: Hallucinations are sensory experiences that seem real but occur in the absence of external stimuli. Individuals with schizophrenia may experience auditory, visual, olfactory, or tactile hallucinations. Delusions, on the other hand, are firmly held beliefs that are not based in reality. They can involve paranoia, grandiosity, or feelings of persecution. These symptoms can significantly impact a person's perception of reality and daily functioning.

Disorganized thinking and speech: Disorganized thinking and speech are common in schizophrenia. Individuals may struggle to connect their thoughts logically, leading to disjointed or incoherent speech patterns. They may exhibit difficulty organizing their thoughts or expressing themselves clearly, which can affect communication and social interactions.

Emotional and social difficulties: Schizophrenia can affect an individual's emotional expression and social functioning. Some individuals may exhibit reduced emotional expression, appearing detached or showing a limited range of emotions. Others may experience heightened emotional states, such as intense anxiety or depression. These emotional difficulties can impact relationships and daily functioning.

Now that we understand the challenges of schizophrenia, let's discuss approaches to treatment and management:

Medication: Medication is a cornerstone of schizophrenia treatment. Antipsychotic medications help manage the symptoms of schizophrenia by reducing hallucinations, delusions, and disorganized thinking. It is important for individuals with schizophrenia to work closely with a healthcare professional to find the right medication and dosage that effectively balances symptom management and potential side effects.

Therapy and psychosocial interventions: In addition to medication, therapy and psychosocial interventions play a crucial role in managing schizophrenia. Cognitive-behavioral therapy (CBT) can help individuals identify and challenge distorted thoughts and beliefs, develop coping strategies, and improve social skills. Family therapy and support groups can provide education, support, and resources for both individuals with schizophrenia and their loved ones.

Recovery-oriented approaches: Recovery-oriented approaches focus on empowering individuals with schizophrenia to live fulfilling lives despite the challenges of the disorder. These approaches emphasize personal strengths, self-advocacy, and goal setting. They promote holistic well-being, including physical health, social connections, meaningful activities, and a sense of purpose.

Supportive services: Accessing supportive services is crucial for individuals with schizophrenia. Case management services can help coordinate treatment, connect individuals with community resources, and provide ongoing support. Vocational rehabilitation programs can assist individuals in finding and maintaining employment. Housing assistance programs can ensure stable and supportive living environments.

Social support: Building a strong support network is vital for individuals with schizophrenia. Surround yourself with understanding and supportive family members, friends, or support groups who can provide empathy, validation, and practical assistance. Engaging in support groups specific to schizophrenia can offer a sense of belonging, reduce isolation, and provide valuable insights and resources.

Lifestyle modifications: Incorporating lifestyle modifications can contribute to overall well-being and symptom management. Engaging in regular physical activity, maintaining a balanced diet, getting enough restful sleep, and reducing stress levels can positively impact both physical and mental health. It is important to consult with healthcare professionals to ensure that any lifestyle changes align with individual needs and treatment plans.

Early intervention and ongoing care: Early intervention is crucial in managing schizophrenia. Timely diagnosis, appropriate treatment, and ongoing care can help minimize the impact of symptoms and improve long-term outcomes. Regular monitoring, medication management, and therapy sessions can help individuals maintain stability and address any emerging challenges.

Education and self-advocacy: Educating oneself about schizophrenia, its symptoms, and treatment options can empower individuals to become active participants in their own care. Learning about the disorder can help individuals better understand their experiences, reduce stigma, and advocate for their needs within the healthcare system and wider community.

So, schizophrenia is a complex mental health disorder characterized by a range of symptoms that significantly impact an individual's perception of reality, thinking patterns, emotions, and behavior. Through a combination of medication, therapy, psychosocial interventions, recovery-oriented approaches, supportive services, social support, lifestyle modifications, early intervention, ongoing care, education, and self-advocacy, individuals with schizophrenia can effectively manage symptoms, foster well-being, and work towards a future where stability and quality of life thrive. Embrace the journey of self-discovery and resilience, surround yourself with support, and remember that there is hope for healing and growth.

Chapter 24: Autism Spectrum Disorder (ASD) and Mental Health Considerations

In this chapter, we will delve into the intricacies of ASD, explore its impact on individuals' lives, and discuss the importance of addressing mental health needs.

Autism spectrum disorder is a neurodevelopmental condition characterized by challenges in social interaction, communication, and restricted or repetitive behaviors. Individuals with ASD may have unique strengths and differences in how they perceive and interact with the world. While living with ASD can present unique challenges, it is important to approach this topic with empathy, understanding, and acceptance.

Let's explore autism spectrum disorder and its mental health considerations more closely:

Social interaction challenges: Individuals with ASD may experience difficulties with social interaction and communication. They may have challenges with understanding social cues, engaging in reciprocal conversations, or interpreting nonverbal communication. These social interaction challenges can lead to feelings of isolation, frustration, and potential mental health concerns.

Sensory sensitivities: Many individuals with ASD have heightened sensory sensitivities, making them more sensitive to sensory stimuli such as loud noises, bright lights, or certain textures. These sensitivities can be overwhelming and may contribute to anxiety, stress, or difficulties with emotional regulation.

Restricted interests and repetitive behaviors: Individuals with ASD often have intense interests in specific topics and engage in repetitive behaviors or routines. While these interests and behaviors can provide comfort and structure, they may also limit flexibility and social engagement. The frustration that can arise from disruptions to these routines or difficulty pursuing these interests may impact mental well-being.

Now that we understand the basics of ASD and its mental health considerations, let's discuss the importance of addressing mental health needs:

Early identification and intervention: Early identification of ASD and associated mental health needs is essential. Early intervention services can provide support and resources to address social, communication, and behavioral challenges. Recognizing and addressing mental health needs early can contribute to better outcomes and improved well-being.

Individualized approach: Each individual with ASD is unique, and it is important to take an individualized approach to address their mental health needs. Recognize and respect their strengths, interests, and challenges. Collaborate with healthcare professionals, educators, and therapists to develop an individualized plan that addresses their specific mental health concerns.

Sensory accommodations: Creating sensory-friendly environments and providing accommodations for individuals with ASD can help reduce sensory overload and promote well-being. This may involve minimizing sensory distractions, providing sensory tools or spaces for self-regulation, and considering individual sensory sensitivities when designing environments or activities.

Communication support: Individuals with ASD may benefit from specific communication supports to express their emotions and mental health needs. Augmentative and alternative communication (AAC) systems, visual supports, or social stories can facilitate effective communication and emotional expression. Encourage the use of these tools and provide opportunities for open and meaningful communication.

Emotional regulation strategies: Teach and support individuals with ASD in developing effective emotional regulation strategies. This may include visual schedules, deep breathing exercises, mindfulness techniques, or engaging in preferred activities as a way to manage stress and anxiety. Providing tools and strategies for emotional regulation can enhance well-being and coping skills.

Social skills development: Social skills training can play a crucial role in addressing mental health needs in individuals with ASD. Teach and practice social skills through structured activities, role-playing, or social groups. Focus on building skills such as turn-taking, perspective-taking, and understanding social cues to promote social engagement and reduce feelings of isolation.

Mental health support services: Access to mental health support services is vital for individuals with ASD. This may involve working with therapists or counselors experienced in working with individuals on the autism spectrum. These professionals can provide strategies for managing anxiety, addressing depression, or addressing other mental health concerns that may arise.

Family and community support: Family and community support play a crucial role in addressing mental health needs in individuals with ASD. Families can provide emotional support, advocate for their loved ones, and connect with support groups or organizations dedicated to autism and mental health. Engaging in community activities and building social connections can also contribute to overall well-being. So, autism spectrum disorder is a neurodevelopmental condition that presents unique challenges in social interaction, communication, and behavior. By recognizing the mental health considerations associated with ASD and addressing them through early identification, individualized approaches, sensory accommodations, communication support, emotional regulation strategies, social skills development, mental health support services, and family and community support, individuals with ASD can thrive and experience enhanced well-being. Embrace the journey of understanding, acceptance, and support, and remember that everyone deserves to live a fulfilling and meaningful life.

Chapter 25: Attention-Deficit/Hyperactivity Disorder (ADHD): Strategies for Management

Attention-deficit/hyperactivity disorder is a neurodevelopmental condition that affects both children and adults. It is characterized by persistent patterns of inattention, hyperactivity, and impulsivity that can impact various aspects of life, including academics, work, relationships, and overall well-being. While living with ADHD can present unique challenges, it is important to approach this topic with empathy, understanding, and a positive outlook.

Let's explore ADHD and strategies for its management more closely:

Inattention: Individuals with ADHD often struggle with maintaining attention and focus, particularly in tasks or activities that require sustained mental effort. They may become easily distracted, have difficulty organizing tasks, lose important items, or have trouble following through on instructions. These challenges can impact productivity and academic or professional performance.

Hyperactivity: Hyperactivity is another hallmark of ADHD, particularly in children. Individuals with ADHD may exhibit excessive motor activity, such as fidgeting, restlessness, or difficulty staying seated. They may also have difficulty engaging in quiet activities or waiting their turn. Hyperactivity can disrupt daily routines and cause frustration for both the individual with ADHD and those around them.

Impulsivity: Impulsivity refers to acting without thinking about the consequences. Individuals with ADHD may have difficulty inhibiting their immediate reactions or responses, leading to impulsive behaviors. This can manifest as interrupting others, making impulsive decisions, or engaging in risky behaviors. Impulsivity can have social and emotional consequences and may contribute to challenges in relationships and self-regulation.

Now, let's discuss strategies for managing ADHD:

Education and self-awareness: Learning about ADHD and understanding its impact can empower individuals to better manage their symptoms. Educate yourself about ADHD, its characteristics, and its effects. Recognize your strengths and challenges and develop a positive mindset about your abilities. Understanding how ADHD manifests in your life is the first step toward developing effective strategies.

Establish routines and organization systems: Create structured routines and organizational systems to help manage time, tasks, and responsibilities. Break tasks into smaller, manageable steps, and use visual reminders or digital tools to stay organized. Establishing consistent routines can provide a sense of predictability and reduce the likelihood of forgetting or becoming overwhelmed.

Use visual aids and reminders: Visual aids and reminders can be helpful in maintaining focus and staying on track. Utilize calendars, to-do lists, or smartphone apps to keep track of deadlines, appointments, and tasks. Visual cues can serve as reminders and help with time management and prioritization.

Break tasks into manageable chunks: Breaking down tasks into smaller, more manageable chunks can make them less overwhelming. Focus on one step at a time, and reward yourself for completing each step. This approach can increase productivity, reduce procrastination, and provide a sense of accomplishment along the way.

Manage distractions: Minimize distractions in your environment to enhance focus. Create a designated workspace or study area that is free from clutter and noise. Use noise-cancelling headphones or white noise machines to help filter out distractions. Additionally, consider using website blockers or apps that limit access to social media during designated work or study periods.

Develop time-management skills: Time management is essential for individuals with ADHD. Break tasks or activities into time blocks, setting specific start and end times. Use timers or alarms to stay on schedule and provide a visual representation of time passing. Experiment with different strategies to find what works best for you, whether it's using a planner, digital reminders, or other time-management techniques.

Seek support and accommodations: Reach out for support from family, friends, or support groups for individuals with ADHD. Share your experiences, challenges, and successes with others who can provide empathy and understanding. Additionally, consider seeking accommodations in academic or work settings, such as extended time for tasks or access to quiet spaces for improved concentration.

Practice self-care and stress management: Prioritize self-care activities to support your overall well-being. Engage in regular exercise, get enough restful sleep, maintain a balanced diet, and incorporate stress-management techniques such as mindfulness or relaxation exercises. Taking care of your physical and mental health can help manage ADHD symptoms and enhance your overall functioning.

Consider therapy and coaching: Therapy or coaching can provide valuable support for individuals with ADHD. Cognitive-behavioral therapy (CBT) can help identify and challenge negative thinking patterns and develop coping strategies. ADHD coaching can provide guidance, accountability, and practical tools for managing ADHD-related challenges.

Celebrate successes and practice self-compassion: Celebrate your successes, no matter how small. Acknowledge your efforts, progress, and accomplishments along the way. Practice self-compassion and embrace a positive mindset. Remember that managing ADHD is a continuous journey, and setbacks are a natural part of the process.

So, attention-deficit/hyperactivity disorder is a neurodevelopmental condition that presents challenges in attention, hyperactivity, and impulsivity. By employing strategies such as education and self-awareness, establishing routines and organization systems, using visual aids and reminders, breaking tasks into manageable chunks, managing distractions, developing time-management skills, seeking support and accommodations, practicing self-care and stress management, considering therapy, or coaching, and celebrating successes, individuals with ADHD can effectively manage their symptoms and thrive in various aspects of life. Embrace your strengths, explore strategies that work for you, and remember that with the right support and strategies, you can navigate life successfully with ADHD.

Chapter 26: Understanding and Treating Personality Disorders

In this chapter, we will delve into the intricacies of personality disorders, explore different types, and discuss approaches to treatment and support.

Personality disorders are characterized by patterns of inflexible and maladaptive thinking, feeling, and behaving that deviate from societal norms. These patterns often manifest across different life areas, causing distress and impairing social, occupational, or interpersonal functioning. It is important to approach this topic with empathy, understanding, and non-judgment, as individuals with personality disorders can experience significant challenges in their lives.

Let's explore personality disorders more closely:

Different types of personality disorders: There are various types of personality disorders, each with its own distinct features and patterns of behavior. Some common types include borderline personality disorder (BPD), narcissistic personality disorder (NPD), antisocial personality disorder (ASPD), and avoidant personality disorder (AvPD). Each type has unique characteristics and poses specific challenges for individuals.

Core features of personality disorders: Personality disorders are characterized by enduring patterns of behavior and thinking that significantly deviate from cultural norms. These patterns may involve difficulties in self-identity, emotional regulation, establishing and maintaining healthy relationships, and managing stress. The severity and impact of these features can vary among individuals.

Now, let's discuss approaches to understanding and treating personality disorders:

Accurate diagnosis and assessment: Accurate diagnosis and assessment are crucial for understanding personality disorders and tailoring appropriate treatment plans. Mental health professionals use clinical interviews, self-report measures, and observation to gather information and assess symptoms. A comprehensive evaluation helps identify the specific personality disorder and any co-occurring mental health conditions.

Psychotherapy: Psychotherapy, particularly long-term and evidence-based approaches, is a primary treatment modality for personality disorders. Various therapeutic approaches can be effective, such as dialectical behavior therapy (DBT) for BPD, cognitive-behavioral therapy (CBT), schema therapy, or transference-focused therapy. These therapies aim to address maladaptive thoughts, beliefs, and behaviors, enhance emotion regulation skills, improve interpersonal functioning, and promote overall well-being.

Medication, if necessary: While there is no specific medication approved for personality disorders, medications may be prescribed to manage co-occurring symptoms, such as depression, anxiety, or mood instability. Antidepressants, mood stabilizers, or antipsychotic medications may be used on a case-by-case basis. Medication is often combined with psychotherapy to address both the underlying personality disorder and any co-occurring conditions.

Supportive and structured environments: Creating supportive and structured environments can be beneficial for individuals with personality disorders. Residential treatment programs, day treatment programs, or therapeutic communities can offer a structured setting where individuals can learn and practice coping skills, receive support, and engage in therapeutic activities. These environments provide a safe and supportive space for individuals to work on their recovery.

Group therapy and support: Group therapy can be particularly helpful for individuals with personality disorders, as it provides an opportunity to learn from others, practice interpersonal skills, and receive support. Group therapy can help individuals develop healthier relationship patterns, gain perspective from others with similar experiences, and reduce feelings of isolation. Support groups specifically tailored for personality disorders can also be valuable sources of understanding and empathy.

Self-help and self-care: Engaging in self-help strategies and practicing self-care can contribute to the management of personality disorders. These may include activities such as journaling, engaging in hobbies or creative outlets, practicing mindfulness or relaxation techniques, maintaining a balanced lifestyle, seeking social support, and educating oneself about the specific personality disorder. These self-care practices can enhance well-being and empower individuals in their recovery journey.

Collaborative treatment and care coordination: Collaborative treatment and care coordination involve the involvement of various healthcare professionals, such as psychiatrists, psychologists, therapists, and social workers, to provide comprehensive care. This approach ensures that different aspects of an individual's treatment are addressed, including medication management, therapy, support services, and social or vocational support. Collaboration among healthcare providers promotes a holistic and integrated approach to treatment.

Patience and understanding: Treating personality disorders requires patience and understanding, both from the individual with the disorder and their support network. Recovery from personality disorders takes time, and progress may be gradual. It is essential to foster a non-judgmental and empathetic environment, offering support and encouragement throughout the process. Celebrating small victories and milestones can help maintain motivation and optimism.

So, personality disorders encompass a range of mental health conditions characterized by enduring patterns of maladaptive thoughts, feelings, and behaviors. Through accurate diagnosis and assessment, psychotherapy, medication if necessary, supportive and structured environments, group therapy and support, self-help and self-care practices, collaborative treatment, and care coordination, individuals with personality disorders can work towards managing their symptoms, improving their interpersonal functioning, and fostering overall well-being. Embrace the journey of understanding, provide support, and remember that with proper care, individuals can experience growth, resilience, and a meaningful life.

Chapter 27: The Role of Therapy in Supporting Mental Health

Therapy, also known as psychotherapy or counseling, is a collaborative process between a trained mental health professional and an individual seeking support. It provides a safe and confidential space for individuals to explore their thoughts, feelings, and experiences, with the goal of improving their mental well-being and overall quality of life. Therapy is not just for those with diagnosed mental health conditions; it can benefit anyone seeking personal growth, self-exploration, or support during challenging times.

Let's explore the role of therapy in supporting mental health more closely:

Creating a safe and non-judgmental space: One of the fundamental aspects of therapy is the creation of a safe and non-judgmental space. This environment allows individuals to express themselves openly, without fear of criticism or rejection. Therapists are trained to provide empathy, understanding, and support, fostering a trusting relationship that enables individuals to explore their thoughts, emotions, and experiences.

Promoting self-awareness and insight: Therapy can help individuals gain a deeper understanding of themselves and their unique experiences. Through guided self-reflection and exploration, therapists assist individuals in uncovering patterns, beliefs, and emotions that may contribute to their current challenges. Increased self-awareness allows individuals to make more informed choices, identify areas for personal growth, and make positive changes in their lives.

Developing coping strategies and skills: Therapy equips individuals with practical coping strategies and skills to navigate life's challenges more effectively. Therapists teach techniques such as relaxation exercises, mindfulness practices, and communication skills. These tools enable individuals to manage stress, regulate their emotions, improve relationships, and enhance overall well-being.

Addressing mental health conditions: Therapy is a valuable resource for individuals with diagnosed mental health conditions.

Therapists are trained to understand various mental health disorders and provide evidence-based treatments tailored to the specific needs of each individual. They can assist individuals in managing symptoms, reducing distress, and improving their daily functioning. Common therapeutic approaches include cognitive-behavioral therapy (CBT), dialectical behavior therapy (DBT), and psychodynamic therapy.

Facilitating personal growth and self-empowerment: Therapy supports personal growth and self-empowerment by providing individuals with the tools and guidance to overcome obstacles and achieve their goals. Therapists act as supportive partners, helping individuals tap into their strengths, identify their values, and develop strategies to live a more fulfilling and authentic life. Therapy empowers individuals to take charge of their mental health and make positive changes in various areas of their lives.

Enhancing interpersonal relationships: Therapy can greatly benefit individuals in their relationships with others. Therapists can help individuals improve communication skills, navigate conflicts, and develop healthier relationship patterns. Through exploration of past experiences and patterns, therapy helps individuals gain insights into how their behaviors and beliefs impact their interactions with others. This self-awareness can lead to more fulfilling and satisfying relationships.

Providing support during life transitions and crises: Life transitions and crises can be challenging to navigate on our own. Therapy provides a supportive space for individuals to process emotions, gain clarity, and develop strategies for coping during difficult times. Whether it's a job loss, a relationship breakdown, or the loss of a loved one, therapy can offer guidance, validation, and practical support to help individuals navigate these transitions and emerge stronger.

Tailoring therapy to individual needs: Therapy is a highly individualized process, tailored to meet each person's unique needs and goals. Therapists work collaboratively with individuals to develop personalized treatment plans. They take into account factors such as cultural background, personal preferences, and specific mental health concerns to ensure therapy is effective and relevant. The flexibility of therapy allows for a personalized approach that honors the diversity and uniqueness of each individual.

Normalizing experiences and reducing stigma: Therapy helps to normalize mental health experiences and reduce the stigma surrounding seeking support. By providing a safe and accepting space, therapy validates individuals' experiences, assuring them that their struggles are valid and that they are not alone. Engaging in therapy encourages open conversations about mental health, promoting a culture of understanding and compassion.

So, therapy plays a vital role in supporting mental health and well-being. Through creating a safe and non-judgmental space, promoting self-awareness and insight, developing coping strategies and skills, addressing mental health conditions, facilitating personal growth and self-empowerment, enhancing interpersonal relationships, providing support during life transitions and crises, tailoring therapy to individual needs, and normalizing experiences, therapy empowers individuals to navigate their mental health journeys with resilience and strength. Embrace the opportunity to seek support, remember that it is a sign of strength, and allow therapy to guide you towards a healthier and more fulfilling life.

Chapter 28: Medication and Psychopharmacology in Mental Health Treatment

Medication, in conjunction with other treatment modalities such as therapy, can play an essential role in managing various mental health conditions. It is important to approach this topic with empathy, understanding, and an open mind, as medication is a personal decision that requires careful consideration and collaboration with healthcare professionals.

Let's explore the role of medication and psychopharmacology in mental health treatment more closely:

Understanding psychopharmacology: Psychopharmacology is the branch of medicine that focuses on the use of medications to treat mental health conditions. It involves the study of how different medications interact with the brain and nervous system to alleviate symptoms and improve overall well-being. Psychopharmacology aims to restore the balance of chemicals in the brain that may be disrupted in various mental health disorders.

Medications for mental health: There is a wide range of medications available to treat different mental health conditions. Antidepressants, mood stabilizers, antipsychotics, anxiolytics, and stimulants are among the commonly prescribed medications. Each medication works in a specific way to target symptoms associated with particular disorders. It is important to note that medication selection depends on factors such as the specific diagnosis, individual symptoms, and personal considerations.

Now, let's discuss the role of medication and psychopharmacology in mental health treatment:

Symptom management: Medication can help alleviate symptoms associated with mental health conditions, providing relief from distressing experiences. For example, antidepressants are commonly prescribed to help regulate mood and reduce symptoms of depression. Mood stabilizers can help manage mood swings in individuals with bipolar disorder. Antipsychotics can help reduce hallucinations and delusions in individuals with schizophrenia. Medication can serve as a valuable tool in managing symptoms and improving overall functioning.

Enhancing therapy outcomes: Medication can complement therapy and enhance its effectiveness. For some individuals, medication can help alleviate symptoms that may interfere with therapy, such as severe anxiety or depressive symptoms. By reducing the intensity of symptoms, individuals may be better able to engage in therapy, absorb insights, and apply coping strategies. Medication can support individuals on their journey of self-discovery and personal growth.

Improving quality of life: Medication can significantly improve an individual's quality of life by reducing the impact of symptoms on daily functioning. For instance, stimulant medications, such as those prescribed for attention-deficit/hyperactivity disorder (ADHD), can help improve focus, attention, and impulse control, allowing individuals to better navigate academic or work-related tasks. Medication can restore stability, enhance well-being, and promote an improved quality of life.

Personalized approach: Medication is not a one-size-fits-all solution. It requires a personalized approach in collaboration with healthcare professionals. The choice of medication, dosage, and duration of treatment depends on factors such as the specific mental health condition, individual symptoms, medical history, potential side effects, and personal preferences. It is essential to work closely with a healthcare professional to find the medication that is most effective and well-tolerated for each individual.

Considerations and potential side effects: Like any medical intervention, medication comes with considerations and potential side effects. It is important to have open and honest discussions with healthcare professionals about potential risks, benefits, and side effects. Common side effects may include drowsiness, changes in appetite, weight gain, gastrointestinal symptoms, or sexual side effects. However, not everyone experiences side effects, and they are often temporary and manageable. Regular communication with healthcare professionals is crucial to monitor progress, adjust medication as needed, and address any concerns.

Collaborative decision-making: The decision to use medication should be a collaborative process involving the individual, their healthcare professional, and potentially their support network. It is important to have a thorough understanding of the benefits and potential risks of medication. Ask questions, express concerns, and share any relevant information about personal medical history, allergies, or other medications being taken. Collaborative decision-making ensures that the individual's unique needs, preferences, and values are taken into account.

Ongoing monitoring and follow-up: Once medication is initiated, ongoing monitoring and follow-up are essential. Regular check-ins with healthcare professionals allow for adjustments to medication dosages, addressing any emerging side effects, and monitoring treatment progress. Open and honest communication is key in order to optimize the benefits of medication and ensure its continued effectiveness.

Integrating holistic approaches: Medication is often most effective when integrated with other holistic approaches to mental health. Therapy, lifestyle modifications, self-care practices, and social support all play important roles in promoting overall well-being. It is important to view medication as one tool among many, rather than the sole solution. Combining medication with other strategies can create a comprehensive and multifaceted approach to mental health treatment. So, medication and psychopharmacology can be valuable tools in supporting mental health. By alleviating symptoms, enhancing therapy outcomes, improving quality of life, and promoting personalized and collaborative care, medication can be an important part of an individual's mental health journey. It is crucial to approach medication decisions with thorough consideration, in collaboration with healthcare professionals, while also integrating holistic approaches. Embrace the opportunity to have open and informed discussions, and remember that the goal of medication is to support individuals in achieving optimal mental well-being and living fulfilling lives.

Chapter 29: Integrating Mindfulness and Meditation into Mental Health Care

Mindfulness and meditation have gained increasing recognition in recent years as valuable tools for promoting mental well-being. These practices involve cultivating present-moment awareness and developing a non-judgmental and accepting attitude toward one's thoughts, emotions, and experiences. Incorporating mindfulness and meditation into mental health care can have transformative effects, allowing individuals to navigate their inner landscapes with greater clarity, resilience, and compassion.

Let's explore the integration of mindfulness and meditation into mental health care more closely:

Understanding mindfulness and meditation: Mindfulness involves paying attention to the present moment without judgment. It involves intentionally directing your awareness to the sensations, thoughts, and emotions that arise in the present moment. Meditation, on the other hand, refers to a set of practices that cultivate mindfulness, typically through focused attention or open awareness. These practices can involve focusing on the breath, bodily sensations, or specific mental imagery.

Benefits of mindfulness and meditation: Mindfulness and meditation have been found to have a wide range of benefits for mental health and overall well-being. They can help reduce stress, enhance emotional regulation, improve attention and focus, promote self-compassion, increase resilience, and cultivate a greater sense of overall calm and contentment. These practices also have the potential to reduce symptoms of anxiety, depression, and other mental health conditions.

Now, let's discuss the integration of mindfulness and meditation into mental health care:

Cultivating self-awareness: Mindfulness and meditation provide individuals with the opportunity to cultivate self-awareness, gaining a deeper understanding of their thoughts, emotions, and patterns of behavior. By developing the ability to observe their inner experiences without judgment, individuals can gain insights into their triggers, automatic reactions, and the underlying causes of their mental health challenges. This increased self-awareness is a valuable foundation for personal growth and healing.

Embracing the present moment: Mental health challenges often arise from dwelling on past events or worrying about the future. Mindfulness and meditation help individuals anchor their attention in the present moment, allowing them to let go of regrets or anxieties and focus on what is happening right now. By embracing the present moment, individuals can cultivate a sense of peace and reduce the tendency to ruminate or catastrophize, leading to improved mental well-being.

Reducing stress and promoting relaxation: Mindfulness and meditation are powerful tools for stress reduction and relaxation. These practices help activate the relaxation response, which counteracts the body's stress response. Regular practice of mindfulness and meditation can lead to a reduction in cortisol (the stress hormone) levels, lower blood pressure, and a decreased heart rate. The ability to tap into a state of relaxation can contribute to improved mental health and overall physiological well-being.

Enhancing emotional regulation: Mindfulness and meditation foster emotional regulation by increasing awareness of one's emotions and developing a non-reactive stance towards them. By observing emotions as they arise without judgment, individuals can cultivate a greater capacity to respond to emotional triggers in a balanced and adaptive manner. These practices allow individuals to navigate difficult emotions with greater clarity and compassion, leading to improved emotional well-being.

Developing self-compassion and acceptance: Mindfulness and meditation promote self-compassion and acceptance, which are vital components of mental health care. These practices encourage individuals to cultivate a kind and non-judgmental attitude toward themselves, embracing imperfections and acknowledging their inherent worth. By fostering self-compassion and acceptance, individuals can reduce self-criticism, increase self-esteem, and develop a greater sense of self-acceptance and self-love.

Integrating mindfulness into daily life: The benefits of mindfulness and meditation extend beyond the formal practice. It is essential to integrate mindfulness into daily life, bringing a sense of presence and awareness to routine activities. This can be achieved by engaging in mindful eating, mindful walking, or simply taking moments throughout the day to pause, breathe, and reconnect with the present moment. By infusing mindfulness into daily life, individuals can sustain the benefits of the practice and enhance their overall well-being.

Combining mindfulness and therapy: Mindfulness can be integrated into various forms of therapy, enhancing their effectiveness. Therapists can incorporate mindfulness techniques into cognitive-behavioral therapy (CBT), dialectical behavior therapy (DBT), acceptance and commitment therapy (ACT), and other therapeutic approaches. Mindfulness-based interventions, such as mindfulness-based stress reduction (MBSR) and mindfulness-based cognitive therapy (MBCT), have also been developed and shown to be effective in addressing specific mental health conditions.

Accessing resources and guidance: Mindfulness and meditation can be learned and practiced independently, but accessing resources and guidance can enhance the experience. Many mindfulness apps, online programs, and guided meditation resources are available, offering structured practices and teachings. Joining mindfulness groups, attending retreats, or seeking the guidance of a qualified mindfulness teacher can provide additional support and deepen the practice.

So, integrating mindfulness and meditation into mental health care can bring about transformative effects, supporting mental well-being, and promoting personal growth. By cultivating self-awareness, embracing the present moment, reducing stress, enhancing emotional regulation, developing self-compassion, and integrating mindfulness into daily life, individuals can navigate their mental health journeys with greater resilience, clarity, and inner peace. Embrace the opportunity to explore mindfulness and meditation, and remember that the practice is a journey of self-discovery and self-care.

Chapter 30: Exploring the Benefits of Art and Music Therapy in Mental Health

Art and music have long been recognized as powerful forms of self-expression and communication. Art therapy and music therapy harness the transformative potential of these creative mediums to address emotional, psychological, and cognitive challenges. These therapies offer individuals alternative channels for self-discovery, healing, and personal exploration in a safe and supportive environment.

Let's explore the benefits of art and music therapy in mental health more closely:

Art therapy: Art therapy involves the use of visual arts, such as painting, drawing, sculpting, or collage, as a means of self-expression and therapeutic exploration. Through art-making, individuals can externalize their thoughts and emotions, gaining insights into their inner experiences and fostering self-awareness.

Music therapy: Music therapy utilizes the inherent qualities of music, including rhythm, melody, and harmony, to address emotional, cognitive, and social needs. Music therapists facilitate therapeutic experiences through singing, playing instruments, composing, or simply listening to music. Music therapy can be particularly effective in engaging individuals who may struggle with verbal expression.

Now, let's discuss the benefits of art and music therapy in mental health:

Emotional expression and regulation: Art and music therapy provide a non-verbal and creative outlet for emotional expression. Individuals can use colors, shapes, lines, or musical elements to represent their feelings, experiences, and inner narratives. The act of creating art or engaging in music-making can help release emotions, reduce emotional distress, and enhance emotional regulation skills. These therapies provide individuals with a safe space to express themselves authentically and process challenging emotions.

Self-exploration and self-discovery: Engaging in art and music therapy invites individuals to explore their inner world, reflect on their experiences, and gain insights into their thoughts, beliefs, and patterns of behavior. The creative process allows for self-reflection, providing individuals with opportunities to explore their identities, values, and personal narratives. Through art and music, individuals can discover new aspects of themselves and develop a deeper understanding of their own stories.

Enhancing communication and social skills: Art and music therapy can improve communication and social skills, particularly for individuals who may struggle with verbal expression or have difficulty engaging in traditional talk therapy. The creative process allows for alternative modes of communication, enabling individuals to express themselves and connect with others through art and music. These therapies can enhance social interactions, foster collaboration, and promote a sense of belonging and connectedness.

Stress reduction and relaxation: Engaging in art and music therapy can promote relaxation, reduce stress, and create a sense of calm. The creative process can serve as a form of mindfulness, allowing individuals to focus their attention on the present moment and experience a state of flow. The rhythmic and repetitive nature of art-making or music-playing can induce a relaxation response, leading to a decrease in anxiety, improved mood, and an overall sense of well-being.

Building self-esteem and self-confidence: Art and music therapy provide opportunities for individuals to experience a sense of accomplishment and build self-esteem. The act of creating something tangible and meaningful can boost self-confidence and foster a sense of mastery. The non-judgmental and supportive environment of therapy encourages individuals to embrace their creative abilities, fostering a positive self-image and a greater appreciation for their unique talents and strengths.

Processing trauma and promoting healing: Art and music therapy can be particularly effective in processing trauma and supporting individuals on their healing journeys. The creative process allows for the expression of complex and difficult emotions that may be challenging to articulate verbally. Through art and music, individuals can explore traumatic experiences, gain a sense of control, and promote emotional integration and healing.

Cognitive stimulation and rehabilitation: Art and music therapy can stimulate cognitive processes and support cognitive rehabilitation.

Engaging in art-making or music-playing can enhance attention, concentration, memory, and problem-solving skills. These therapies can be particularly beneficial for individuals with cognitive impairments, neurodevelopmental disorders, or neurological conditions.

Integrating art and music into daily life: The benefits of art and music therapy extend beyond the therapy sessions. Individuals can integrate art and music into their daily lives as creative outlets for self-expression, stress reduction, and personal enjoyment. Engaging in art or music as a hobby or leisure activity can provide ongoing support for mental well-being and serve as a source of fulfillment and joy.

So, art and music therapy offer unique and powerful avenues for self-expression, personal growth, and healing in mental health care. Through emotional expression and regulation, self-exploration, communication enhancement, stress reduction, building self-esteem, trauma processing, cognitive stimulation, and integration into daily life, these therapies can support individuals in navigating their mental health journeys. Embrace the opportunity to engage in art and music as tools for self-discovery and self-care, and remember that the creative process holds transformative potential for fostering well-being and fostering personal growth.

Chapter 31: Animal-Assisted Therapy: The Healing Power of Animals

Animals have an innate ability to connect with humans on an emotional level, offering unconditional love, companionship, and a sense of comfort. Animal-assisted therapy harnesses the unique bond between humans and animals to promote emotional healing, reduce stress, and enhance overall well-being. Whether it's interacting with dogs, cats, horses, or other animals, the therapeutic presence of these animals can have profound effects on individuals' mental health journeys.

Let's explore the healing power of animals and the practice of animal-assisted therapy more closely:

What is animal-assisted therapy: Animal-assisted therapy (AAT) involves the inclusion of animals in therapeutic interventions to achieve specific treatment goals. Trained animals, such as dogs or horses, work alongside mental health professionals to provide support and facilitate therapeutic experiences. AAT is a collaborative process that recognizes and utilizes the unique bond between humans and animals to enhance overall well-being.

Benefits of animal-assisted therapy: Animal-assisted therapy offers a range of benefits for mental health and well-being. Interacting with animals can help reduce anxiety, alleviate symptoms of depression, provide comfort and companionship, decrease feelings of loneliness, improve social interactions, and promote emotional regulation. The presence of animals has also been shown to reduce physiological indicators of stress, such as blood pressure and heart rate. These benefits can contribute to an enhanced therapeutic experience and support individuals on their path to healing.

Now, let's discuss the benefits and considerations of animal-assisted therapy in more detail:

Emotional support and companionship: Animals provide unconditional love, support, and companionship, which can be particularly beneficial for individuals experiencing feelings of loneliness, isolation, or low self-esteem. The presence of animals can create a sense of comfort, promote a feeling of being understood, and provide a source of emotional support during therapeutic sessions. The bond formed with animals can help individuals feel accepted and valued, fostering a positive therapeutic relationship.

Stress reduction and relaxation: Interacting with animals has been shown to reduce stress and induce a sense of calm. The tactile experience of petting or grooming animals can promote the release of oxytocin, a hormone associated with relaxation and bonding. Spending time with animals can also encourage individuals to focus on the present moment, diverting attention from stressors and promoting a state of mindfulness. The soothing presence of animals can lower blood pressure, decrease heart rate, and facilitate a sense of overall relaxation.

Enhanced social interactions and communication: Animals can serve as social catalysts, making it easier for individuals to engage in social interactions and communication. The non-judgmental and accepting nature of animals can create a safe space for individuals to practice social skills, build confidence, and develop trust. Animals can act as bridges between individuals, facilitating connections and fostering a sense of belonging and community.

Emotional regulation and self-expression: Animals can assist individuals in regulating their emotions and expressing themselves. Interacting with animals can provide a safe outlet for expressing difficult emotions, reducing anxiety, and promoting emotional release. Animals can help individuals develop emotional awareness, increase empathy, and improve their ability to identify and manage their feelings. The presence of animals can also create a nurturing and calming environment, allowing individuals to explore and process emotions more effectively.

Motivation and engagement: Animals have a natural ability to motivate and engage individuals, even when they may be struggling with low motivation or apathy. The joy and enthusiasm displayed by animals can be contagious, sparking a sense of playfulness and increasing motivation to participate in therapeutic activities. Animals can help individuals feel energized, inspired, and more open to exploration and personal growth.

Considerations and ethical considerations: While animal-assisted therapy can be highly beneficial, it is essential to consider the ethical considerations and ensure the well-being of the animals involved. The therapy animals should be carefully selected, appropriately trained, and receive regular veterinary care. The therapy sessions should prioritize the safety and comfort of both the individuals and the animals. A qualified mental health professional and an animal handler should be present during sessions to ensure the well-being of all involved parties.

Integrating animals into therapeutic interventions: Animals can be integrated into various therapeutic interventions, such as individual therapy, group therapy, or family therapy. For example, in individual therapy, animals may provide a calming presence during discussions of sensitive topics or assist in developing coping strategies. In group therapy, animals can facilitate communication and promote a sense of camaraderie among group members. The specific roles and activities of animals in therapy will depend on the therapeutic goals and the needs of the individuals involved.

Animal-assisted interventions beyond therapy: The benefits of animals extend beyond formal therapy sessions. Engaging with animals outside of therapy, such as interacting with a personal pet, volunteering at an animal shelter, or participating in equine-assisted activities, can also contribute to mental well-being. These interactions provide ongoing support, connection, and opportunities for growth and healing.

So, animal-assisted therapy harnesses the healing power of animals to promote emotional support, stress reduction, enhanced social interactions, emotional regulation, motivation, and engagement in therapeutic settings. Through the presence of animals, individuals can experience companionship, relaxation, and a sense of acceptance, leading to improved mental well-being and overall quality of life. It is important to approach animal-assisted therapy with ethical considerations, ensuring the well-being of the animals involved and maintaining a safe and supportive environment for all participants.

Embrace the opportunity to experience the healing power of animals in your mental health journey. Whether through formal animal-assisted therapy or engaging with animals in your daily life, the presence of these remarkable creatures can provide comfort, connection, and support. Remember to approach animals with respect, care, and appreciation for the unique bond they offer. Open your heart to the healing power of animals and allow their presence to guide you towards a brighter, more fulfilling path of well-being and emotional growth.

Chapter 32: Peer Support and Its Impact on Mental Health Recovery

Mental health recovery is a deeply personal and unique process. While professional support from therapists and healthcare providers is crucial, the support and understanding of peers who have shared similar experiences can be equally transformative. Peer support involves individuals with lived experience of mental health challenges coming together to provide empathy, encouragement, and practical guidance to one another.

Let's explore the impact of peer support on mental health recovery more closely:

What is peer support? Peer support involves individuals who have faced mental health challenges providing support and guidance to others who are on a similar journey. These individuals are often referred to as peer supporters, peers, or peer specialists. They offer lived experience, empathy, and practical insights to help others navigate their own mental health challenges.

Benefits of peer support: Peer support offers a range of benefits for mental health recovery. Connecting with peers who have faced similar experiences can provide a sense of validation, reduce feelings of isolation and stigma, increase hope, and foster a sense of belonging. Peer support can also enhance self-esteem, promote personal empowerment, and inspire individuals to take an active role in their own recovery.

Now, let's discuss the impact of peer support on mental health recovery in more detail:

Validation and understanding: Peer support creates an environment where individuals feel understood and validated. Peers share common experiences, challenges, and emotions, which can help individuals realize that they are not alone in their struggles. The shared understanding of peers can offer a sense of relief, as individuals no longer feel isolated or judged. This validation can be a powerful catalyst for healing and personal growth.

Reduction of stigma and self-judgment: Peer support helps combat the stigma associated with mental health challenges. Peers provide a non-judgmental space where individuals can openly discuss their experiences without fear of stigma or discrimination. By sharing their stories, peers challenge societal stereotypes and promote acceptance, self-acceptance, and self-compassion. Through peer support, individuals can develop a more positive and empowered perspective on their own mental health journey.

Increased hope and inspiration: Peer support instills hope by showcasing stories of resilience, recovery, and personal growth. Peers who have overcome similar challenges serve as living examples of what is possible, providing inspiration and motivation to others. By witnessing the progress and achievements of peers, individuals can develop a renewed sense of hope and believe in their own capacity for recovery.

Practical guidance and coping strategies: Peers offer practical guidance and coping strategies based on their own experiences. They can share insights on navigating the mental healthcare system, accessing community resources, and developing effective self-care practices. Peer supporters may provide information on therapy options, medication management, or alternative healing modalities. This practical guidance can empower individuals to make informed decisions and take proactive steps in their recovery.

Building a sense of belonging and community: Peer support creates a sense of belonging and community, which is crucial for mental health recovery. By connecting with others who have faced similar challenges, individuals can find acceptance, understanding, and a supportive network. Peer support groups, online communities, and in-person meetings offer opportunities to develop meaningful relationships, share experiences, and offer mutual encouragement. The sense of community can provide individuals with ongoing support and a sense of belonging on their recovery journey.

Empowerment and taking an active role in recovery: Peer support encourages individuals to take an active role in their own recovery. Peers promote self-advocacy, empowering individuals to voice their needs, seek appropriate support, and make informed choices. By witnessing the personal growth and resilience of peers, individuals gain confidence in their ability to navigate challenges, set goals, and make positive changes in their lives.

Peer support as a complement to professional treatment: Peer support is not a substitute for professional treatment but rather a valuable complement to it. Peers can work collaboratively with therapists, counselors, and healthcare providers to create a comprehensive and holistic approach to mental health care. The combination of professional expertise and lived experience can provide individuals with a well-rounded support system that addresses their unique needs.

Becoming a peer supporter: Engaging in peer support can be a transformative experience for both the person receiving support and the peer supporter. Some individuals may choose to become peer supporters themselves, using their lived experience to help others on their mental health journeys. Becoming a peer supporter offers opportunities for personal growth, deepened understanding, and a sense of purpose in supporting others. Training programs and certifications are available for individuals interested in pursuing a formal role as a peer supporter.

So, peer support plays a vital role in mental health recovery by offering validation, reducing stigma, fostering hope, providing practical guidance, building a sense of belonging, promoting empowerment, and complementing professional treatment. Connecting with peers who have faced similar challenges can be a transformative experience, offering support, understanding, and inspiration on the path to recovery. Embrace the power of peer support and seek opportunities to connect with others who can offer empathy, encouragement, and practical insights. Remember that together, as a community of peers, we can create a safe and supportive space for healing, growth, and resilience.

Chapter 33: Tackling Loneliness and Isolation for Improved Mental Health

Loneliness and isolation are universal human experiences that can profoundly impact our mental health. Despite living in a highly interconnected world, many individuals struggle with feelings of loneliness and a lack of meaningful connections. Understanding the effects of loneliness and isolation and implementing strategies to combat these challenges can contribute to improved mental well-being and overall life satisfaction.

Let's explore the impact of loneliness and isolation on mental health and strategies to tackle these issues more closely:

Understanding loneliness and isolation: Loneliness refers to the subjective feeling of being alone, disconnected, or lacking companionship, despite being surrounded by others. Isolation, on the other hand, is the objective state of being physically or socially separated from others. Loneliness and isolation often go hand in hand, but it is possible to feel lonely even in the presence of others or to experience isolation without feeling lonely. Both experiences can have negative consequences for mental health.

The effects of loneliness and isolation on mental health: Loneliness and isolation can have a significant impact on mental well-being. Prolonged periods of loneliness and isolation are associated with increased risk of developing mental health conditions such as depression, anxiety, and substance abuse. They can also contribute to decreased self-esteem, impaired cognitive function, and poor sleep quality. Addressing these challenges is essential for promoting mental health and overall well-being.

Now, let's discuss strategies to tackle loneliness and isolation and improve our mental health:

Cultivating meaningful connections: Building meaningful connections with others is a fundamental aspect of overcoming loneliness and isolation. This can involve reaching out to friends, family members, or colleagues to initiate conversations, plan activities, or simply spend quality time together. Engaging in shared interests, hobbies, or joining community groups or clubs can provide opportunities to meet like-minded individuals and forge new connections.

Nurturing existing relationships: It is important to invest time and effort into nurturing existing relationships. This can involve regularly checking in with loved ones, expressing gratitude for their presence in our lives, and actively listening and showing interest in their experiences. Small gestures of kindness and support can go a long way in maintaining strong and meaningful connections.

Seeking social support: Don't be afraid to reach out for support when you need it. Sharing your feelings of loneliness or isolation with trusted friends, family members, or mental health professionals can provide validation and help alleviate the burden. Support groups or online communities focused on mental health can also be valuable sources of connection and understanding.

Engaging in community activities: Participating in community activities or volunteering can be a great way to combat loneliness and isolation while making a positive impact. Getting involved in local initiatives, charities, or volunteering for causes that resonate with you can provide a sense of purpose, expand your social network, and create opportunities for meaningful connections.

Exploring online communities: The digital age offers numerous opportunities to connect with others through online communities and social media platforms. Engaging in online forums or groups focused on shared interests, hobbies, or mental health can help foster connections and provide a sense of belonging. However, it is essential to strike a balance and ensure that online interactions complement real-world connections rather than replacing them entirely.

Developing self-compassion and self-care practices: Loneliness and isolation can be emotionally challenging, but developing self-compassion and prioritizing self-care can help navigate these difficulties. Practice self-compassion by treating yourself with kindness, acknowledging your emotions without judgment, and engaging in self-care activities that nourish your mind, body, and spirit. This can include activities such as exercise, mindfulness, journaling, engaging in hobbies, or spending time in nature.

Seeking professional help: If feelings of loneliness and isolation persist and significantly impact your mental health, seeking professional help is a crucial step. Mental health professionals can provide guidance, support, and therapeutic interventions tailored to your specific needs. They can help explore the underlying causes of loneliness and isolation and develop strategies to address them effectively.

Embracing solitude and self-reflection: While loneliness and isolation can be challenging, there can also be value in embracing solitude and using it as an opportunity for self-reflection and personal growth. Spending time alone can allow for self-discovery, introspection, and the development of a deeper understanding of oneself. Engage in activities that promote self-reflection, such as meditation, journaling, or pursuing creative endeavors.

Practice active listening and empathy: When interacting with others, practice active listening and empathy. Show genuine interest in their experiences, validate their emotions, and seek to understand their perspective. Cultivating empathy creates a sense of connection and fosters deeper, more meaningful relationships.

Be open to new experiences: Step outside your comfort zone and be open to new experiences and opportunities for connection. Say yes to social invitations, explore new hobbies or interests, or join classes or workshops where you can meet people who share similar passions. Embracing novelty can help break the cycle of loneliness and isolation and broaden your social horizons.

So, tackling loneliness and isolation is crucial for improving mental health and overall well-being. By cultivating meaningful connections, nurturing existing relationships, seeking social support, engaging in community activities, exploring online communities, developing self-compassion, seeking professional help when needed, embracing solitude and self-reflection, practicing active listening and empathy, and being open to new experiences, we can gradually overcome these challenges and cultivate a sense of belonging and connectedness. Remember that building and maintaining meaningful connections is a journey, and it requires effort, vulnerability, and perseverance. By taking proactive steps and embracing opportunities for connection, we can create a supportive network and improve our mental health and overall quality of life.

Chapter 34: The Power of Positive Psychology in Enhancing Mental Well-being

Positive psychology is a field of study that focuses on the positive aspects of human experiences, such as happiness, well-being, resilience, and personal growth. It offers a fresh perspective that goes beyond merely treating mental illness to promote flourishing and thriving in individuals. By understanding and harnessing the power of positive emotions, character strengths, and meaningful connections, positive psychology empowers individuals to cultivate resilience, optimize well-being, and lead a more fulfilling life.

Let's explore the principles and benefits of positive psychology in enhancing mental well-being more closely:

Understanding positive psychology: Positive psychology shifts the focus from pathology and dysfunction to strengths, virtues, and positive experiences. It aims to understand what enables individuals to live meaningful and fulfilling lives and explores the factors that contribute to happiness, resilience, and overall well-being. By studying positive emotions, character strengths, positive relationships, and purposeful engagement, positive psychology offers evidence-based strategies for enhancing mental health.

The benefits of positive psychology: Incorporating positive psychology principles into our lives can have profound effects on our mental well-being. Research has shown that practicing positive psychology interventions can lead to increased happiness, greater life satisfaction, improved physical health, enhanced resilience, and reduced symptoms of depression and anxiety. By focusing on our strengths and cultivating positive emotions, we can experience a higher quality of life and develop the tools to navigate life's challenges more effectively.

Now, let's discuss how to apply positive psychology in enhancing mental well-being:

Cultivating gratitude: Gratitude is a powerful positive emotion that can shift our focus towards appreciation for the present moment. Engaging in gratitude practices, such as keeping a gratitude journal or expressing gratitude to others, can help reframe our mindset and foster a sense of contentment and well-being. Taking time each day to reflect on the things we are grateful for can cultivate a positive outlook and increase our overall happiness.

Building resilience through optimism: Optimism plays a crucial role in resilience—the ability to bounce back from adversity. By adopting an optimistic mindset and reframing challenges as opportunities for growth and learning, we can build resilience and navigate difficulties with a sense of hope and determination. Recognizing our own ability to overcome obstacles and cultivating a belief in our capacity for positive change can enhance our mental well-being and empower us to face life's challenges.

Discovering and utilizing strengths: Identifying and utilizing our strengths is a fundamental aspect of positive psychology. By recognizing and leveraging our unique character strengths—such as creativity, perseverance, kindness, or curiosity—we can engage in activities that align with our strengths, leading to a greater sense of fulfillment and accomplishment. Reflecting on our strengths and finding ways to incorporate them into our daily lives can boost our confidence, increase motivation, and improve overall well-being.

Nurturing positive relationships: Positive relationships are essential for our mental well-being. Cultivating and nurturing supportive and meaningful connections with family, friends, and communities can provide a sense of belonging, support, and fulfillment. Actively investing in our relationships, practicing empathy, and engaging in acts of kindness can foster positive connections and create a social support system that enhances our overall happiness and well-being.

Engaging in meaningful activities: Meaningful engagement in activities that align with our values and interests is a cornerstone of positive psychology. Pursuing activities that provide a sense of purpose, accomplishment, and joy can enhance our well-being and foster a sense of fulfillment. This can include hobbies, volunteer work, creative pursuits, or engaging in activities that contribute to a greater cause. By aligning our actions with our values, we can experience a greater sense of meaning and satisfaction in our lives.

Practicing mindfulness and savoring the present moment: Mindfulness involves being fully present in the moment and cultivating an awareness of our thoughts, feelings, and sensations without judgment. By practicing mindfulness, we can reduce stress, increase self-awareness, and enhance our ability to savor and appreciate the present moment. Engaging in mindfulness techniques, such as meditation or deep breathing exercises, can foster a sense of calm, improve our overall well-being, and help us cultivate a more positive perspective on life.

Fostering a growth mindset: Developing a growth mindset involves embracing challenges, seeing failures as learning opportunities, and believing in our capacity for growth and development. By cultivating a growth mindset, we can approach life's obstacles with resilience and view setbacks as temporary and surmountable. Embracing a growth mindset allows us to overcome self-limiting beliefs, expand our abilities, and foster a sense of personal growth and fulfillment.

Engaging in acts of kindness: Engaging in acts of kindness and altruism can have a positive impact on both our mental well-being and the well-being of others. Simple acts of kindness, such as offering a helping hand, expressing gratitude, or practicing random acts of kindness, can create a ripple effect of positivity and enhance our overall sense of connection and happiness.

So, positive psychology offers a refreshing perspective on mental well-being by focusing on strengths, positive emotions, meaningful connections, and purposeful engagement. By incorporating positive psychology principles into our lives, we can cultivate gratitude, build resilience, discover, and utilize our strengths, nurture positive relationships, engage in meaningful activities, practice mindfulness, foster a growth mindset, and engage in acts of kindness. Embracing the principles of positive psychology empowers us to lead more fulfilling lives, enhance our mental well-being, and navigate challenges with optimism and resilience. Remember, the power to cultivate positivity and well-being lies within each of us.

Chapter 35: Holistic Approaches to Mental Health: Yoga, Ayurveda, and Traditional Medicine

Holistic approaches recognize the interconnectedness of the mind, body, and spirit and emphasize the importance of addressing all aspects of an individual's well-being to promote optimal health. By integrating practices that focus on physical, mental, emotional, and spiritual well-being, holistic approaches offer a comprehensive framework for enhancing mental health and nurturing overall wellness.

Let's explore the principles and benefits of yoga, Ayurveda, and traditional medicine in supporting mental well-being more closely:

Yoga: Yoga is an ancient practice that originated in India and encompasses physical postures (asanas), breath control (pranayama), and meditation. It is a holistic discipline that integrates the body, mind, and spirit. The practice of yoga promotes physical strength, flexibility, and balance while also cultivating mental clarity, emotional stability, and inner peace.

Ayurveda: Ayurveda is a traditional system of medicine that originated in India over 5,000 years ago. It emphasizes the balance between mind, body, and spirit for optimal health and well-being. Ayurveda views each individual as unique, with a specific mind-body constitution (dosha). It utilizes various techniques, including dietary adjustments, herbal remedies, lifestyle modifications, and therapeutic practices, to restore balance and promote overall wellness.

Traditional medicine: Traditional medicine refers to the diverse range of healing practices and systems that have been developed and used by different cultures throughout history. Traditional medicine often integrates natural remedies, herbal medicines, acupuncture, energy healing, and other modalities to address physical, mental, and spiritual well-being. These practices recognize the interconnectedness of all aspects of health and strive to restore harmony and balance within the individual.

Now, let's discuss how to apply these holistic approaches in supporting mental well-being:

Yoga for mental health: The practice of yoga offers numerous benefits for mental well-being. By combining physical movement, breath awareness, and meditation, yoga helps reduce stress, anxiety, and depression. Regular yoga practice promotes relaxation, improves focus and concentration, enhances self-awareness, and cultivates a sense of inner peace and emotional balance. It provides a safe and nurturing space to connect with oneself and develop resilience in the face of life's challenges.

Ayurveda for mental well-being: Ayurveda offers a holistic approach to mental well-being by considering an individual's mind-body constitution (dosha) and addressing imbalances that may contribute to mental health challenges. Through dietary adjustments, herbal remedies, lifestyle modifications, and practices such as meditation and yoga, Ayurveda aims to restore balance and harmony in the body and mind. Ayurvedic treatments can help reduce stress, improve sleep, enhance cognitive function, and promote emotional stability.

Traditional medicine for mental well-being: Traditional medicine encompasses a wide range of healing practices that can support mental well-being. Herbal remedies, acupuncture, energy healing, and other modalities can be used to address imbalances in the body and promote mental and emotional equilibrium. Traditional medicine often emphasizes the connection between physical health and mental well-being, recognizing that nurturing the body can have profound effects on mental health.

Integrating holistic practices into daily life: Incorporating holistic practices into our daily lives can support our mental well-being. Engaging in a regular yoga practice, even for a few minutes a day, can have a significant impact. Setting aside time for meditation, breathwork, or mindful movement can help reduce stress and promote emotional balance. Embracing Ayurvedic principles in our dietary choices, sleep routines, and self-care rituals can contribute to overall well-being. Exploring traditional healing practices that resonate with us and seeking guidance from qualified practitioners can further enhance our mental health journey.

Seeking guidance and support: It is essential to approach holistic practices with guidance from experienced teachers, practitioners, or healthcare professionals. They can provide personalized recommendations based on individual needs and circumstances. When seeking support from holistic approaches, it is important to communicate openly, share relevant medical history, and work collaboratively with professionals to ensure safe and effective integration of these practices into one's overall mental health care.

Embracing self-care and self-compassion: Holistic approaches to mental well-being emphasize the importance of self-care and self-compassion. Nurturing oneself through practices such as yoga, Ayurveda, and traditional medicine is an act of self-love and kindness. Embrace self-care rituals that resonate with you, whether it's practicing mindfulness, taking relaxing baths, spending time in nature, or engaging in creative activities. Remember to be gentle with yourself, honoring your unique needs and journey towards mental well-being.

Integrating multiple approaches: Holistic approaches are not mutually exclusive, and integrating multiple practices can offer a synergistic effect. For example, combining yoga and meditation with Ayurvedic dietary adjustments can provide comprehensive support for mental well-being. Explore different modalities and find the combination that resonates with you, recognizing that each person's journey is unique and may require a tailored approach.

So, holistic approaches such as yoga, Ayurveda, and traditional medicine offer powerful tools for enhancing mental well-being. By embracing these practices, we can cultivate physical strength, mental clarity, emotional stability, and spiritual connection. Remember that incorporating holistic approaches is a journey of self-discovery and self-care. Embrace the principles and practices that resonate with you, seek guidance from qualified professionals, and approach these modalities with an open mind and heart. By nurturing our mind, body, and spirit, we can foster a sense of balance, harmony, and resilience in our lives, leading to improved mental well-being and overall vitality.

Chapter 36: Examining the Role of Nutrition in Mental Health

It is becoming increasingly clear that what we eat plays a vital role in our mental health. The food we consume provides the building blocks for our brain's structure and function, influences our neurotransmitter production, and affects the overall balance of chemicals in our brain. By understanding the impact of nutrition on mental health, we can make informed choices to support our well-being.

Let's explore the relationship between nutrition and mental health in more detail:

The gut-brain connection: The gut and the brain are intricately connected through a bidirectional communication network known as the gut-brain axis. The gut is home to trillions of microbes that form the gut microbiota, which plays a crucial role in regulating brain function and mental health. Research suggests that imbalances in the gut microbiota can contribute to mental health conditions such as anxiety, depression, and stress. Nurturing a healthy gut through proper nutrition is essential for promoting optimal mental well-being.

Key nutrients for mental health: Several key nutrients have been identified for their importance in supporting mental health: a. Omega-3 fatty acids: Omega-3 fatty acids, found in fatty fish (such as salmon and sardines), walnuts, flaxseeds, and chia seeds, are essential for brain health. They contribute to the structure and function of brain cell membranes and are involved in neurotransmitter production. Omega-3 fatty acids have been linked to reduced risk of depression and improved cognitive function. b. B vitamins: B vitamins, including folate, B6, and B12, are crucial for proper brain function and the synthesis of neurotransmitters. Foods rich in B vitamins include leafy greens, legumes, whole grains, eggs, and lean meats. Deficiencies in B vitamins have been associated with mood disorders and cognitive decline. c. Antioxidants: Antioxidants, such as vitamin C, vitamin E, and flavonoids, protect the brain from oxidative stress and inflammation. They are found in colorful fruits and vegetables, nuts, seeds, and dark chocolate. Antioxidants have been shown to support cognitive function and reduce the risk of mental decline. d. Magnesium: Magnesium is an essential mineral involved in over 300 biochemical reactions in the body, including neurotransmitter production and stress regulation. Good sources of magnesium include leafy greens, nuts, seeds, whole grains, and legumes. Magnesium deficiency has been linked to increased risk of anxiety and depression. e. Probiotics: Probiotics are beneficial bacteria that support a healthy gut microbiota. They can be found in fermented foods such as yogurt, kefir, sauerkraut, and kimchi. Research suggests that probiotics can improve mood, reduce anxiety, and support overall mental well-being.

The impact of sugar and processed foods: Consumption of excessive sugar and highly processed foods has been associated with negative effects on mental health. High sugar intake can lead to blood sugar spikes and crashes, causing mood swings, fatigue, and impaired cognitive function. Processed foods often lack essential nutrients and are high in additives, preservatives, and unhealthy fats, which can contribute to inflammation and negatively impact brain health. Opting for whole, unprocessed foods and minimizing added sugars can support mental well-being.

Mindful eating and the connection to emotional well-being: Mindful eating involves being fully present and aware while eating, paying attention to the taste, texture, and sensations of food. It also involves tuning into hunger and satiety cues and eating in response to physical rather than emotional cues. Practicing mindful eating can foster a healthier relationship with food, reduce emotional eating, and promote a sense of balance and satisfaction.

Personalizing nutrition for mental health: Each person is unique, and individual nutrient needs may vary based on factors such as age, sex, genetics, and overall health. Working with a healthcare professional, such as a registered dietitian or nutritionist, can help personalize nutrition recommendations to support mental health goals. They can provide guidance on optimizing nutrient intake, addressing deficiencies, and developing a balanced meal plan that suits individual needs.

The importance of a balanced and varied diet: A balanced and varied diet that includes a wide range of nutrient-dense foods is essential for supporting mental health. Emphasize whole foods such as fruits, vegetables, whole grains, lean proteins, nuts, and seeds. Aim for a colorful plate to ensure a variety of nutrients. Consider incorporating plant-based meals and reducing the consumption of processed and fried foods. Hydration is also important, so remember to drink plenty of water throughout the day.

Sustaining a healthy eating pattern: Consistency is key when it comes to nutrition and mental health. Rather than relying on short-term diets or restrictive eating patterns, focus on sustainable habits that promote long-term well-being. Establish regular meal times, prioritize nourishing foods, and practice mindful eating. Remember that small, gradual changes can have a significant impact on mental health over time.

The role of nutrition in conjunction with other mental health interventions: It is important to note that nutrition is not a standalone treatment for mental health conditions. It plays a complementary role alongside other mental health interventions such as therapy, medication, and self-care practices. Integrating nutrition into a comprehensive approach can enhance the effectiveness of overall mental health management.

So, nutrition plays a critical role in supporting mental health and well-being. By incorporating key nutrients, nurturing a healthy gut, reducing sugar and processed food intake, practicing mindful eating, personalizing nutrition, and maintaining a balanced and varied diet, we can optimize our mental well-being. Remember that nutrition is a lifelong journey, and small changes in dietary habits can have a significant impact on mental health over time. Embrace the power of nourishing your body and mind through wholesome, nutrient-dense foods, and seek guidance from healthcare professionals for personalized recommendations. By prioritizing nutrition, we can support our mental well-being and pave the way for a healthier and happier life.

Chapter 37: The Link Between Exercise and Improved Mental Health

It is widely recognized that engaging in regular exercise not only benefits our physical health but also has a profound impact on our mental well-being. Exercise has been shown to reduce symptoms of stress, anxiety, and depression while improving mood, cognitive function, and overall quality of life. Let's explore the link between exercise and mental health in more detail:

The benefits of exercise for mental health: Regular exercise has numerous positive effects on mental well-being. It stimulates the release of endorphins, our body's natural mood-elevating chemicals, which can enhance feelings of happiness and reduce symptoms of depression and anxiety. Exercise also improves sleep quality, boosts self-esteem, enhances cognitive function, reduces stress levels, and provides a healthy outlet for emotional release. These benefits contribute to an overall sense of well-being and improved mental health.

The underlying mechanisms: Exercise influences several physiological and psychological processes that contribute to improved mental health: a. Neurotransmitter regulation: Exercise affects the levels and functioning of neurotransmitters, such as serotonin, dopamine, and norepinephrine, which play crucial roles in mood regulation. Regular exercise can increase the availability of these neurotransmitters, leading to improved mood and reduced symptoms of depression and anxiety. b. Stress reduction: Exercise has a powerful impact on stress reduction. It helps lower levels of the stress hormone cortisol while promoting the release of endorphins, which act as natural stress relievers. Engaging in physical activity provides a healthy outlet for managing and reducing stress, leading to improved mental well-being. c. Neuroplasticity and cognitive function: Exercise has been shown to enhance neuroplasticity—the brain's ability to adapt and reorganize itself. Regular exercise promotes the growth of new neurons and increases the connectivity between brain regions, leading to improved cognitive function, memory, and attention. d. Self-esteem and body image: Engaging in regular exercise can improve self-esteem and body image. Physical activity can help individuals feel stronger, more confident, and in control of their bodies. This positive self-perception can have a significant impact on mental well-being and overall self-worth. e. Social interaction: Exercise often provides opportunities for social interaction and connection. Participating in group activities, sports, or fitness classes can foster a sense of community, support, and belonging. Social engagement is crucial for mental health and can enhance overall well-being.

Finding the right exercise for you: The key to incorporating exercise into your life is to find activities that you enjoy and that fit your lifestyle. Whether it's walking, jogging, swimming, cycling, dancing, yoga, or team sports, there is a wide range of options to choose from. Experiment with different activities and find what brings you joy and fulfillment. Remember, consistency is more important than intensity. Start with small, achievable goals and gradually increase the duration and intensity of your exercise routine over time.

Creating a routine: Establishing a regular exercise routine can significantly contribute to the mental health benefits of physical activity. Set aside dedicated time in your schedule for exercise, just as you would for any other important commitment. Consider finding an exercise buddy or joining a class to stay motivated and accountable. Remember, even short bursts of physical activity can be beneficial, so find opportunities to incorporate movement into your daily life, such as taking the stairs instead of the elevator or going for a walk during your lunch break.

Mind-body practices: Mind-body practices, such as yoga, tai chi, and qigong, offer a unique combination of physical activity, mindfulness, and relaxation. These practices not only improve physical fitness but also promote mental calmness, stress reduction, and emotional well-being. Incorporating mind-body practices into your exercise routine can provide a holistic approach to supporting your mental health.

Nature and outdoor activities: Engaging in physical activity outdoors can amplify the mental health benefits of exercise. Spending time in nature, whether it's walking in a park, hiking in the mountains, or swimming in the ocean, has been shown to reduce stress, improve mood, and enhance feelings of well-being. Take advantage of outdoor spaces and incorporate nature-based activities into your exercise routine whenever possible.

Overcoming barriers and staying motivated: It's natural to encounter barriers and challenges when it comes to exercise. Lack of time, motivation, or access to facilities can hinder our efforts. It's important to identify and address these barriers proactively. Break down your goals into smaller, achievable steps, and focus on the positive feelings and benefits you experience after each exercise session. Consider seeking support from friends, family, or a fitness professional to stay motivated and accountable. Remember that any form of movement is better than none, and even small steps can make a significant difference in your mental well-being.

Integrating exercise with other mental health practices: Exercise can complement and enhance other mental health practices such as therapy, medication, and self-care. It is not a standalone solution but rather a valuable component of a comprehensive approach to mental well-being. Consider integrating exercise with other practices that support mental health, such as mindfulness, stress management, and cultivating positive relationships.

So, exercise is a powerful tool for improving mental health and overall well-being. By engaging in regular physical activity, we can reduce symptoms of stress, anxiety, and depression, boost mood, enhance cognitive function, and improve self-esteem. Find activities that you enjoy, create a routine, embrace mind-body practices, connect with nature, and stay motivated. Remember that exercise is a journey, and it's important to listen to your body, respect your limits, and celebrate the progress you make. Incorporate exercise as a vital part of your self-care routine, and enjoy the transformative benefits it brings to your mental health and overall quality of life.

Chapter 38: Mind-Body Practices for Stress Reduction and Emotional Balance

In our fast-paced and demanding lives, stress has become a common experience for many of us. Chronic stress can take a toll on our well-being, impacting both our physical and mental health. Mind-body practices offer a holistic approach to managing stress and promoting emotional balance. These practices integrate the mind and body, allowing us to cultivate a deeper sense of awareness, relaxation, and inner peace. Let's explore some of the most popular mind-body practices and their benefits:

Meditation: Meditation is a practice that involves training the mind to focus and redirect thoughts, promoting a state of mental clarity and emotional calmness. There are various forms of meditation, including mindfulness meditation, loving-kindness meditation, and transcendental meditation. Research has shown that regular meditation practice can reduce stress, anxiety, and depression, improve attention and concentration, increase self-awareness, and promote overall emotional well-being.

Yoga: Yoga is an ancient practice that combines physical postures, breath control, and meditation. It integrates the mind and body, fostering a sense of balance, flexibility, and relaxation. The physical movements in yoga, combined with deep breathing and mindful awareness, can help reduce stress, increase body awareness, improve flexibility and strength, and promote a sense of calmness and well-being.

Tai Chi: Tai Chi is a gentle martial art that originated in ancient China. It involves slow, flowing movements combined with deep breathing and meditation. Tai Chi promotes relaxation, balance, and a sense of inner peace. Regular practice of Tai Chi has been shown to reduce stress, improve flexibility and balance, enhance cognitive function, and support emotional well-being.

Qigong: Qigong is an ancient Chinese practice that combines gentle movements, deep breathing, and meditation to cultivate and balance the body's vital energy or "qi." Qigong exercises promote relaxation, improve energy flow, reduce stress, and enhance overall well-being. It is often used as a self-care practice to manage stress and foster emotional balance.

Breathing exercises: Deep breathing exercises are simple yet powerful tools for stress reduction and emotional balance. These exercises involve consciously slowing down and deepening the breath, allowing the body to relax and the mind to calm. Deep breathing activates the body's relaxation response, reduces the production of stress hormones, and promotes a state of calmness and centeredness.

Now, let's discuss how to incorporate these mind-body practices into our lives for stress reduction and emotional balance:

Start small and be consistent: Begin by dedicating a few minutes each day to a mind-body practice of your choice. Whether it's meditation, yoga, Tai Chi, or breathing exercises, consistency is key. Set realistic goals and gradually increase the duration and frequency of your practice over time. Remember that even a few minutes of practice each day can yield significant benefits for your well-being.

Create a peaceful space: Designate a quiet and peaceful space in your home where you can practice your chosen mind-body practice. Make this space inviting and clutter-free, with soft lighting, comfortable cushions or a yoga mat, and any props or tools that support your practice. Creating a dedicated space can help set the tone for relaxation and focus.

Find guided resources: If you are new to mind-body practices, consider using guided resources such as meditation apps, online yoga classes, or instructional videos. These resources can provide structure, guidance, and inspiration as you explore and deepen your practice. There are numerous free or low-cost options available, making mind-body practices accessible to everyone.

Listen to your body: Pay attention to your body's signals and adjust your practice accordingly. Mind-body practices should feel comfortable and nurturing. If a particular posture or technique causes discomfort or strain, modify it to suit your needs. Honor your body's limits and practice self-compassion as you explore and develop your mind-body practice.

Incorporate mindfulness into daily life: Mindfulness is a fundamental aspect of mind-body practices. Embrace the practice of mindfulness in your everyday life by bringing awareness to your thoughts, emotions, and physical sensations throughout the day. Practice being present and fully engaged in each moment, whether it's eating a meal, walking in nature, or engaging in daily activities. Cultivating mindfulness in daily life can enhance your overall sense of well-being and emotional balance.

Seek community and support: Consider joining a local class or group that practices mind-body techniques. Engaging in these practices with others can provide a sense of community, support, and accountability. Sharing experiences and insights with like-minded individuals can deepen your practice and foster a sense of connection.

Be patient and compassionate: Mind-body practices are a journey of self-discovery and growth. Be patient with yourself as you develop your practice. Understand that progress may come in small increments, and each moment spent in practice is valuable. Practice self-compassion and embrace the process of learning and deepening your mind-body practice.

Integrate mind-body practices with other self-care strategies: Mind-body practices work synergistically with other self-care strategies to promote overall well-being. Incorporate them into a holistic self-care routine that includes nourishing food, quality sleep, regular physical activity, social connection, and meaningful activities. By cultivating a comprehensive self-care approach, you can enhance your ability to manage stress, foster emotional balance, and nurture your mental and physical health.

So, mind-body practices offer transformative tools for stress reduction and emotional balance. By incorporating practices such as meditation, yoga, Tai Chi, Qigong, and breathing exercises into our lives, we can cultivate a deeper sense of awareness, relaxation, and inner peace. Start small, be consistent, create a peaceful space, and find guided resources to support your practice. Listen to your body, incorporate mindfulness into daily life, seek community and support, and practice patience and compassion. Remember that mind-body practices are a journey of self-discovery and growth, and each moment spent in practice is valuable.

By integrating these practices with other self-care strategies, you can enhance your ability to manage stress, foster emotional balance, and nurture your mental and physical well-being. Embrace the transformative power of mind-body practices, and embark on a path of greater self-awareness, relaxation, and overall well-being.

Chapter 39: Building Healthy Relationships for Better Mental Health

In this chapter, we will delve into the intricate ways in which our relationships impact our well-being, discuss the characteristics of healthy relationships, provide insights on effective communication and conflict resolution, and offer practical tips on cultivating and nurturing meaningful connections in our lives.

Humans are social beings, and the quality of our relationships has a profound impact on our mental health and overall well-being. Healthy relationships provide support, connection, and a sense of belonging, while toxic or unhealthy relationships can lead to stress, anxiety, and emotional turmoil. Let's explore the key aspects of building and maintaining healthy relationships:

The impact of relationships on mental health: Our relationships, whether with family, friends, romantic partners, or colleagues, significantly influence our mental health. Positive and supportive relationships can promote feelings of happiness, reduce stress, and increase resilience. On the other hand, toxic or unhealthy relationships can cause emotional distress, contribute to anxiety and depression, and hinder personal growth. Recognizing the impact of relationships on our well-being empowers us to prioritize healthy connections in our lives.

Characteristics of healthy relationships: Healthy relationships are built on a foundation of mutual respect, trust, and open communication. They foster a sense of safety and emotional support, allowing individuals to express themselves authentically without fear of judgment or rejection. Healthy relationships also involve shared values, empathy, and the ability to navigate conflicts in a constructive manner. These relationships contribute to a positive sense of self-worth, provide a support system during challenging times, and enhance overall mental well-being.

Effective communication: Communication is the cornerstone of healthy relationships. It involves active listening, expressing oneself honestly and assertively, and maintaining open dialogue. Effective communication fosters understanding, builds trust, and nurtures emotional connection. Practicing active listening, validating each other's feelings, and expressing oneself with clarity and empathy are essential skills for cultivating healthy communication in relationships.

Conflict resolution: Conflict is a natural part of any relationship, but healthy relationships require effective conflict resolution. It involves addressing conflicts openly and respectfully, actively seeking solutions, and compromising when necessary. Healthy conflict resolution focuses on finding common ground, understanding each other's perspectives, and working together to find mutually beneficial outcomes. Embracing conflict as an opportunity for growth and learning can strengthen relationships and contribute to improved mental well-being.

Setting boundaries: Healthy relationships involve setting and respecting personal boundaries. Boundaries define what is acceptable and what is not in terms of behavior, communication, and personal space. Establishing and communicating boundaries with clarity and assertiveness is crucial for maintaining healthy relationships. Respecting each other's boundaries fosters a sense of safety, autonomy, and emotional well-being.

Nurturing meaningful connections: Cultivating and nurturing meaningful connections is essential for building healthy relationships. It involves investing time and effort in building rapport, fostering emotional intimacy, and showing appreciation for one another. Engage in activities together, create shared experiences, and celebrate each other's achievements. Show genuine interest and care in each other's lives, and prioritize spending quality time together. Meaningful connections provide a sense of belonging and support, fostering positive mental health outcomes.

Recognizing toxic relationships: It is important to be aware of toxic or unhealthy relationships that can negatively impact our mental health. Toxic relationships involve patterns of disrespect, manipulation, emotional abuse, or control. If you find yourself consistently feeling drained, anxious, or unhappy in a relationship, it may be necessary to reevaluate its dynamics. Prioritizing your mental health may involve setting boundaries, seeking professional help, or even considering distancing yourself from toxic individuals.

Seeking support and professional help: Building and maintaining healthy relationships can be challenging at times. Seeking support from trusted friends, family members, or support groups can provide perspective, validation, and guidance. Additionally, professional help, such as couples therapy or individual counseling, can offer valuable tools and insights for navigating relationship challenges and enhancing communication skills.

Self-reflection and personal growth: Healthy relationships are not solely reliant on the actions of others; they also require self-reflection and personal growth. Engaging in self-reflection allows us to gain insight into our own needs, emotions, and patterns of behavior. It helps us understand our strengths and areas for improvement, fostering self-awareness and personal growth. Taking responsibility for our own actions and working on personal development contributes to healthier and more fulfilling relationships.

Embracing diversity and inclusivity: Healthy relationships thrive on diversity and inclusivity. Embrace and celebrate differences in backgrounds, perspectives, and experiences. Practice empathy and seek to understand and learn from one another. By valuing and respecting diversity, we create an inclusive environment that fosters growth, acceptance, and stronger relationships.

So, building healthy relationships is a fundamental aspect of supporting our mental health and overall well-being. Prioritize relationships that are built on mutual respect, trust, effective communication, and healthy conflict resolution. Set and respect personal boundaries, nurture meaningful connections, and seek support when needed. Recognize the signs of toxic relationships and take necessary steps to protect your mental health. Engage in self-reflection, embrace personal growth, and value diversity and inclusivity in your relationships. Remember that building healthy relationships is an ongoing process that requires effort, understanding, and compassion. By prioritizing and cultivating healthy relationships, you can create a supportive network that enhances your mental well-being and contributes to a happier and more fulfilling life.

Chapter 40: Exploring the Connection Between Creativity and Mental Health

Creativity is a powerful and innate human trait that allows us to express ourselves, think outside the box, and explore new possibilities. It encompasses a wide range of activities, including art, music, writing, dancing, crafting, and problem-solving. Engaging in creative endeavors not only provides a source of enjoyment and self-expression but also offers numerous benefits for our mental health. Let's explore the connection between creativity and mental health in more detail:

Self-expression and emotional release: Creativity provides a channel for self-expression and emotional release. When we engage in creative activities, we can express our thoughts, feelings, and experiences in a non-verbal and cathartic way. It allows us to explore and process complex emotions, release pent-up stress, or tension, and gain a sense of emotional clarity and relief.

Flow state and mindfulness: Creativity often leads to a state of flow, where we become fully absorbed in the activity at hand. Flow is characterized by a sense of timelessness, complete focus, and a feeling of being "in the zone." This state of mind is akin to mindfulness, where we are fully present and immersed in the present moment. Flow and mindfulness have been shown to reduce stress, increase happiness, and promote overall well-being.

Sense of accomplishment and self-confidence: Engaging in creative pursuits can provide a sense of accomplishment and boost self-confidence. Whether it's completing a painting, writing a poem, or mastering a musical piece, the act of creating something tangible instills a sense of pride and achievement. These positive feelings contribute to a healthy self-image and can counteract feelings of self-doubt or low self-esteem.

Coping with adversity and promoting resilience: Creativity can serve as a powerful tool for coping with adversity and promoting resilience. During challenging times, engaging in creative activities can provide a much-needed outlet for processing emotions, finding solace, and gaining a sense of control. Creativity allows us to transform our experiences into something meaningful, fostering resilience and helping us navigate through difficult circumstances.

Enhanced problem-solving and cognitive flexibility: Creative thinking enhances problem-solving abilities and cognitive flexibility. When we engage in creative activities, we train our brains to think outside conventional boundaries, explore multiple perspectives, and generate innovative solutions. These skills are not only beneficial in artistic pursuits but also applicable to various aspects of life, including work, relationships, and personal growth.

Connection and social support: Creativity can foster connection and provide opportunities for social support. Engaging in creative endeavors allows us to connect with like-minded individuals, join communities or classes, and participate in collaborative projects. These social connections provide a sense of belonging, support, and inspiration, which are vital for our mental well-being.

Mindful and therapeutic art practices: Mindful art practices, such as art therapy or mindful coloring, combine the benefits of creativity with mindfulness techniques. These practices emphasize the process of creating rather than the final outcome, promoting self-exploration, relaxation, and emotional well-being. Engaging in mindful art practices can be particularly helpful for individuals experiencing stress, anxiety, or trauma.

Embracing and nurturing creativity in our lives:

Give yourself permission to create: Many of us may hold self-limiting beliefs or fears of judgment when it comes to expressing our creativity. Give yourself permission to create without judgment or expectations. Embrace the process rather than focusing solely on the end result. Remember that creativity is a deeply personal and subjective journey.

Explore various creative outlets: Creativity comes in many forms. Explore different creative outlets to find what resonates with you. Experiment with painting, writing, dancing, playing a musical instrument, photography, or any other creative activity that piques your interest. Embrace the joy of trying new things and discovering hidden talents.

Create a dedicated space: Create a space in your home or workplace where you can engage in creative activities. Whether it's a corner with art supplies, a writing desk, or a quiet room for meditation and reflection, having a dedicated space can inspire and encourage regular creative practice.

Prioritize regular creative time: Make creativity a regular part of your life by scheduling dedicated time for creative pursuits. Set aside specific blocks of time each week to engage in your chosen creative activities. Consistency is key to nurturing your creative spirit and reaping the mental health benefits.

Embrace imperfection and experimentation: Release the need for perfection and embrace the spirit of experimentation. Remember that creativity is about exploration, growth, and self-expression. Allow yourself to make mistakes, try new techniques, and learn from the process. Embracing imperfection can lead to unexpected discoveries and greater personal satisfaction.

Seek inspiration from others: Surround yourself with sources of inspiration. Seek out the work of artists, writers, musicians, or creators whose work resonates with you. Attend exhibitions, read books, listen to music, and engage with creative communities to fuel your own creativity. Inspiration can come from various sources, and exposing yourself to different forms of art and expression can broaden your creative horizons.

Practice self-care and balance: Creativity thrives in an environment of self-care and balance. Prioritize your well-being by taking care of your physical and mental health. Get enough rest, eat nourishing food, engage in regular physical activity, and manage stress effectively. By taking care of yourself, you create the optimal conditions for your creative energy to flow.

Collaborate and share with others: Engage in collaborative projects or share your creative work with others. Collaborating with fellow creatives can spark new ideas, deepen connections, and provide a sense of camaraderie. Sharing your work with friends, family, or the broader community can bring a sense of fulfillment and contribute to a sense of purpose and belonging.

Embrace creative blocks as opportunities: Creative blocks are a natural part of the creative process. Instead of becoming discouraged, view these blocks as opportunities for reflection and growth. Step away from your creative work for a while, engage in other activities, or seek inspiration from different sources. Trust that the creative spark will return in its own time.

Practice gratitude for the creative journey: Cultivate gratitude for the gift of creativity and the opportunity to express yourself. Embrace the ups and downs of the creative journey, appreciating the moments of inspiration and the lessons learned along the way. Gratitude nurtures a positive mindset and enhances the overall enjoyment of the creative process.

So, embracing, and nurturing creativity in our lives can have profound benefits for our mental health and overall well-being. Whether through art, music, writing, or any other creative outlet, engaging in creative activities allows us to express ourselves, find emotional release, enhance problem-solving skills, and cultivate resilience. Embrace your creative spirit, prioritize regular creative practice, and create a space for self-expression. By embracing creativity, we invite joy, self-discovery, and a deeper connection with ourselves and the world around us.

Chapter 41: Addressing Mental Health Disparities in Underserved Communities

Mental health disparities refer to the unequal distribution of mental health resources, access to care, and quality of care among different populations. Underserved communities, including low-income individuals, racial and ethnic minorities, LGBTQ+ individuals, and rural populations, often face significant barriers when it comes to accessing mental health services. Let's explore this issue in more detail:

Understanding mental health disparities: Mental health disparities are influenced by a range of factors, including socioeconomic status, systemic inequalities, discrimination, stigma, and cultural factors. These disparities manifest in various ways, such as limited access to mental health services, a lack of culturally competent care, higher rates of untreated mental health conditions, and poorer mental health outcomes within underserved communities.

Socioeconomic factors: Socioeconomic factors play a significant role in mental health disparities. Individuals in underserved communities often face higher rates of poverty, unemployment, housing instability, and limited access to education. These socioeconomic stressors can contribute to increased rates of mental health conditions, as well as barriers to accessing mental health care due to financial constraints.

Systemic inequalities and discrimination: Systemic inequalities and discrimination exacerbate mental health disparities. Marginalized communities, including racial and ethnic minorities, LGBTQ+ individuals, and immigrants, often experience higher levels of discrimination, prejudice, and societal stressors. These factors can lead to increased rates of mental health conditions and limited access to culturally competent and inclusive mental health care.

Stigma and cultural factors: Stigma surrounding mental health, both within communities and in society at large, can prevent individuals from seeking help and accessing appropriate care. Cultural factors, such as beliefs about mental health, language barriers, and mistrust of healthcare systems, can also contribute to disparities in mental health care utilization.

Addressing mental health disparities in underserved communities:

Increasing access to mental health services: One key step in addressing mental health disparities is increasing access to mental health services in underserved communities. This can be achieved by improving the availability and affordability of mental health services, expanding telehealth options, integrating mental health care into primary care settings, and establishing community-based mental health programs. It is crucial to prioritize resources and funding to ensure that mental health services are accessible to all individuals, regardless of their socioeconomic status or location.

Promoting cultural competence: Culturally competent care is essential for addressing mental health disparities. Mental health professionals should receive training and education on providing culturally sensitive care that takes into account the unique experiences, beliefs, and needs of diverse populations. This includes understanding cultural nuances, addressing language barriers, and incorporating community values and practices into treatment approaches.

Community outreach and education: Engaging in community outreach and education is vital for reducing stigma and increasing awareness of mental health within underserved communities. Education campaigns can debunk myths surrounding mental health, promote help-seeking behaviors, and provide information about available resources and support. Community organizations, faith-based groups, and grassroots initiatives can play a crucial role in disseminating information and fostering dialogue around mental health.

Collaboration and partnerships: Addressing mental health disparities requires collaboration among various stakeholders, including healthcare providers, community organizations, policymakers, and advocacy groups. Building partnerships can facilitate the development of targeted interventions, resource allocation, and policy changes to improve mental health outcomes in underserved communities. By working together, we can amplify our impact and create lasting change.

Empowering individuals and fostering resilience: Empowering individuals within underserved communities is essential for promoting mental health and resilience. This can be achieved through community empowerment initiatives, peer support programs, and promoting self-care practices. Encouraging individuals to become advocates for their own mental health and providing them with tools and resources to navigate challenges can lead to improved mental health outcomes.

Research and data collection: Collecting accurate data on mental health disparities and their impact on underserved communities is crucial for driving change and advocating for policy reforms. Robust research can help identify specific areas of need, understand the underlying causes of disparities, and evaluate the effectiveness of interventions. By prioritizing research and data collection, we can make evidence-based decisions and allocate resources where they are most needed.

Policy advocacy: Advocating for policy changes at the local, regional, and national levels is instrumental in addressing mental health disparities. Policies that prioritize mental health funding, ensure insurance coverage for mental health services, promote workforce diversity, and integrate mental health into broader healthcare systems can contribute to reducing disparities and improving access to quality care.

So, addressing mental health disparities in underserved communities is a multifaceted and ongoing endeavor that requires collective effort and commitment. By increasing access to mental health services, promoting cultural competence, engaging in community outreach and education, fostering collaboration and partnerships, empowering individuals, prioritizing research, and data collection, and advocating for policy changes, we can work towards achieving mental health equity for all. Let us stand together in creating a society where everyone has access to the care and support they need to thrive mentally and emotionally.

Chapter 42: Traumatic Brain Injury and its Psychological Impact

Traumatic brain injury refers to an injury to the brain caused by a sudden, external force. It can occur as a result of various incidents, such as falls, motor vehicle accidents, sports-related injuries, or assaults. TBI can range from mild concussions to severe brain damage, and its consequences extend beyond physical impairments to encompass significant psychological challenges. Let's explore the psychological impact of TBI in more detail:

Emotional and behavioral changes: TBI can lead to emotional and behavioral changes that affect an individual's mood, personality, and social interactions. These changes may include irritability, impulsivity, agitation, anger outbursts, depression, anxiety, and difficulties with emotional regulation. It is important to recognize that these changes are often a result of the physical damage to the brain and not a reflection of the individual's character.

Cognitive difficulties: TBI can also result in cognitive difficulties that impact memory, attention, concentration, problem-solving, and decision-making abilities. Individuals may experience challenges with organizing thoughts, processing information, and multitasking. These cognitive impairments can affect academic or work performance, daily activities, and overall quality of life.

Social and relationship challenges: TBI can strain social relationships and lead to social isolation. Individuals may struggle to communicate effectively, experience difficulties with empathy or understanding social cues, and face challenges in maintaining social connections. Friends, family members, and partners may need support and education on how to navigate these changes and provide appropriate support.

Adjustment and coping difficulties: Adjusting to life after TBI can be challenging. Individuals may experience frustration, grief, and a sense of loss due to the changes in their abilities and lifestyle. Coping with the physical, emotional, and cognitive changes requires resilience and adaptation. Support from healthcare professionals, rehabilitation services, and peer support groups can play a crucial role in helping individuals navigate this adjustment period.

Impact on mental health: TBI can increase the risk of developing mental health conditions, such as depression, anxiety disorders, post-traumatic stress disorder (PTSD), and substance abuse. The psychological impact of TBI can be long-lasting and may require ongoing support and intervention to address mental health concerns effectively.

Supporting individuals affected by TBI in their journey towards recovery:

Education and awareness: Education is vital in understanding the effects of TBI and its psychological impact. Educate yourself, family members, and friends about TBI and its potential psychological consequences. This knowledge will foster empathy, reduce stigma, and create a supportive environment for individuals affected by TBI.

Collaborative treatment approach: TBI rehabilitation typically involves a multidisciplinary approach, including healthcare professionals, psychologists, occupational therapists, and speech therapists. Collaborate with healthcare professionals to develop a comprehensive treatment plan that addresses both physical and psychological aspects of recovery. This may involve cognitive rehabilitation, psychotherapy, medication management, and other supportive interventions.

Psychological therapy: Psychotherapy can be beneficial for individuals with TBI to address the psychological impact and enhance coping strategies. Cognitive-behavioral therapy (CBT), which focuses on identifying and modifying unhelpful thoughts and behaviors, can be particularly effective. Additionally, therapy can provide a safe space for individuals to process emotions, manage stress, and develop strategies for rebuilding their lives after TBI.

Social support: Encourage individuals with TBI to seek social support and connect with others who have had similar experiences. Support groups, both in-person and online, can provide a sense of belonging, empathy, and valuable insights. Sharing experiences and learning from others can be empowering and help individuals navigate the challenges of TBI more effectively.

Family and caregiver support: Family members and caregivers play a crucial role in supporting individuals with TBI. Encourage open communication, patience, and understanding within the family unit. Offer emotional support, educate yourself about TBI, and seek guidance from healthcare professionals on how to best support your loved one's recovery and psychological well-being.

Promote self-care: Self-care is essential for individuals with TBI to support their overall well-being. Encourage activities that promote relaxation, stress reduction, and emotional well-being, such as mindfulness exercises, gentle physical exercise, engaging in hobbies, and maintaining a balanced lifestyle. Encourage individuals to pace themselves, prioritize rest, and engage in activities they enjoy.

Advocate for accommodations: Individuals with TBI may benefit from accommodations and modifications to support their cognitive and emotional well-being in various settings, such as work, school, or social environments. Encourage individuals to advocate for their needs and explore available resources and accommodations that can facilitate their success and inclusion.

Foster a positive and supportive environment: Foster a positive and supportive environment for individuals with TBI by focusing on their strengths, providing encouragement, and celebrating milestones in their recovery journey. Avoid judgment and support their efforts towards independence and reintegration into daily life.

So, traumatic brain injury can have significant psychological consequences that impact individuals' emotional well-being, cognition, social interactions, and overall quality of life. Understanding the psychological impact of TBI and providing appropriate support, education, and resources is crucial in helping individuals navigate the challenges they face. By fostering a supportive environment, promoting collaborative treatment approaches, and embracing empathy and understanding, we can empower individuals affected by TBI to achieve psychological well-being and lead fulfilling lives.

Chapter 43: Understanding Dual Diagnosis: Mental Health and Substance Use Disorders

Dual diagnosis occurs when an individual experiences both a mental health disorder and a substance use disorder concurrently. These disorders can interact and exacerbate one another, making diagnosis and treatment complex. Let's explore the topic of dual diagnosis in more detail:

Understanding the relationship: Mental health disorders and substance use disorders often coexist due to various factors. Some individuals may turn to substances as a way to self-medicate or alleviate the symptoms of mental health conditions. In turn, substance use can worsen mental health symptoms or trigger the onset of new mental health issues. This complex relationship requires an integrated and holistic approach to treatment.

Common co-occurring disorders: Several mental health disorders commonly co-occur with substance use disorders. These may include depression, anxiety disorders, bipolar disorder, post-traumatic stress disorder (PTSD), borderline personality disorder, and schizophrenia. It's important to note that any mental health disorder can potentially coexist with a substance use disorder.

The impact of dual diagnosis: Dual diagnosis presents unique challenges for individuals. The co-occurrence of mental health and substance use disorders can lead to increased severity of symptoms, poorer treatment outcomes, higher relapse rates, and decreased overall functioning. It can be a complex cycle, as substance use can temporarily alleviate mental health symptoms but ultimately worsen the underlying condition.

Integrated treatment approach: Effective treatment for dual diagnosis requires an integrated approach that addresses both the mental health and substance use aspects. Ideally, mental health and addiction professionals collaborate to develop a comprehensive treatment plan. Integrated treatment may include individual therapy, group therapy, medication management, psychoeducation, and support groups tailored to the individual's specific needs.

Stigma and barriers to treatment: Individuals with dual diagnosis often face stigma and encounter barriers to treatment. Stigma surrounding mental health and substance use can lead to feelings of shame, self-judgment, and reluctance to seek help. Additionally, the fragmented nature of the healthcare system, limited access to specialized services, and societal misconceptions can create challenges in accessing appropriate and timely care.

Addressing both disorders simultaneously: Treatment for dual diagnosis should address both the mental health and substance use disorders simultaneously. It's essential to identify and address the underlying factors contributing to both conditions. Therapy can help individuals develop coping skills, manage triggers, and explore healthier ways of managing emotions. Additionally, support groups or peer counseling can provide a sense of connection and understanding.

Motivation and readiness for change: Motivation and readiness for change play a significant role in the recovery process for individuals with dual diagnosis. Building motivation involves highlighting the benefits of treatment, setting realistic goals, and focusing on the individual's personal values and aspirations. Recognizing the potential impact on overall well-being can serve as a driving force in seeking and maintaining treatment.

Building a support network: Having a strong support network is crucial for individuals with dual diagnosis. Surrounding oneself with understanding and supportive individuals can provide encouragement, accountability, and guidance throughout the recovery journey. This network may include family, friends, support groups, and healthcare professionals who specialize in dual diagnosis treatment.

Self-care and relapse prevention: Self-care is essential for individuals with dual diagnosis to maintain stability and prevent relapse. Engaging in activities that promote physical and mental well-being, such as exercise, meditation, healthy eating, and pursuing hobbies, can contribute to overall recovery. Developing relapse prevention strategies, identifying triggers, and implementing healthy coping mechanisms are also vital components of long-term recovery.

Ongoing support and aftercare: Recovery from dual diagnosis is a lifelong journey. Ongoing support and aftercare are crucial for sustained well-being. After completing formal treatment, individuals may benefit from continued therapy, participation in support groups, and accessing community resources. Regular check-ins with healthcare professionals can ensure that progress is maintained and any emerging challenges are addressed promptly.

So, dual diagnosis presents unique challenges as individuals navigate the complexities of mental health and substance use disorders simultaneously. Understanding the relationship between these disorders and adopting an integrated treatment approach is essential for effective care. By addressing both the mental health and substance use aspects, providing a supportive environment, and focusing on long-term recovery, individuals with dual diagnosis can find hope, stability, and a fulfilling life. Let us strive to break down the barriers, reduce stigma, and ensure that comprehensive and compassionate care is available for those with dual diagnosis.

Chapter 44: Supporting Veterans' Mental Health: Challenges and Solutions

Veterans, individuals who have served in the military, often face a range of mental health challenges as a result of their experiences. The transition from military to civilian life, exposure to combat or traumatic events, and the strain of deployment can have a profound impact on their psychological well-being. Let's explore the topic of supporting veterans' mental health in more detail:

Unique challenges faced by veterans: Veterans encounter unique challenges that can impact their mental health. These challenges may include post-traumatic stress disorder (PTSD), depression, anxiety, traumatic brain injury (TBI), substance abuse, and difficulties with transitioning to civilian life. It is important to understand the complexities and nuances of these challenges in order to effectively support veterans.

Post-traumatic stress disorder (PTSD): PTSD is a common mental health condition among veterans. It can develop after exposure to traumatic events, such as combat, military sexual trauma, or witnessing life-threatening situations. Symptoms of PTSD may include intrusive memories, nightmares, flashbacks, hypervigilance, avoidance of triggers, and emotional distress. Providing appropriate assessment, treatment, and support is crucial for managing PTSD in veterans.

Depression and anxiety: Veterans may also experience depression and anxiety as a result of their military experiences. The transition from the structured and cohesive military environment to civilian life can be challenging, leading to feelings of isolation, loss of identity, and difficulties in establishing a sense of purpose. Providing mental health services that address depression and anxiety is essential for veterans' overall well-being.

Traumatic brain injury (TBI): TBI, often caused by blasts or other head injuries during military service, can have long-lasting effects on veterans' mental health. It can result in cognitive impairments, memory problems, difficulties with concentration, and changes in mood and behavior. Comprehensive assessment and treatment, including cognitive rehabilitation and psychological support, are important for managing the psychological impact of TBI.

Substance abuse and addiction: Veterans may be at increased risk of substance abuse and addiction due to the unique stressors they face. Self-medication, coping mechanisms, and difficulties in transitioning to civilian life can contribute to substance abuse issues. Providing access to specialized treatment programs, addressing co-occurring mental health disorders, and implementing preventive measures are important steps in supporting veterans with substance use disorders.

Transitioning to civilian life: The transition from military to civilian life can be challenging for veterans. They may experience difficulties in adjusting to new routines, establishing social connections, finding employment, and navigating the healthcare system. Offering comprehensive support services, including career counseling, educational opportunities, and assistance with accessing healthcare, can help ease this transition and promote veterans' mental well-being.

Building a supportive community: Building a supportive community is essential for veterans' mental health. This can be achieved through initiatives that foster a sense of belonging and camaraderie among veterans, such as veteran support groups, peer mentoring programs, and community events. Encouraging social connections and creating a safe space for veterans to share their experiences and support one another is crucial in promoting their mental well-being.

Improving access to mental health services: Ensuring accessible and timely mental health services for veterans is paramount. This includes increasing awareness of available resources, reducing stigma around seeking help, and improving the availability of mental health professionals who are knowledgeable about veterans' specific needs. Telehealth options can also play a significant role in overcoming geographical barriers and ensuring access to care, particularly for veterans in rural areas.

Enhancing cultural competency: Understanding the unique experiences and cultural aspects of military service is crucial for providing effective mental health support to veterans. Mental health professionals should receive training in military culture and be knowledgeable about the specific challenges faced by veterans. Culturally competent care promotes trust, understanding, and a better therapeutic alliance between veterans and healthcare providers.

Collaboration and partnerships: Addressing the mental health needs of veterans requires collaboration among various stakeholders, including government agencies, healthcare providers, community organizations, and veteran advocacy groups. Collaboration can lead to the development of comprehensive programs, policies, and resources that support veterans' mental health and ensure continuity of care.

So, supporting veterans' mental health requires a comprehensive and compassionate approach that addresses their unique challenges and provides them with the care they deserve. By understanding the specific mental health issues veterans face, improving access to mental health services, building a supportive community, and enhancing cultural competency, we can work together to promote the well-being of those who have served our country. Let us honor their sacrifices by providing them with the support they need to live healthy and fulfilling lives after their military service.

Chapter 45: Promoting Mental Health in Schools: Strategies for Students and Educators

Schools play a vital role in nurturing the overall well-being of students. Promoting mental health in the educational setting is crucial for creating a supportive environment that fosters learning, resilience, and positive social-emotional development. Let's explore strategies for students and educators to promote mental health in schools:

Creating a safe and inclusive environment: Foster a safe and inclusive environment where students feel accepted, valued, and respected. Promote a zero-tolerance policy for bullying, discrimination, and harassment. Encourage open dialogue, empathy, and understanding among students to create a sense of belonging and reduce the stigma surrounding mental health.

Providing mental health education: Integrate mental health education into the school curriculum. Offer age-appropriate lessons on topics such as stress management, emotional regulation, self-care, healthy relationships, and coping strategies. Educating students about mental health empowers them with knowledge, reduces stigma, and equips them with the skills to take care of their own well-being.

Implementing social-emotional learning programs: Social-emotional learning (SEL) programs provide students with the tools to develop self-awareness, empathy, emotional regulation, and positive relationships. Collaborate with educators, counselors, and administrators to implement evidence-based SEL programs that support students' social and emotional development. These programs can enhance students' resilience, self-esteem, and overall mental well-being.

Fostering open communication: Encourage open communication between students, educators, and parents regarding mental health. Provide opportunities for students to express their concerns, seek guidance, and share their experiences. Educators should create a safe space for students to discuss their feelings, concerns, and challenges without judgment. Regularly communicate with parents about mental health initiatives, resources, and support available within the school.

Offering counseling and support services: Ensure access to school-based counseling services staffed by qualified professionals. Counselors can provide individual or group counseling, crisis intervention, and referrals to outside resources when needed. Establish a confidential and non-judgmental environment where students can seek support for their mental health concerns.

Encouraging self-care and stress reduction: Teach students the importance of self-care and stress reduction techniques. Promote activities such as mindfulness exercises, physical exercise, creative outlets, and time for relaxation. Educate students on the benefits of self-care practices and encourage them to prioritize their mental well-being.

Creating peer support networks: Establish peer support networks within the school community. Peer mentoring programs, support groups, or buddy systems can provide students with the opportunity to connect, share experiences, and offer support to one another. Encourage students to be aware of their peers' well-being and foster a culture of kindness and empathy.

Providing professional development for educators: Offer professional development opportunities for educators to enhance their understanding of mental health, recognize signs of distress, and learn strategies for supporting students. Training should focus on creating a trauma-informed and culturally sensitive classroom environment, fostering resilience, and utilizing appropriate referral processes for students in need.

Collaborating with external resources: Establish partnerships with community organizations and mental health providers to ensure a comprehensive support network for students. These partnerships can provide additional resources, referrals, and expert advice. Collaborating with external resources strengthens the support system available to students and enables schools to address a wide range of mental health needs effectively.

Engaging parents and guardians: Involve parents and guardians in mental health initiatives. Offer workshops, seminars, or support groups that address common parenting concerns related to mental health. Encourage parents to communicate with educators and collaborate on strategies to support their children's mental well-being at home and in school.

So, promoting mental health in schools is essential for creating a nurturing environment where students can thrive academically, socially, and emotionally. By implementing strategies such as creating a safe and inclusive environment, providing mental health education, implementing social-emotional learning programs, fostering open communication, offering counseling and support services, encouraging self-care, creating peer support networks, providing professional development for educators, collaborating with external resources, and engaging parents and guardians, we can collectively prioritize and support mental well-being in schools. Let us work together to create an environment where every student feels valued, understood, and equipped with the skills to navigate life's challenges while maintaining good mental health.

Chapter 46: The Role of Parenting in Nurturing Children's Mental Health

Parenting has a profound influence on children's mental health and development. The way parents interact with their children, communicate, set boundaries, and provide support can significantly impact their children's emotional well-being. Let's explore the role of parenting in nurturing children's mental health in more detail:

Nurturing a secure attachment: Building a secure attachment with your child is a cornerstone of their mental well-being. Responding sensitively to your child's needs, providing comfort and reassurance, and being emotionally available create a sense of security and trust. This secure attachment lays the foundation for healthy emotional development and positive relationships throughout their lives.

Creating a positive and supportive environment: Foster a positive and supportive environment at home. Encourage open communication, active listening, and validation of your child's feelings and experiences. Show empathy and understanding, and provide a safe space for your child to express themselves without judgment. This creates an atmosphere where children feel valued, heard, and supported.

Promoting emotional literacy: Help your child develop emotional literacy by teaching them to recognize and express their emotions. Encourage them to identify and label their feelings, and validate their emotions by acknowledging their experiences. Teach them healthy ways to manage and regulate their emotions, such as deep breathing, engaging in calming activities, or seeking support from trusted adults.

Setting clear and consistent boundaries: Establish clear and consistent boundaries for your child. Boundaries provide structure and predictability, which can contribute to a child's sense of safety and security. Consistently enforcing boundaries helps children understand expectations and develop self-discipline. It is important to balance boundaries with warmth and flexibility, allowing for open dialogue and age-appropriate autonomy.

Encouraging autonomy and independence: Support your child's autonomy and encourage their growing independence. Allow them to make age-appropriate choices, take on responsibilities, and learn from their mistakes. This helps children develop confidence, self-esteem, and a sense of competence, all of which are crucial for their mental well-being.

Modeling healthy coping strategies: Children learn by observing their parents' behavior. Model healthy coping strategies, such as problem-solving, effective communication, stress management, and self-care. Demonstrate resilience in the face of challenges and show them that it's okay to ask for help when needed. By modeling healthy coping strategies, you provide your child with valuable tools to navigate life's ups and downs.

Fostering a positive parent-child relationship: Cultivate a positive and loving relationship with your child. Spend quality time together, engage in activities they enjoy, and show genuine interest in their lives. Celebrate their achievements, provide encouragement, and show unconditional love. A strong parent-child bond serves as a protective factor against mental health challenges and promotes overall well-being.

Promoting healthy lifestyle habits: Support your child's physical and mental well-being by promoting healthy lifestyle habits. Encourage regular physical activity, a balanced diet, and sufficient sleep. Limit screen time and encourage outdoor play and social interactions. A healthy lifestyle contributes to better mental health, emotional regulation, and overall resilience.

Creating a sense of belonging: Foster a sense of belonging and connection within the family unit. Create traditions, rituals, and opportunities for shared experiences. Encourage positive sibling relationships and facilitate connections with extended family members and community groups. A sense of belonging enhances a child's self-esteem, self-worth, and overall mental well-being.

Seeking support when needed: Recognize that parenting can be challenging, and seeking support when needed is a sign of strength. Reach out to other parents, join parenting support groups, or seek guidance from professionals. Being open to learning and growing as a parent contributes to a nurturing environment for your child's mental health.

So, parenting plays a pivotal role in nurturing children's mental health. By building a secure attachment, creating a positive and supportive environment, promoting emotional literacy, setting clear boundaries, encouraging autonomy and independence, modeling healthy coping strategies, fostering a positive parent-child relationship, promoting healthy lifestyle habits, creating a sense of belonging, and seeking support when needed, parents can create an environment that supports their children's mental well-being. Let us strive to prioritize our children's mental health, provide them with love, guidance, and support, and equip them with the skills they need to thrive emotionally and lead fulfilling lives.

Chapter 47: Mental Health Considerations for Older Adults

As individuals age, their mental health becomes increasingly important. Older adults may face unique challenges such as loss of loved ones, changes in physical health, retirement, and social isolation, which can impact their mental well-being. Let's explore the mental health considerations for older adults in more detail:

Understanding the importance of mental health in aging: Mental health is crucial for overall well-being at any stage of life, including the older adult years. Good mental health enables individuals to maintain independence, enjoy meaningful relationships, and engage in activities they find fulfilling. Prioritizing mental health in older adults is essential for promoting healthy aging and a higher quality of life.

Common mental health challenges: Older adults may experience various mental health challenges, including depression, anxiety, loneliness, grief, cognitive decline, and substance abuse. It is important to recognize that mental health conditions are not a normal part of aging and should be addressed with compassion and appropriate care.

Depression and anxiety: Depression and anxiety are prevalent mental health concerns among older adults. They can be triggered by factors such as chronic health conditions, social isolation, loss of independence, or the death of a loved one. Recognizing the signs and symptoms of depression and anxiety, such as persistent sadness, lack of interest, changes in sleep or appetite, excessive worry, or restlessness, is essential for early intervention and effective treatment.

Loneliness and social isolation: Older adults are at risk of experiencing loneliness and social isolation, which can have a significant impact on their mental health. Loss of friends and family members, retirement, mobility limitations, and changing social dynamics can contribute to feelings of loneliness. It is crucial to address social isolation by fostering connections, encouraging participation in community activities, and promoting intergenerational interactions.

Grief and loss: Older adults may experience multiple losses, including the death of friends, family members, or their spouse. Grief can manifest in various ways and may contribute to depression and feelings of emptiness. Providing support, understanding, and creating spaces for individuals to express their grief can aid in the healing process and promote emotional well-being.

Cognitive decline and dementia: Cognitive decline, including conditions such as Alzheimer's disease and other forms of dementia, can impact older adults' mental health. Memory loss, confusion, and changes in behavior can cause distress and affect overall well-being. It is important to provide appropriate support, resources, and access to healthcare professionals who specialize in working with older adults experiencing cognitive decline.

Substance abuse and medication management: Older adults may be at risk of substance abuse, including the misuse of prescription medications or ..... It is important to monitor medication use and ensure that older adults understand proper dosage and potential side effects. Encouraging open communication with healthcare providers and offering education on substance abuse prevention are key components of supporting mental health in this population.

Maintaining social connections: Supporting older adults in maintaining social connections is vital for their mental well-being. Encouraging participation in community groups, senior centers, and volunteer activities can provide opportunities for social engagement. Technology can also be leveraged to connect older adults with family members, friends, and support networks, particularly for those who face physical limitations or live in remote areas.

Holistic self-care: Promoting holistic self-care practices is beneficial for older adults' mental health. Encouraging regular exercise, proper nutrition, adequate sleep, and engaging in activities that bring joy and fulfillment can contribute to overall well-being. Mind-body practices, such as mindfulness, meditation, and gentle yoga, can also be effective tools for managing stress and promoting mental well-being.

Access to mental health services: Ensuring access to mental health services is critical for older adults. This includes providing information about available resources, reducing stigma around seeking help, and training healthcare providers to be knowledgeable about the specific mental health considerations of older adults. Integrating mental health services into primary care settings can also enhance accessibility and promote early intervention.

So, understanding the mental health considerations for older adults is essential for promoting their well-being and ensuring healthy aging. By recognizing the common mental health challenges faced by older adults, providing support, addressing social isolation, promoting holistic self-care practices, and ensuring access to mental health services, we can support their mental well-being and enhance their overall quality of life. Let us embrace a society that values and prioritizes the mental health of older adults, creating an environment where they can age with dignity, purpose, and joy.

Chapter 48: Cultural Competence in Mental Health Care

Cultural competence is a vital component of delivering quality mental health care. It involves understanding and respecting the unique cultural backgrounds, beliefs, values, and experiences of individuals seeking mental health support. Let's explore the topic of cultural competence in more detail:

Understanding cultural competence: Cultural competence refers to the ability of mental health professionals to effectively work with individuals from diverse cultural backgrounds. It involves acknowledging and respecting the influence of culture on a person's beliefs, attitudes, and behaviors. Cultural competence encompasses awareness, knowledge, and skills that enable professionals to provide culturally responsive and inclusive care.

Embracing diversity: Cultural competence starts with embracing and valuing diversity. Recognize that every individual is shaped by their cultural background, including their ethnicity, language, religion, socioeconomic status, sexual orientation, and more. Understanding that cultural diversity enriches our society and contributes to the unique perspectives and experiences individuals bring to mental health care is crucial.

Challenging biases and stereotypes: Cultural competence requires self-reflection and awareness of our own biases and stereotypes. It is important to challenge and overcome preconceived notions and assumptions about individuals from different cultures. Recognize that cultural competence involves treating each person as an individual rather than making assumptions based on their cultural background.

Building cultural knowledge: Cultivating cultural knowledge is an essential aspect of cultural competence. Mental health professionals should seek to educate themselves about various cultures, traditions, values, and belief systems. This includes understanding the impact of culture on perceptions of mental health, help-seeking behaviors, and coping mechanisms. Engage in continuous learning to expand your cultural knowledge and understanding.

Developing effective communication skills: Communication is key in providing culturally competent care. Mental health professionals should strive to develop effective communication skills that respect diverse cultural norms and preferences. This may involve adapting communication styles, utilizing interpreters or translators when necessary, and being sensitive to non-verbal cues and cultural nuances in communication.

Promoting inclusivity and accessibility: Cultural competence involves creating an inclusive and accessible environment for individuals from diverse cultural backgrounds. This includes considering language barriers, providing translated materials, and ensuring physical spaces are welcoming and culturally sensitive. Make efforts to accommodate individuals' needs and preferences to promote equal access to mental health services.

Building trust and rapport: Building trust and rapport is essential in cultural competence. Mental health professionals should establish a respectful and non-judgmental relationship with their clients. This involves being sensitive to cultural differences, actively listening to clients' concerns, and acknowledging the impact of culture on their mental health experiences. Trust is the foundation for effective therapeutic relationships.

Collaborating with communities and cultural leaders: Engaging with communities and cultural leaders is crucial for cultural competence. Collaborate with community organizations, religious leaders, and cultural groups to gain insights into specific cultural contexts, beliefs, and practices. Seek their guidance to better understand the needs of individuals within these communities and to develop culturally appropriate interventions and support systems.

Addressing cultural stigma and barriers: Cultural competence includes addressing cultural stigma and barriers to mental health care. Stigma surrounding mental health varies across cultures and can impact help-seeking behaviors. Mental health professionals should actively work to reduce stigma by educating communities, promoting open dialogue, and offering culturally sensitive outreach programs.

Advocating for culturally responsive policies and practices: Cultural competence extends beyond individual interactions to advocate for systemic changes in mental health care. Mental health professionals should advocate for policies and practices that promote cultural responsiveness and address disparities in access to care. This may involve advocating for diversity in the mental health workforce, increasing funding for culturally appropriate services, and developing training programs on cultural competence.

So, cultural competence is essential for providing effective and inclusive mental health care. By embracing diversity, challenging biases, building cultural knowledge, developing effective communication skills, promoting inclusivity and accessibility, building trust and rapport, collaborating with communities, addressing cultural stigma and barriers, and advocating for culturally responsive policies and practices, we can enhance cultural competence and better serve diverse populations. Let us strive to create a mental health care system that respects, values, and embraces the diverse cultural backgrounds of individuals, ensuring that everyone receives equitable and effective support for their mental well-being.

Chapter 49: The Impact of Technology on Mental Health Diagnosis and Treatment

Technology has revolutionized various aspects of our lives, and mental health care is no exception. From online therapy platforms to mobile applications, technology has the potential to improve accessibility, efficiency, and effectiveness in diagnosing and treating mental health conditions. Let's explore the impact of technology on mental health diagnosis and treatment in more detail:

Increased accessibility: Technology has significantly improved accessibility to mental health services. Online therapy platforms and telemedicine enable individuals to access mental health support from the comfort of their own homes. This is especially beneficial for individuals who live in remote areas, have limited mobility, or face barriers to seeking in-person care. Technology has bridged the gap and provided access to mental health services for many who previously struggled to receive timely support.

Enhanced self-monitoring: Mobile applications and wearable devices offer tools for self-monitoring and tracking mental health symptoms. These tools allow individuals to monitor their mood, sleep patterns, stress levels, and other relevant factors. Self-monitoring helps individuals gain insight into their mental well-being, identify patterns, and make informed decisions about their care. It empowers individuals to actively participate in their mental health management.

Personalized interventions: Technology enables the development of personalized interventions for mental health care. Mobile applications and online platforms offer tailored content, self-help resources, and therapeutic tools based on individual needs. These interventions can range from cognitive-behavioral therapy exercises and relaxation techniques to guided meditation and stress management techniques. Personalized interventions provide individuals with targeted support, increasing the effectiveness of mental health care.

Real-time support: Technology facilitates real-time support for individuals in crisis or those who need immediate assistance. Crisis helplines, text-based support services, and chatbots provide instant support and guidance. These services can be particularly valuable during times of heightened distress or when traditional face-to-face support may not be readily available. Real-time support through technology ensures that individuals receive timely assistance and can prevent escalating mental health crises.

Data collection and analysis: Technology allows for the collection and analysis of large amounts of data related to mental health. This data can provide valuable insights into trends, treatment outcomes, and population-level mental health needs. Researchers and mental health professionals can use this information to improve diagnosis accuracy, identify risk factors, and develop more effective treatment strategies. Data-driven approaches enhance our understanding of mental health and guide evidence-based practices.

Mental health education and awareness: Technology serves as a powerful tool for mental health education and awareness. Online platforms, social media, and mobile applications offer resources, articles, and educational content that help reduce stigma, raise awareness, and promote mental health literacy. These platforms also provide opportunities for individuals to connect with others who share similar experiences, fostering a sense of community and support.

Challenges and ethical considerations: While technology has numerous benefits, it also presents challenges and ethical considerations. Privacy and data security are of paramount importance when using technology for mental health care. Ensuring the confidentiality of sensitive information and implementing robust security measures is crucial. Additionally, technology should not replace the human connection and therapeutic alliance that is essential in mental health care. It is important to strike a balance between technology-driven interventions and the value of human interaction.

Addressing the digital divide: The digital divide, referring to disparities in access to technology and digital resources, is an important consideration in the impact of technology on mental health care. Not everyone has equal access to the internet, smartphones, or digital literacy. It is essential to address these disparities to ensure equitable access to technology-based mental health care. Efforts should be made to bridge the digital divide and provide support to those who may face barriers to accessing and utilizing technology.

Ethical guidelines and regulations: As technology continues to advance, it is crucial to establish ethical guidelines and regulations for the use of technology in mental health care. Professionals should adhere to ethical principles, such as informed consent, confidentiality, and ensuring the competence of technology-based interventions. Regulatory bodies play a vital role in setting standards and ensuring that technology-driven mental health care meets ethical and quality standards.

Integrating technology with traditional approaches: The most effective approach to mental health care often involves integrating technology with traditional in-person interventions. Technology can supplement face-to-face therapy, provide additional support between sessions, and enhance self-management. The integration of technology with traditional approaches allows for a comprehensive and personalized approach to mental health care.

So, technology has had a transformative impact on mental health diagnosis and treatment. With increased accessibility, enhanced self-monitoring, personalized interventions, real-time support, data collection and analysis, mental health education and awareness, there are significant benefits to leveraging technology in mental health care. However, it is crucial to address challenges, consider ethical considerations, and bridge the digital divide. By harnessing the power of technology while upholding ethical standards and ensuring human connection, we can leverage technology to improve mental health care and empower individuals on their journey toward mental well-being.

Chapter 50: Addressing Suicidal Ideation and Providing Effective Support

Suicidal ideation is a complex and serious issue that requires our attention and compassion. It is essential to approach this topic with sensitivity, empathy, and a commitment to providing the support needed to help individuals in crisis. Let's explore how we can address suicidal ideation and offer effective support:

Understanding suicidal ideation: Suicidal ideation refers to thoughts or contemplation of taking one's own life. It can range from fleeting thoughts to more persistent and intrusive ideation. It is important to recognize that suicidal ideation is a symptom of immense emotional pain and distress, often indicating an underlying mental health condition or overwhelming life circumstances. Understanding the nature of suicidal ideation is crucial for providing appropriate support.

Creating a safe and non-judgmental environment: When someone opens up about their suicidal thoughts, it is essential to create a safe and non-judgmental environment. Listen attentively, avoid making moral judgments, and let the person know that you are there to support them. Cultivate an atmosphere of trust and acceptance, assuring them that their feelings are valid and that they are not alone.

Asking directly about suicidal thoughts: It can be uncomfortable to ask someone directly if they are experiencing suicidal thoughts, but it is an important step in providing effective support. Be direct, yet compassionate, in your approach. Asking questions like, "Are you feeling so overwhelmed that you've had thoughts of ending your life?" can open up a dialogue and allow the person to share their experiences. Remember that discussing suicide does not increase the risk; in fact, it often provides relief for individuals to express their feelings.

Active listening and validation: When someone shares their suicidal thoughts, it is crucial to actively listen and validate their feelings. Avoid dismissing or minimizing their experiences. Validate their emotions by acknowledging their pain and struggles. Reflective listening, paraphrasing, and empathizing can help individuals feel heard and understood, fostering a sense of connection and support.

Assessing the level of risk: It is important to assess the level of risk when addressing suicidal ideation. Inquire about the intensity, frequency, and duration of the thoughts, as well as any plans or access to means. Assessing risk helps determine the appropriate level of support needed. If there is an immediate risk of harm, it is essential to involve emergency services and ensure the person's safety.

Encouraging professional help: Suicidal ideation often requires professional intervention. Encourage the person to seek help from mental health professionals, such as therapists, counselors, or psychiatrists, who are trained to address suicidal ideation. Offer to assist them in finding appropriate resources and provide information about helplines or crisis services that they can contact for immediate support.

Creating a safety plan: A safety plan is a personalized strategy that individuals can use to manage their suicidal thoughts and keep themselves safe. Help the person develop a safety plan that includes identifying triggers, coping strategies, supportive contacts, and emergency resources. A safety plan provides individuals with a tangible tool to turn to during times of crisis.

Offering ongoing support: Supporting someone experiencing suicidal ideation is an ongoing process. Continue to check in with them regularly, expressing your care and concern. Let them know that you are there to listen, offer support, and help them access professional help when needed. Encourage them to engage in self-care activities, maintain a support network, and remind them that seeking help is a sign of strength, not weakness.

Educating yourself and raising awareness: Educating yourself about suicidal ideation, risk factors, warning signs, and available resources is crucial for providing effective support. Attend workshops, read reputable literature, and access online resources to expand your knowledge. Additionally, raise awareness in your community about suicide prevention and the importance of mental health, reducing stigma, and promoting open conversations.

Self-care for supporters: Supporting someone experiencing suicidal ideation can be emotionally challenging. Remember to prioritize your own self-care and seek support from friends, family, or mental health professionals. Establish healthy boundaries, engage in activities that recharge you, and seek out support networks for individuals supporting those experiencing mental health challenges.

So, addressing suicidal ideation and providing effective support requires empathy, active listening, and a commitment to promoting mental well-being. By creating a safe environment, asking directly about suicidal thoughts, actively listening and validating emotions, assessing the level of risk, encouraging professional help, creating a safety plan, offering ongoing support, educating yourself, and prioritizing self-care, you can play a vital role in providing support and helping individuals navigate through their darkest moments. Remember, together, we can create a supportive and compassionate community where individuals feel heard, understood, and valued, fostering hope and resilience in the face of adversity.

Chapter 51: Trauma-Informed Care: Creating Safe Spaces for Healing

Trauma is a widespread experience that can have long-lasting effects on individuals' mental, emotional, and physical well-being. Trauma-informed care is an approach that recognizes the impact of trauma and aims to create safe and supportive environments that promote healing and empowerment. Let's explore the concept of trauma-informed care in more detail:

Understanding trauma: Trauma refers to experiences that are emotionally distressing and overwhelm an individual's ability to cope. It can result from a wide range of events, including physical or sexual abuse, neglect, accidents, natural disasters, or witnessing violence. Trauma can have a profound impact on an individual's mental health, leading to conditions such as post-traumatic stress disorder (PTSD), anxiety, depression, and substance abuse.

The principles of trauma-informed care: Trauma-informed care is based on a set of guiding principles that emphasize safety, trustworthiness, collaboration, empowerment, and cultural sensitivity. These principles provide a framework for creating environments that recognize and respond to the unique needs of individuals who have experienced trauma. By adopting a trauma-informed approach, we can foster healing and recovery while avoiding retraumatization.

Creating safe and supportive environments: A trauma-informed approach starts with creating safe and supportive environments for individuals who have experienced trauma. This involves providing physical and emotional safety, ensuring confidentiality, and offering choices and opportunities for individuals to exercise control over their healing process. Creating a sense of safety and predictability helps individuals feel secure and more open to engaging in the healing process.

Building trust and rapport: Trust is essential in trauma-informed care. Building trust requires establishing a compassionate and non-judgmental relationship with individuals who have experienced trauma. It involves active listening, empathy, and respecting their autonomy and boundaries. By demonstrating trustworthiness and reliability, we can foster a therapeutic alliance that promotes healing and growth.

Recognizing the impact of trauma: Trauma-informed care requires an understanding of the impact of trauma on mental health. Trauma can manifest in various ways, including hypervigilance, emotional dysregulation, dissociation, and avoidance of trauma reminders. Recognizing these symptoms and their connection to past traumatic experiences allows for more accurate assessment and the development of tailored treatment plans.

Promoting choice and collaboration: Trauma-informed care emphasizes collaboration and respects individuals' choices in their healing journey. It involves providing information, options, and involving individuals in decisions regarding their treatment. Empowering individuals to have a voice and agency in their care helps rebuild a sense of control and autonomy that may have been compromised by past trauma.

Understanding the role of culture: Culture plays a significant role in trauma and healing. Trauma-informed care recognizes and respects the cultural backgrounds, beliefs, and values of individuals. It acknowledges the influence of culture on the experience and expression of trauma, as well as the importance of culturally sensitive interventions. Incorporating cultural competence into trauma-informed care helps ensure that healing approaches are appropriate and respectful.

Addressing secondary trauma: Professionals working in trauma-informed care must also address their own potential for experiencing secondary trauma, also known as vicarious trauma. Engaging in self-care practices, seeking support, and maintaining healthy boundaries are essential for professionals to continue providing effective care without being overwhelmed by the traumatic experiences of those they support.

Training and education: Trauma-informed care requires ongoing training and education for professionals. This includes learning about trauma, its impact on mental health, trauma-specific interventions, and self-care strategies. Regular training helps professionals stay informed about the latest research and best practices in trauma-informed care, enhancing the quality of care provided to individuals who have experienced trauma.

Advocacy and policy changes: Trauma-informed care extends beyond individual interactions to advocating for policy changes that support trauma survivors. This includes advocating for trauma-informed practices in healthcare settings, educational institutions, and community organizations. Policy changes that prioritize trauma-informed care can lead to systemic improvements and enhance access to supportive services for individuals who have experienced trauma.

So, trauma-informed care is crucial for creating safe and supportive environments that promote healing and recovery. By understanding the impact of trauma, adopting the principles of trauma-informed care, creating safe spaces, building trust and rapport, recognizing the role of culture, promoting choice and collaboration, addressing secondary trauma, investing in training and education, and advocating for policy changes, we can provide effective support to individuals who have experienced trauma. Let us work together to create a society that embraces trauma-informed care, fosters healing, and empowers individuals on their journey toward recovery and resilience.

Chapter 52: Exploring Resilience in the Face of Adversity

Life is full of ups and downs, and resilience is the quality that enables individuals to bounce back and adapt in the face of adversity. Resilience is not about avoiding difficult situations or pretending that everything is fine. It is about finding inner strength, drawing upon available resources, and developing coping mechanisms to navigate and overcome the obstacles that come our way. Let's explore the concept of resilience in more detail:

Understanding resilience: Resilience can be defined as the ability to adapt, recover, and thrive in the face of adversity, trauma, or significant stress. It is not a fixed trait but rather a dynamic process that can be cultivated and strengthened over time. Resilience involves harnessing our inner resources, building supportive relationships, and developing effective coping strategies to navigate challenges and emerge stronger.

Protective factors: Resilience is influenced by various protective factors that enhance our ability to cope with adversity. These factors include having a supportive network of family and friends, access to resources and opportunities, a positive sense of self-worth, effective problem-solving skills, and the ability to regulate emotions. These protective factors act as a buffer during challenging times and contribute to our overall resilience.

Building self-awareness: Self-awareness is a fundamental aspect of resilience. It involves understanding our strengths, limitations, and emotional reactions to different situations. By cultivating self-awareness, we can identify our triggers, recognize when we are feeling overwhelmed, and develop strategies to manage stress effectively. Self-awareness empowers us to make conscious choices and respond to adversity in a proactive manner.

Developing healthy coping mechanisms: Coping mechanisms play a crucial role in resilience. Healthy coping mechanisms include engaging in physical activity, practicing relaxation techniques such as deep breathing or meditation, seeking social support, expressing emotions through creative outlets like art or writing, and maintaining a healthy lifestyle. By developing a toolbox of healthy coping strategies, we can better navigate challenges and maintain our well-being.

Cultivating optimism and positive mindset: Optimism and a positive mindset can significantly contribute to resilience. It involves reframing challenges as opportunities for growth, focusing on strengths and solutions rather than dwelling on obstacles, and cultivating a sense of hope and belief in our ability to overcome adversity. Adopting an optimistic perspective enables us to face challenges with resilience and maintain a hopeful outlook.

Building strong support networks: Social support is a vital component of resilience. Building strong support networks involves cultivating relationships with family, friends, mentors, or support groups who provide emotional support, encouragement, and practical assistance during difficult times. These connections offer a sense of belonging, reinforce our resilience, and remind us that we are not alone in facing challenges.

Embracing adaptability and flexibility: Resilience involves embracing adaptability and flexibility in the face of change or adversity. It means being open to new perspectives, adjusting our goals or plans when necessary, and finding alternative pathways to achieve our desired outcomes. Embracing adaptability allows us to navigate unexpected situations and setbacks with resilience and resourcefulness.

Cultivating gratitude and practicing mindfulness: Cultivating gratitude and practicing mindfulness can enhance resilience. Gratitude involves acknowledging and appreciating the positive aspects of our lives, even in challenging times. Mindfulness, on the other hand, involves being fully present and non-judgmentally aware of our thoughts, emotions, and sensations. Both gratitude and mindfulness help us cultivate resilience by fostering a sense of perspective, grounding us in the present moment, and promoting psychological well-being.

Learning from setbacks and failures: Resilience is not about avoiding setbacks or failures but rather learning from them. Viewing setbacks as opportunities for growth and self-reflection allows us to develop resilience. It involves analyzing what went wrong, identifying lessons learned, and using those insights to adapt our approach and move forward with renewed determination.

Seeking professional support when needed: Resilience does not mean going through challenges alone. Seeking professional support, such as therapy or counseling, can be a valuable resource during difficult times. Mental health professionals can provide guidance, offer strategies for building resilience, and help individuals navigate the emotional impact of adversity.

So, resilience is a valuable quality that enables individuals to navigate and overcome adversity. By understanding resilience, cultivating self-awareness, developing healthy coping mechanisms, embracing optimism, building strong support networks, embracing adaptability, cultivating gratitude and mindfulness, learning from setbacks, and seeking professional support when needed, we can strengthen our resilience and thrive in the face of challenges. Remember, resilience is a journey, and with each experience, we have the opportunity to grow stronger, wiser, and more resilient.

Chapter 53: Spirituality and Mental Health:

Finding Meaning and Purpose

Spirituality is a deeply personal and unique aspect of human existence. It encompasses our beliefs, values, connection to something greater than ourselves, and the search for meaning and purpose in life. While spirituality is often associated with religious practices, it can also be a broader concept that encompasses a sense of interconnectedness, mindfulness, and inner reflection. Let's explore the relationship between spirituality and mental health in more detail:

Understanding spirituality: Spirituality is a multifaceted concept that varies from person to person. It involves exploring our beliefs, values, and experiences in relation to something beyond the material world. Spirituality can encompass religious traditions, but it can also be independent of any particular religious affiliation. It is a deeply personal journey of self-discovery, seeking connection, and finding meaning and purpose in life.

Finding meaning and purpose: Spirituality plays a vital role in helping individuals find meaning and purpose in their lives. It offers a framework for understanding the bigger picture, contemplating existential questions, and seeking answers to profound life inquiries. By exploring our spirituality, we can tap into a sense of purpose and align our actions with our values, leading to a greater sense of fulfillment and mental well-being.

Connection and community: Spirituality often involves a sense of connection and belonging. Engaging in spiritual practices, participating in religious or spiritual communities, or finding solace in nature can foster a sense of connection to something greater than ourselves. These connections can provide social support, offer opportunities for growth and learning, and provide a sense of belonging that promotes mental well-being.

Mindfulness and self-reflection: Spirituality often emphasizes the importance of mindfulness and self-reflection. Practices such as meditation, prayer, or contemplation enable individuals to cultivate a deeper awareness of their thoughts, emotions, and experiences. By engaging in regular mindfulness practices, we can develop a greater sense of self-awareness, reduce stress, and enhance our overall mental well-being.

Coping with adversity: Spirituality can provide a source of strength and resilience in times of adversity. Engaging in spiritual practices, seeking solace in prayer or meditation, or drawing inspiration from sacred texts or teachings can offer comfort, hope, and a sense of purpose during challenging times. Spirituality provides individuals with tools to cope with stress, navigate loss, and find meaning even in the face of adversity.

Values and ethical considerations: Spirituality often guides individuals in identifying their values and ethical principles. It provides a moral compass for decision-making and actions, promoting a sense of integrity and congruence between one's beliefs and behaviors. Living in alignment with our values can contribute to a greater sense of well-being and mental health.

Cultivating gratitude and compassion: Spirituality often emphasizes cultivating gratitude and compassion for oneself and others. Expressing gratitude for the present moment and acknowledging the blessings in our lives can enhance our overall well-being. Similarly, practicing compassion and kindness toward oneself and others fosters a sense of connection and promotes positive mental health.

Support during life transitions: Spirituality can provide support and guidance during major life transitions, such as birth, death, marriage, or career changes. Engaging in spiritual rituals, seeking guidance from spiritual leaders or mentors, or reflecting on the deeper significance of these transitions can provide comfort, clarity, and a sense of direction during times of change.

Integration of mind, body, and spirit: Spirituality recognizes the interconnectedness of the mind, body, and spirit. It emphasizes the importance of nurturing all aspects of our being to achieve overall well-being. Engaging in practices that promote physical health, emotional well-being, and spiritual growth can lead to a more integrated and holistic approach to mental health care.

Embracing diversity and personal exploration: Spirituality embraces diversity and personal exploration. It encourages individuals to explore their own beliefs, values, and experiences without judgment. It is a deeply personal journey that respects the unique path of each individual. By embracing diversity and personal exploration, we foster a more inclusive and accepting approach to spirituality and mental health. So, spirituality plays a significant role in mental health and well-being. By embracing spirituality, we can find meaning and purpose, cultivate connection and community, practice mindfulness and self-reflection, cope with adversity, live in alignment with our values, cultivate gratitude and compassion, find support during life transitions, integrate mind, body, and spirit, and embrace diversity and personal exploration. Spirituality offers a profound pathway to enhancing our mental health and experiencing a deeper sense of fulfillment and inner peace.

Chapter 54: The Influence of Personality Types on Mental Health

Our personalities shape how we perceive the world, interact with others, and navigate life's challenges. Understanding our unique personality traits can provide valuable insights into our mental health, helping us identify potential strengths, vulnerabilities, and areas for growth. Let's explore the influence of personality types on mental health in more detail:

The concept of personality: Personality refers to the pattern of thoughts, emotions, and behaviors that define an individual. It encompasses various traits, characteristics, and tendencies that shape how we perceive, interpret, and respond to the world around us. While everyone is unique, psychologists have identified common patterns of personality that can be categorized into different types.

The Big Five Personality Traits: One widely recognized model of personality is the Big Five, which includes five broad dimensions of personality:

• Openness to experience: This trait reflects a person's openness to new ideas, curiosity, and imagination. Those high in openness tend to be more adventurous, creative, and open-minded.

• Conscientiousness: Conscientiousness relates to a person's level of organization, responsibility, and self-discipline. Individuals high in conscientiousness are often reliable, organized, and focused on achieving their goals.

• Extraversion: Extraversion refers to the degree to which a person seeks social interaction, enjoys being around others, and is energized by social situations. Extraverts are typically outgoing, assertive, and enjoy being in the spotlight.

• Agreeableness: Agreeableness relates to a person's level of warmth, empathy, and concern for others. Individuals high in agreeableness tend to be cooperative, compassionate, and value harmonious relationships.

• Neuroticism: Neuroticism represents a person's tendency to experience negative emotions such as anxiety, depression, or mood swings. Those high in neuroticism may be more prone to stress, worry, and emotional instability.

Impact on mental health: Different personality traits can influence mental health in various ways. For example:

• Openness to experience: Individuals high in openness may have a greater capacity for creative problem-solving, adaptability, and seeking out new opportunities for personal growth. However, they may also be more susceptible to feelings of overwhelm or sensitivity to emotional stimuli.

• Conscientiousness: High levels of conscientiousness are often associated with better mental health outcomes. Individuals who are conscientious tend to exhibit higher levels of self-control, set, and achieve goals, and maintain healthier lifestyle habits.

• Extraversion: Extraverts generally thrive in social situations and may have a larger support network, leading to improved mental well-being. However, excessive extraversion can sometimes be associated with higher levels of impulsivity or risk-taking behaviors.

• Agreeableness: Individuals high in agreeableness tend to have strong interpersonal relationships, which can contribute to better mental health. However, they may also be prone to putting others' needs before their own, leading to potential difficulties in setting boundaries.

• Neuroticism: Higher levels of neuroticism are associated with a greater likelihood of experiencing anxiety, depression, and other mood disorders. Individuals with high neuroticism may benefit from developing strategies to manage stress, enhance emotional resilience, and seek professional support when needed.

Embracing individual differences: It is essential to note that there is no "ideal" or "correct" personality type. Each personality trait has its strengths and challenges. Embracing our unique combination of traits allows us to appreciate the diversity of human personalities and fosters self-acceptance. Instead of comparing ourselves to others, we can focus on developing our strengths and managing potential vulnerabilities.

Personality and self-care: Understanding our personality can guide us in developing personalized self-care strategies. For example:

• If you are high in conscientiousness, establishing a routine and setting achievable goals can provide a sense of structure and accomplishment.

• If you are introverted, allowing yourself regular alone time to recharge and engage in solitary activities can be crucial for maintaining your mental well-being.

• If you are high in neuroticism, developing stress management techniques, such as mindfulness or relaxation exercises, can help you navigate emotional ups and downs more effectively.

• If you are extraverted, seeking out social connections and engaging in activities that involve collaboration and interaction can boost your mood and provide a sense of fulfillment.

• If you are low in agreeableness, practicing assertiveness and setting boundaries can protect your mental well-being and prevent feelings of being taken advantage of.

The role of therapy: Therapy can be beneficial for individuals seeking a deeper understanding of their personality and its impact on mental health. Therapists can help individuals identify maladaptive patterns, develop coping strategies, and cultivate self-awareness. Therapy provides a safe and non-judgmental space to explore personal growth and enhance overall well-being.

So, personality traits have a significant influence on mental health and well-being. By understanding our unique personality type, we can gain valuable insights into our strengths, vulnerabilities, and areas for growth. Embracing our individual differences, developing personalized self-care strategies, and seeking professional support when needed can contribute to better mental health outcomes. Remember, each personality type is valuable, and by embracing our authentic selves, we can lead more fulfilling and mentally healthy lives.

Chapter 55: Supporting Mental Health During and After Pregnancy

Pregnancy and the postpartum period bring about significant physical, emotional, and social changes. While this can be an exciting and joyous time, it can also present various challenges and potential mental health concerns. It is crucial to prioritize mental health and ensure that individuals receive the support they need during this transformative journey. Let's explore the topic of supporting mental health during and after pregnancy in more detail:

Pregnancy and mental health: Pregnancy is a time of transition and adjustment. Hormonal fluctuations, physical discomfort, and anticipation of the upcoming changes can impact mental well-being. It is essential to recognize that mental health concerns can arise during pregnancy, including anxiety, depression, and perinatal mood and anxiety disorders. Open discussions and awareness surrounding mental health help reduce stigma and encourage seeking support.

Perinatal mood and anxiety disorders: Perinatal mood and anxiety disorders, including postpartum depression and anxiety, are common mental health concerns during and after pregnancy. These conditions can affect anyone, regardless of their background or circumstances. Symptoms may include persistent sadness, feelings of guilt or worthlessness, changes in appetite or sleep patterns, and difficulty bonding with the baby. Early identification and appropriate support are crucial for recovery.

Risk factors and protective factors: It is important to understand both risk factors and protective factors that can influence mental health during and after pregnancy. Risk factors may include a history of mental health issues, lack of social support, stressful life events, or complications during pregnancy. Conversely, protective factors, such as a strong support network, access to healthcare, and positive coping mechanisms, can enhance mental well-being.

Importance of prenatal care: Prenatal care plays a vital role in supporting mental health. Regular check-ups provide an opportunity to discuss emotional well-being, address concerns, and receive appropriate support. Healthcare providers can screen for mental health issues, offer resources, and provide referrals to mental health professionals when necessary. Engaging in prenatal care ensures that individuals receive comprehensive support for both their physical and mental health.

Building a support network: A strong support network is invaluable during and after pregnancy. Family, friends, partners, and healthcare professionals can offer emotional support, practical assistance, and a listening ear. Engaging in prenatal classes, support groups, or online communities can connect individuals with others who are experiencing similar challenges and foster a sense of belonging.

Self-care and stress management: Self-care is crucial for maintaining mental well-being during and after pregnancy. It involves prioritizing activities that promote relaxation, stress reduction, and self-nurturing. Engaging in activities such as gentle exercise, mindfulness practices, seeking alone time, and pursuing hobbies can help individuals recharge and maintain a positive mindset.

Open communication: Encouraging open communication is essential. Creating an environment where individuals feel comfortable discussing their emotions, fears, and concerns is crucial for destigmatizing mental health issues. Partners, family members, and friends can play an active role by actively listening, validating feelings, and offering non-judgmental support.

Seeking professional help: Professional support should be readily available and destigmatized. Mental health professionals with expertise in perinatal mental health can offer specialized care and evidence-based interventions. Therapy, counseling, and, if necessary, medication can be beneficial in managing perinatal mood and anxiety disorders. Seeking help is a sign of strength and prioritizing one's well-being.

Postpartum support: Postpartum support is essential during the early months after birth. This includes emotional support, assistance with practical tasks, and education about the challenges of parenthood. Community resources, such as postpartum support groups or home visiting programs, can provide guidance and reduce feelings of isolation.

Partner involvement: Partners play a crucial role in supporting mental health during and after pregnancy. Open communication, shared responsibilities, and understanding the challenges faced by the birthing parent can strengthen the support system. Partners can educate themselves about perinatal mental health, actively participate in prenatal care, and offer emotional support throughout the journey.

So, supporting mental health during and after pregnancy is crucial for the well-being of individuals and their families. By prioritizing mental health, building a support network, engaging in self-care, fostering open communication, seeking professional help when needed, and involving partners in the journey, we can create a supportive and nurturing environment. Remember, it is normal to experience a range of emotions during this transformative time, and seeking support is a proactive step toward ensuring the best possible mental health outcomes for both parent and child.

Chapter 56: Peer Pressure and its Impact on Adolescent Mental Health

Adolescence is a time of significant physical, emotional, and social development. During this period, the opinions and actions of peers become increasingly influential. While peer interactions can be positive and supportive, they can also create pressure to conform, engage in risky behaviors, or adopt unhealthy habits. It is important to understand the dynamics of peer pressure and empower adolescents to make choices that prioritize their mental well-being. Let's explore this topic in more detail:

Understanding peer pressure: Peer pressure refers to the influence exerted by peers on an individual's thoughts, attitudes, and behaviors. It can be both direct (explicitly expressed) or indirect (implicit or perceived pressure). Peers can shape adolescents' choices regarding appearance, social activities, academic performance, substance use, and other aspects of their lives.

Types of peer pressure: Peer pressure can take different forms:

• Positive peer pressure: Positive peer pressure encourages healthy and constructive behaviors. It can motivate adolescents to excel academically, participate in extracurricular activities, or engage in positive social interactions. Positive peer influence can foster personal growth, self-esteem, and resilience.

• Negative peer pressure: Negative peer pressure involves pressure to engage in behaviors that may be risky, unhealthy, or against an individual's values. This can include substance abuse, bullying, skipping school, or engaging in other harmful activities. Negative peer pressure can lead to increased stress, anxiety, and compromised mental health.

Impact on mental health: Peer pressure can have a significant impact on adolescent mental health:

• Self-esteem and self-worth: Adolescents may feel pressured to conform to certain standards set by their peers, which can negatively affect their self-esteem and self-worth. Constantly seeking validation from others and feeling the need to fit in can contribute to anxiety, depression, and low self-confidence.

•	Stress and anxiety: The pressure to conform to peer expectations can create stress and anxiety for adolescents. Fear of social rejection or exclusion can lead to constant worry and a heightened sense of self-consciousness. This can impact mental well-being and contribute to feelings of isolation or inadequacy.

•	Substance use and risky behaviors: Negative peer pressure can influence adolescents to experiment with substances, engage in risky sexual behaviors, or participate in dangerous activities. These behaviors can have long-lasting effects on mental health, leading to addiction, emotional distress, and compromised decision-making abilities.

•	Academic pressure: Peer pressure can extend to academic performance, with adolescents feeling pressured to achieve high grades or engage in cheating. The fear of academic failure or the inability to meet peer expectations can contribute to stress, anxiety, and an unhealthy focus on performance rather than personal growth.

Navigating peer pressure: Adolescents can adopt strategies to navigate peer pressure in a way that supports their mental health:

•	Building self-confidence: Encouraging adolescents to develop a strong sense of self-worth and self-acceptance can provide a foundation for resisting negative peer pressure. Fostering a positive self-image and emphasizing personal values can help them make decisions aligned with their well-being.

•	Developing assertiveness skills: Adolescents can learn assertiveness skills to express their opinions, set boundaries, and make independent choices. Being assertive allows them to resist negative peer pressure without succumbing to the fear of social rejection.

•	Cultivating a supportive network: Encouraging adolescents to build relationships with peers who share similar values and goals can provide a supportive network. These connections can offer validation, encouragement, and an alternative influence that promotes positive mental health.

•	Educating about risks and consequences: Providing adolescents with information about the risks and consequences of engaging in risky behaviors can empower them to make informed decisions. Understanding the potential negative outcomes can help them weigh the short-term desires against their long-term well-being.

•	Encouraging open communication: Creating an open and non-judgmental environment at home, school, or within the community encourages adolescents to seek guidance and express their concerns. Active listening and validating their experiences can help them navigate peer pressure more effectively.

•	Developing resilience and coping skills: Teaching adolescents resilience and healthy coping skills equips them with tools to manage stress and adversity. Resilience enables them to bounce back from negative experiences, make independent choices, and maintain mental well-being in the face of peer pressure.

Seeking professional support: If peer pressure significantly impacts an adolescent's mental health or leads to harmful behaviors, seeking professional support is crucial. Mental health professionals can provide guidance, counseling, and interventions tailored to the individual's needs.

So, peer pressure can have a profound impact on adolescent mental health. By understanding the dynamics of peer pressure, fostering self-confidence, developing assertiveness skills, cultivating a supportive network, educating about risks and consequences, encouraging open communication, and promoting resilience and coping skills, adolescents can navigate peer pressure in ways that prioritize their mental well-being. Remember, adolescents have the power to make choices that align with their values and promote positive mental health, and with the right support and guidance, they can confidently navigate the challenges of peer pressure.

Chapter 57: The Role of Artistic Expression in Mental Health Recovery

Artistic expression has long been recognized as a powerful tool for healing and self-discovery. Whether it's through painting, writing, music, dance, or any other form of creative outlet, engaging in art can have a profound impact on our mental and emotional well-being. Let's explore the role of artistic expression in mental health recovery in more detail:

The healing power of art: Artistic expression provides a unique platform for individuals to express and explore their thoughts, emotions, and experiences in a non-verbal and creative way. It offers an outlet for self-expression, a means to communicate feelings that may be difficult to articulate, and a safe space for personal exploration and healing.

Self-discovery and self-expression: Engaging in artistic activities allows individuals to tap into their inner selves and discover new aspects of their identities. Through art, they can express their authentic selves, break free from societal expectations, and embrace their unique perspectives and experiences. This process of self-discovery can be empowering and contribute to mental health recovery.

Emotional release and catharsis: Artistic expression provides a healthy and constructive avenue for emotional release and catharsis. It allows individuals to externalize and process their emotions, transforming inner turmoil into tangible and expressive creations. This release of emotions can provide a sense of relief, release tension, and promote emotional well-being.

Promoting mindfulness and presence: Engaging in art often requires focused attention and concentration. Whether it's painting, playing an instrument, or engaging in other creative activities, the process of creation can be meditative, grounding individuals in the present moment. This mindful state promotes relaxation, reduces stress, and enhances overall mental well-being.

Building resilience and coping skills: Artistic expression fosters resilience by providing individuals with a creative outlet to cope with and navigate life's challenges. It offers a constructive way to process difficult experiences, manage stress, and develop adaptive coping strategies. Engaging in art can help individuals build resilience and enhance their ability to face adversity.

Fostering connection and social support: Artistic expression can facilitate connection and community. Participating in group art activities, workshops, or joining creative communities can foster a sense of belonging and provide a supportive network of like-minded individuals. This social support can be invaluable in the journey of mental health recovery.

Enhancing self-esteem and confidence: Engaging in art and witnessing the growth and progress in one's creative abilities can boost self-esteem and confidence. Creating something meaningful and receiving validation for artistic achievements can instill a sense of accomplishment and pride. This enhanced self-esteem can contribute to improved mental well-being.

Integrating the mind and body: Artistic expression integrates the mind and body, allowing for a holistic approach to mental health recovery. Physical engagement in artistic activities, such as dancing or sculpting, can enhance body awareness, promote self-acceptance, and foster a positive body-image. This integration contributes to a sense of wholeness and well-being.

Accessible to all: One of the beautiful aspects of artistic expression is its accessibility. Engaging in art does not require any specific skill level or expertise. It is a personal and subjective journey, open to anyone who wishes to explore and express themselves creatively. Everyone can find their own unique way to engage in art and experience its therapeutic benefits.

Incorporating art into daily life: To harness the therapeutic benefits of artistic expression, it is important to incorporate art into daily life. This can be done by setting aside dedicated time for creative activities, establishing a creative routine, or integrating art into existing daily practices. Finding joy and inspiration in the creative process can contribute to sustained mental health recovery.

So, artistic expression plays a vital role in mental health recovery. Through art, individuals can embark on a journey of self-discovery, emotional release, and healing. Artistic expression promotes mindfulness, resilience, connection, self-esteem, and a holistic approach to well-being. Whether it's painting, writing, music, dance, or any other creative outlet, engaging in art has the power to transform and support mental health recovery. So, unleash your creativity, embrace the therapeutic benefits of art, and embark on a journey of self-expression and healing.

Chapter 58: Understanding Body Image and Its Effect on Mental Well-being

Body image refers to the thoughts, feelings, and perceptions we have about our bodies. It encompasses how we view our physical appearance, as well as our thoughts and emotions related to our bodies. Body image is deeply intertwined with our sense of self-worth, confidence, and overall mental well-being. Let's explore the topic of body image and its effect on mental well-being in more detail:

The perception of body image: Body image is a subjective experience that is influenced by a variety of factors, including societal ideals, media representations, cultural norms, personal experiences, and individual characteristics. It is important to recognize that body image is not solely based on objective appearance, but also on our own thoughts, beliefs, and interpretations.

Societal and media influences: Societal ideals of beauty and media representations play a significant role in shaping our body image perceptions. The media often promotes narrow and unrealistic beauty standards, emphasizing the importance of a certain body shape, size, or appearance. Constant exposure to these ideals can lead to comparison, dissatisfaction, and a negative impact on mental well-being.

Cultural influences: Cultural norms and values surrounding body image vary across different societies. Some cultures prioritize specific body ideals, while others embrace diversity and a broader definition of beauty. Understanding and challenging cultural norms can help individuals develop a healthier and more inclusive perspective on body image.

Personal experiences and traumas: Personal experiences, such as past trauma, body shaming, or negative comments from others, can significantly impact body image. These experiences can create negative beliefs about one's body, leading to low self-esteem, body dissatisfaction, and increased vulnerability to mental health concerns.

Body image and mental well-being: Body image concerns can have a profound effect on mental health:

• Body dissatisfaction: Feeling dissatisfied with one's body can contribute to diminished self-esteem, depression, anxiety, and disordered eating behaviors. Negative body image can lead to a preoccupation with appearance, constant comparison to others, and a persistent sense of inadequacy.

• Eating disorders: Body image concerns are closely linked to the development of eating disorders, such as anorexia nervosa, bulimia nervosa, and binge eating disorder. Distorted body image perceptions can contribute to an unhealthy relationship with food, excessive exercise, and an intense desire to control or change one's body.

• Depression and anxiety: Negative body image can be a significant risk factor for depression and anxiety. Constant negative self-evaluation and a focus on perceived flaws can contribute to feelings of hopelessness, social withdrawal, and heightened anxiety in social situations.

• Low self-esteem and self-worth: Body image concerns can erode self-esteem and self-worth. Constantly comparing oneself to societal ideals or feeling inadequate based on appearance can undermine confidence and hinder overall mental well-being.

Cultivating a positive body image:

• Practice self-acceptance: Embrace the concept of self-acceptance, recognizing that our worth extends far beyond our physical appearance. Focus on valuing your unique qualities, strengths, and accomplishments.

• Challenge societal beauty ideals: Critically analyze and challenge societal beauty ideals. Surround yourself with diverse representations of beauty, both in media and in your personal life. Celebrate different body shapes, sizes, and appearances.

• Focus on self-care: Prioritize self-care activities that nourish your mind, body, and spirit. Engage in regular physical activity that you enjoy, not as a means of changing your body, but for the joy of movement and overall well-being.

• Develop a healthy relationship with food: Shift your focus from restrictive or obsessive eating patterns to a balanced approach to nutrition. Listen to your body's hunger and fullness cues and engage in mindful eating practices.

• Surround yourself with positive influences: Surround yourself with supportive and body-positive individuals who promote acceptance, inclusivity, and self-love. Engage in communities that celebrate diversity and challenge societal beauty standards.

• Seek professional support: If body image concerns significantly impact your mental well-being, consider seeking support from mental health professionals. Therapists, counselors, or support groups can provide guidance, coping strategies, and interventions tailored to your specific needs.

Mindful self-compassion: Practice mindful self-compassion by treating yourself with kindness, understanding, and forgiveness. Be gentle with yourself and challenge negative self-talk. Focus on developing a positive inner dialogue that uplifts and encourages self-acceptance.

So, body image plays a significant role in our mental well-being. By understanding the factors that influence body image perceptions, challenging societal beauty ideals, practicing self-acceptance, engaging in self-care, surrounding ourselves with positive influences, and seeking professional support when needed, we can cultivate a positive body image that enhances our mental well-being. Remember, embracing our unique bodies and valuing ourselves beyond appearance is a powerful step towards fostering a healthy and positive relationship with our bodies and ultimately supporting our overall mental well-being. Let's embrace body positivity, challenge societal standards, and celebrate the diversity and beauty of every body.

Chapter 59: Combating Perfectionism and Cultivating Self-compassion

Perfectionism is a common mindset characterized by setting excessively high standards for oneself and striving for flawlessness in all areas of life. While striving for excellence can be a positive trait, perfectionism often comes with self-criticism, fear of failure, and an unrelenting pursuit of unattainable ideals. Let's explore the topic of perfectionism and the importance of self-compassion in more detail:

Understanding perfectionism: Perfectionism is rooted in the belief that self-worth is contingent upon meeting high standards and achieving flawless performance. It often manifests as an all-or-nothing mindset, where any perceived imperfection is deemed unacceptable. Perfectionists place immense pressure on themselves, seeking validation through external achievements and fearing criticism or rejection.

The impact of perfectionism on mental well-being: Perfectionism can have a detrimental impact on mental health:

• Anxiety and stress: The relentless pursuit of perfection can lead to heightened anxiety and chronic stress. Perfectionists are often plagued by self-doubt, fear of failure, and excessive worry about meeting their own impossibly high standards.

• Depression and self-esteem: Perfectionists are more prone to depression due to the constant self-criticism and self-imposed pressure. The discrepancy between their idealized expectations and perceived failures can erode self-esteem, leading to a negative self-image and feelings of inadequacy.

• Procrastination and paralysis: The fear of making mistakes or falling short of perfection can lead to procrastination and avoidance. Perfectionists may become paralyzed by the fear of failure, preventing them from taking necessary risks or pursuing their goals.

• Relationship challenges: Perfectionism can impact relationships, as the constant need for control and unrealistic expectations can strain personal connections. Perfectionists may have difficulty accepting others' imperfections and struggle to show compassion or empathy.

Cultivating self-compassion: Self-compassion is the antidote to perfectionism, offering a kinder and more balanced perspective. It involves treating oneself with understanding, warmth, and acceptance in the face of perceived shortcomings or mistakes. Here are strategies for cultivating self-compassion:

•   Mindfulness and self-awareness: Practice mindfulness to become aware of self-critical thoughts and perfectionistic tendencies. Recognize the impact these thoughts have on your well-being and challenge their validity.

•   Challenge perfectionistic beliefs: Question the beliefs underlying perfectionism. Replace self-critical thoughts with more realistic and compassionate ones. Remind yourself that no one is perfect, and that it's okay to make mistakes and learn from them.

•   Set realistic goals and expectations: Establish goals that are challenging yet attainable. Break larger tasks into smaller, manageable steps. Embrace the idea that progress and growth are more important than flawless outcomes.

•   Embrace imperfections and failures: Instead of viewing imperfections or failures as personal shortcomings, reframe them as opportunities for learning and growth. Embrace the lessons and insights gained from setbacks, and celebrate the courage to try again.

•   Practice self-kindness: Treat yourself with kindness, just as you would treat a loved one. Offer supportive and encouraging self-talk, acknowledging your efforts and progress. Celebrate achievements, no matter how small.

•   Cultivate gratitude: Focus on appreciating the positives in your life and expressing gratitude for your unique qualities and strengths. Gratitude can shift your perspective and help you recognize the value in imperfections and failures.

•   Seek support and connection: Reach out to trusted friends, family, or mental health professionals for support. Sharing your experiences and challenges with others can provide validation, perspective, and encouragement.

•   Prioritize self-care: Engage in activities that nurture your physical, mental, and emotional well-being. Take time for relaxation, self-reflection, hobbies, and self-care practices that bring you joy and rejuvenation.

Embracing growth and progress: Shift your focus from rigid perfectionism to a growth-oriented mindset. Embrace the journey of personal growth, recognizing that mistakes and imperfections are opportunities for learning and development.

Celebrating self-acceptance: Embrace self-acceptance as a lifelong practice. Accept that you are a human being with strengths and limitations. Value your inherent worth beyond achievements and external validation.

Seeking professional help: If perfectionism significantly impacts your mental well-being or interferes with your daily life, consider seeking support from a mental health professional. Therapists can provide guidance, strategies, and interventions tailored to your specific needs.

So, combating perfectionism and cultivating self-compassion is a transformative journey toward greater mental well-being. By challenging perfectionistic beliefs, embracing self-compassion, setting realistic expectations, practicing self-kindness, and embracing growth and progress, we can free ourselves from the shackles of perfectionism and embrace a more fulfilling and balanced life. Remember, self-compassion is a lifelong practice that allows us to embrace our imperfect, authentic selves, and flourish in all areas of our lives.

Chapter 60: Exploring the Connection Between Chronic Pain and Mental Health

Living with chronic pain can be an overwhelming and challenging experience that affects not only the body but also the mind. Chronic pain refers to persistent pain that lasts for more than three months and can stem from various conditions or injuries. Let's explore the connection between chronic pain and mental health in more detail:

The impact of chronic pain on mental well-being: Chronic pain can have a profound effect on mental health:

• Emotional distress: Living with persistent pain can lead to emotional distress, including feelings of frustration, sadness, irritability, or anxiety. Coping with the constant discomfort and limitations can take a toll on one's overall emotional well-being.

• Depression: Chronic pain is strongly linked to the development of depression. The experience of ongoing pain can lead to a loss of pleasure, decreased motivation, and a sense of hopelessness. Chronic pain and depression often coexist and can worsen each other's symptoms.

• Anxiety: The unpredictability and chronic nature of pain can create anxiety about when the next flare-up will occur or how it may impact daily life. Chronic pain can also disrupt sleep, which further contributes to anxiety symptoms.

• Social isolation: The limitations imposed by chronic pain can lead to social withdrawal and feelings of isolation. Engaging in social activities may become more challenging, and individuals may experience a loss of connection with others, which can negatively impact mental well-being.

• Impact on self-esteem: Chronic pain can erode self-esteem, as individuals may struggle with feelings of inadequacy or worthlessness due to their perceived inability to engage in activities or perform tasks as they once did.

The biopsychosocial model: Understanding the connection between chronic pain and mental health requires adopting a biopsychosocial perspective. This model recognizes that chronic pain is influenced by biological, psychological, and social factors. It acknowledges that mental and emotional factors can both contribute to and be influenced by the experience of chronic pain.

The vicious cycle of chronic pain and mental health: Chronic pain and mental health concerns often perpetuate each other in a vicious cycle:

• Pain amplification: Mental health issues, such as stress, anxiety, and depression, can amplify the perception of pain. These factors can contribute to a heightened sensitivity to pain and make it more challenging to cope with.

• Coping mechanisms: Individuals may turn to maladaptive coping mechanisms, such as excessive use of pain medications, ..., or other substances, to manage their pain and emotional distress. These coping strategies can further exacerbate mental health concerns.

• Reduced physical activity: Chronic pain can limit one's ability to engage in physical activities, leading to a more sedentary lifestyle. The lack of physical activity can negatively impact mood, contribute to weight gain or loss, and further complicate the management of both physical and mental health.

The importance of a multidisciplinary approach: Managing chronic pain and its impact on mental health requires a multidisciplinary approach:

• Medical interventions: Consult with healthcare professionals, such as pain specialists or physiotherapists, to explore medical interventions aimed at reducing pain and improving physical functioning. This may include medications, physical therapy, or other treatments tailored to your specific condition.

• Psychological support: Seek support from mental health professionals, such as therapists or psychologists, who specialize in pain management. Psychological interventions, such as cognitive-behavioral therapy (CBT) or mindfulness-based techniques, can help individuals develop coping strategies, manage stress, and address the emotional impact of chronic pain.

• Social support: Connect with support groups or individuals who share similar experiences. Sharing your challenges and finding

understanding can alleviate feelings of isolation and provide practical tips for managing daily life with chronic pain.
•	Lifestyle modifications: Explore lifestyle modifications that may complement medical and psychological interventions. This may include adopting a balanced and nutritious diet, engaging in gentle exercise or movement that suits your abilities, and prioritizing activities that bring joy and purpose.
•	Self-care practices: Incorporate self-care practices into your routine to support both your physical and mental well-being. This may include relaxation techniques, mindfulness, journaling, engaging in hobbies, or seeking moments of solitude to recharge.

Embracing a holistic approach: Adopting a holistic approach to managing chronic pain and mental health involves recognizing the interconnectedness of mind, body, and social factors. It entails addressing physical symptoms, managing emotional distress, cultivating social support, and engaging in self-care practices that promote overall well-being.

Seeking professional help: If chronic pain significantly impacts your mental well-being or interferes with your daily life, consider seeking support from a multidisciplinary team of healthcare professionals. They can provide personalized guidance, treatment options, and interventions to help you effectively manage both your physical and mental health.

So, chronic pain and mental health are intricately connected. Understanding and addressing this connection is crucial for individuals experiencing chronic pain. By adopting a multidisciplinary approach, embracing a holistic perspective, seeking support from healthcare professionals, and implementing self-care practices, individuals can enhance their overall well-being and effectively manage the challenges of chronic pain. Remember, you are not alone in this journey, and with the right support and strategies, it is possible to live a fulfilling and meaningful life, even in the presence of chronic pain.

Chapter 61: Gender Dysphoria: Navigating Mental Health Challenges

Gender dysphoria refers to the distress experienced by individuals whose gender identity does not align with the sex they were assigned at birth. It encompasses feelings of discomfort, dissatisfaction, and distress related to the incongruence between one's experienced gender and their assigned sex. Let's explore the topic of gender dysphoria and its impact on mental health in more detail:

Understanding gender dysphoria: Gender dysphoria is a deeply personal and individual experience. It involves a disconnect between one's internal sense of gender identity and the external gender assigned at birth. It is important to recognize that gender dysphoria is not a mental illness but rather a response to societal expectations and norms that may not align with one's true gender identity.

Impact on mental well-being: Gender dysphoria can have a significant impact on mental health:

• Depression and anxiety: The distress associated with gender dysphoria can contribute to symptoms of depression and anxiety. The mismatch between one's internal sense of self and societal expectations can lead to feelings of isolation, fear of rejection, and discrimination, which can exacerbate mental health challenges.

• Body image concerns: Body dysphoria, a specific aspect of gender dysphoria, involves dissatisfaction with one's physical characteristics that do not align with their gender identity. This can lead to body image concerns, self-consciousness, and emotional distress.

• Social and interpersonal challenges: Individuals with gender dysphoria may face challenges in their relationships and social interactions. The fear of judgment or rejection can lead to social isolation, difficulty forming authentic connections, and a lack of support.

• Minority stress: Experiencing discrimination, prejudice, or stigma due to gender identity can contribute to minority stress, which increases the risk of mental health concerns. It is important to address systemic and societal factors that contribute to minority stress and work towards creating inclusive and accepting environments.

Navigating mental health challenges:

• Seek support: Connecting with supportive individuals, such as friends, family, or members of the LGBTQ+ community, can provide a sense of understanding and validation. Support groups, therapy, or online communities can offer a safe space for sharing experiences, gaining support, and accessing resources.

• Find a knowledgeable healthcare provider: It is crucial to work with healthcare professionals who are knowledgeable and affirming in their approach to gender dysphoria. They can provide appropriate medical and mental health support, including hormone therapy, gender-affirming surgeries, or referrals to specialists.

• Educate yourself: Learning about gender identity, gender expression, and transgender experiences can help individuals better understand their own journey and navigate the challenges they may face. Educating oneself can also empower individuals to advocate for their rights and educate others about gender diversity.

• Practice self-care: Engaging in self-care activities that promote mental and emotional well-being is essential. This may include engaging in activities that bring joy, practicing mindfulness or meditation, seeking moments of solitude, and prioritizing physical well-being through exercise, nutrition, and adequate rest.

• Develop coping strategies: Developing healthy coping strategies can help manage the stressors associated with gender dysphoria. This may involve mindfulness techniques, journaling, creative outlets, or engaging in supportive friendships and communities.

• Access mental health support: If gender dysphoria significantly impacts your mental well-being, seeking professional mental health support is crucial. Mental health professionals with experience in transgender issues can provide therapy, support, and strategies to cope with the challenges and develop resilience.

Building resilience and self-acceptance: Building resilience is a key aspect of navigating mental health challenges associated with gender dysphoria:

• Self-acceptance: Embracing and affirming your gender identity is an important step toward self-acceptance. Recognize that your gender identity is valid and deserving of respect and understanding, both from yourself and others.

• Surround yourself with support: Cultivate a support network of understanding and affirming individuals who respect and validate your gender identity. Engage with LGBTQ+ organizations and communities that provide resources, advocacy, and a sense of belonging.

• Advocate for yourself: Empower yourself by advocating for your needs and rights. Educate others about gender diversity, challenge stereotypes and biases, and work towards creating inclusive environments where all individuals can thrive.

• Celebrate milestones and progress: Celebrate your personal milestones and achievements on your journey of self-discovery and self-acceptance. Acknowledge and honor the courage and resilience it takes to live authentically.

Continued self-growth and learning: Remember that gender identity is a personal and ongoing journey. It is essential to embrace continuous self-growth, self-compassion, and ongoing learning about gender diversity, as well as nurturing your mental and emotional well-being.

So, gender dysphoria presents unique challenges to an individual's mental well-being. By seeking support, finding knowledgeable healthcare providers, educating oneself, practicing self-care, accessing mental health support, and building resilience and self-acceptance, individuals can navigate these challenges and foster their mental health and well-being. Remember, your gender identity is valid, and you deserve to live authentically and with self-compassion. Together, we can work towards creating a more inclusive and accepting world for all genders.

Chapter 62: Mental Health Considerations for Individuals with Chronic Illnesses

Living with a chronic illness presents numerous physical, emotional, and social challenges that can significantly impact mental well-being. Chronic illnesses are long-term health conditions that require ongoing management and can include conditions such as diabetes, multiple sclerosis, fibromyalgia, or autoimmune disorders. Let's explore the topic of mental health considerations for individuals with chronic illnesses in more detail:

The impact of chronic illness on mental well-being: Chronic illnesses can have a profound effect on mental health:

• Emotional distress: The experience of living with a chronic illness can evoke a range of emotions, including sadness, grief, frustration, anger, or anxiety. Coping with the uncertainties, limitations, and changes in lifestyle that accompany chronic illness can contribute to emotional distress.

• Loss and adjustment: Individuals with chronic illnesses often experience various losses, including loss of physical abilities, loss of independence, or changes in personal and professional roles. Adjusting to these losses and adapting to a new reality can be emotionally challenging.

• Anxiety and depression: The chronic nature of the illness, along with its associated symptoms and treatment regimens, can lead to increased anxiety and depression. Uncertainty about the future, fear of worsening symptoms, or the impact of the illness on daily life can contribute to these mental health concerns.

• Social isolation: The limitations imposed by chronic illnesses, such as physical symptoms, fatigue, or reduced mobility, can lead to social isolation. Difficulty participating in social activities, maintaining relationships, or engaging in work or school can contribute to feelings of loneliness and disconnection.

• Identity and self-esteem: Chronic illnesses can challenge an individual's sense of identity and self-worth. The changes in physical appearance, abilities, or roles can impact self-esteem and lead to feelings of inadequacy or loss of identity.

Common challenges faced by individuals with chronic illnesses:

• Managing physical symptoms: Chronic illnesses often present physical symptoms that can be distressing and impact daily functioning. Managing pain, fatigue, nausea, or other symptoms requires energy and resilience, which can affect overall well-being.

• Treatment adherence: Following complex treatment regimens, including medications, therapies, or lifestyle modifications, can be challenging and may contribute to feelings of frustration or overwhelm.

• Uncertainty and fear: The unpredictable nature of chronic illnesses can create uncertainty about the future and fear of symptom exacerbation or disease progression. This uncertainty can contribute to anxiety and stress.

• Self-advocacy and navigating healthcare systems: Individuals with chronic illnesses often need to advocate for their healthcare needs and navigate complex healthcare systems. This can be overwhelming and may require learning new skills and assertively communicating with healthcare providers.

• Financial and practical considerations: Chronic illnesses can bring financial burdens, such as medical expenses, treatments, or adaptations to living environments. Managing these practical considerations can contribute to stress and anxiety.

Strategies for supporting mental health while managing chronic illness:

• Self-care: Prioritize self-care practices that promote physical, mental, and emotional well-being. This may include engaging in activities that bring joy, practicing relaxation techniques, maintaining a balanced diet, getting regular exercise, and prioritizing adequate rest and sleep.

• Seek support: Connect with individuals who understand and can provide support. This may include family, friends, support groups, or online communities. Sharing experiences, exchanging information, and receiving validation can help alleviate feelings of isolation and provide a sense of belonging.

•   Mental health support: Consider seeking professional help from mental health providers experienced in working with individuals with chronic illnesses. Therapy can provide a safe space to explore emotions, develop coping strategies, and address the psychological impact of the illness.

•   Develop a support network: Build a network of healthcare providers who specialize in your specific chronic illness. Having a team of supportive professionals can provide comprehensive care and help navigate the challenges associated with managing the illness.

•   Educate yourself: Knowledge is empowering. Learn about your chronic illness, treatment options, and self-management strategies. Being informed can help you actively participate in your healthcare decisions and communicate effectively with your healthcare providers.

•   Set realistic goals: Adjust your expectations and set realistic goals that align with your current capabilities and limitations. This may involve pacing yourself, breaking tasks into manageable steps, and celebrating small achievements along the way.

•   Practice stress management techniques: Explore stress management techniques such as mindfulness, meditation, deep breathing exercises, or engaging in creative outlets. These techniques can help reduce anxiety, promote relaxation, and enhance overall well-being.

•   Foster resilience and acceptance: Cultivate resilience by embracing a mindset focused on adapting to challenges and bouncing back from setbacks. Acceptance of your chronic illness as part of your life journey can contribute to a sense of empowerment and psychological well-being.

Celebrate small victories and self-compassion: Acknowledge and celebrate your achievements, no matter how small. Practice self-compassion by being kind to yourself and recognizing that managing a chronic illness is a courageous and ongoing process.

Engage in advocacy and awareness: Consider getting involved in advocacy efforts to raise awareness and support for individuals with chronic illnesses. By sharing your story, you can help reduce stigma, improve understanding, and advocate for improved healthcare access and support systems.

So, managing a chronic illness is a complex journey that impacts both physical and mental well-being. By prioritizing self-care, seeking support, accessing mental health resources, developing a support network, educating oneself, setting realistic goals, practicing stress management techniques, fostering resilience and acceptance, and engaging in advocacy efforts, individuals can navigate the challenges of chronic illness while supporting their mental health and well-being. Remember, you are not defined by your illness, and with the right support and strategies, it is possible to lead a fulfilling and meaningful life.

Chapter 63: Building Emotional Intelligence for Improved Mental Health

Emotional intelligence refers to the ability to recognize, understand, and manage our own emotions, as well as the ability to recognize, understand, and influence the emotions of others. It encompasses a set of skills that enable us to navigate the complexities of our emotions and relationships. Let's explore the topic of building emotional intelligence and its connection to mental health in more detail:

The importance of emotional intelligence: Emotional intelligence plays a crucial role in our overall well-being and mental health:

• Self-awareness: Developing self-awareness allows us to understand our emotions, thoughts, and behaviors. It helps us recognize patterns, triggers, and underlying reasons behind our reactions, empowering us to make informed choices and respond more effectively to challenging situations.

• Emotional regulation: The ability to regulate our emotions is essential for maintaining mental balance. It involves recognizing and managing both positive and negative emotions in a healthy and constructive manner. By regulating our emotions, we can reduce stress, enhance resilience, and cultivate a greater sense of well-being.

• Empathy and understanding: Emotional intelligence enables us to empathize with others and understand their emotions and perspectives. This skill fosters healthier and more meaningful relationships, promotes effective communication, and contributes to a sense of connection and belonging.

• Conflict resolution: Emotional intelligence equips us with the skills to navigate conflicts and disagreements in a constructive and respectful manner. By understanding our own emotions and the emotions of others involved, we can find common ground, seek mutually beneficial solutions, and foster healthier relationships.

• Stress management: Developing emotional intelligence supports effective stress management. By recognizing and understanding our stressors, we can employ strategies to reduce their impact, such as practicing relaxation techniques, setting boundaries, seeking support, or engaging in self-care activities.

Developing emotional intelligence:

•	Cultivating self-awareness: Start by paying attention to your emotions and their triggers. Reflect on your thoughts, behaviors, and their connection to your emotional experiences. Regular self-reflection and journaling can help deepen your understanding of yourself.

•	Mindfulness practice: Engaging in mindfulness activities, such as meditation or deep breathing exercises, can help you become more present and aware of your emotions in the present moment. Mindfulness enhances your ability to observe and accept your emotions without judgment.

•	Practicing empathy: Put yourself in others' shoes and try to understand their perspectives and emotions. Practice active listening and validate their feelings. Empathy can be developed through curiosity, open-mindedness, and a genuine interest in others' experiences.

•	Recognizing and managing emotions: Learn to identify and label your emotions accurately. Notice the physical sensations and thoughts associated with each emotion. Once you recognize your emotions, explore healthy ways to express and process them, such as through journaling, talking to a trusted friend, or engaging in creative outlets.

•	Effective communication: Develop your communication skills by expressing your emotions clearly and assertively. Practice active listening and be attentive to non-verbal cues. Effective communication facilitates understanding and fosters healthier relationships.

•	Building resilience: Cultivate resilience by developing a positive mindset, reframing challenges as opportunities for growth, and maintaining optimism in the face of adversity. Resilience helps us bounce back from setbacks, cope with stress, and adapt to change.

•	Seeking feedback: Seek feedback from trusted individuals who can provide honest and constructive insights about your emotional intelligence. Their perspectives can help you identify areas for growth and improvement.

•	Continuous learning and growth: Emotional intelligence is a lifelong journey. Engage in personal development activities, read books on emotional intelligence, attend workshops or seminars, and seek opportunities for self-growth. Embrace the mindset of continuous learning and improvement.

Applying emotional intelligence to mental health:

•	Stress reduction: Use your emotional intelligence skills to identify and manage stressors effectively. By understanding your emotions and developing healthy coping mechanisms, you can reduce the impact of stress on your mental health.

•	Building resilience: Emotional intelligence supports the development of resilience, which is crucial for maintaining mental well-being. By recognizing and managing your emotions, you can bounce back from challenges, adapt to change, and maintain a positive outlook.

•	Enhancing relationships: Cultivating emotional intelligence helps foster healthier and more meaningful relationships. By understanding and empathizing with others, practicing effective communication, and managing conflicts constructively, you can create and maintain positive connections with those around you.

•	Self-care and self-compassion: Emotional intelligence encourages self-care and self-compassion. By recognizing and responding to your own emotional needs, you can prioritize self-care activities that promote your mental well-being. Treat yourself with kindness, understanding, and self-compassion.

•	Mental health management: Emotional intelligence enhances your ability to recognize signs of mental health challenges in yourself and others. By being attuned to your emotions, seeking support when needed, and advocating for your mental health, you can take proactive steps to maintain your well-being.

Embracing a lifelong journey: Building emotional intelligence is an ongoing process. It requires patience, self-reflection, and a commitment to personal growth. Remember that developing emotional intelligence is not about achieving perfection but rather about cultivating awareness, understanding, and healthier ways of relating to yourself and others.

So, building emotional intelligence is a valuable endeavor that can positively impact mental health and well-being. By developing self-awareness, practicing mindfulness, cultivating empathy, recognizing, and managing emotions, improving communication skills, building resilience, seeking feedback, and embracing continuous learning, individuals can enhance their emotional intelligence and support their mental health. Remember, emotional intelligence is a lifelong journey of self-discovery and growth, and with practice, it can lead to improved emotional well-being and more fulfilling relationships.

Chapter 64: The Impact of Social Support on Mental Health Outcomes

Social support refers to the assistance, comfort, and resources provided by our social networks, including family, friends, peers, and community. It plays a vital role in our mental health, providing a sense of belonging, validation, and emotional and practical assistance during challenging times. Let's explore the topic of social support and its connection to mental health in more detail:

The importance of social support: Social support is crucial for our overall well-being and mental health:

• Emotional support: Having someone who listens, understands, and validates our feelings can alleviate emotional distress, reduce feelings of loneliness, and provide a sense of comfort and connection. Emotional support can come from close relationships, such as family and friends, or from support groups or online communities.

• Practical support: Practical assistance, such as help with daily tasks, transportation, or childcare, can ease the burden and stress of daily life. Knowing that we have reliable support when needed allows us to focus on our mental well-being and manage life's challenges more effectively.

• Informational support: Access to accurate information and guidance from trusted sources can empower us to make informed decisions about our mental health. It can involve seeking advice from professionals, attending educational workshops, or engaging in discussions with knowledgeable individuals who can provide valuable insights.

• Appraisal support: Feedback and constructive input from others can provide perspective and help us reframe our thoughts and emotions. Trusted individuals can offer alternative viewpoints, challenge negative self-perceptions, and contribute to our personal growth and self-awareness.

• Social connection and belonging: Being part of a supportive social network fosters a sense of belonging and identity. Connecting with others who share similar experiences or challenges can provide a supportive and non-judgmental space for validation, understanding, and empathy.

Types of social support:

• Family support: Family members, including parents, siblings, or extended family, can provide a strong foundation of support. They often offer unconditional love, understanding, and practical assistance during difficult times.

• Friends and peer support: Friends play a crucial role in our social support network. They provide companionship, emotional support, and a sense of belonging. Peer support groups, both in-person and online, offer opportunities to connect with others who share similar experiences and challenges.

• Community support: Engaging with the broader community, such as through volunteering, participating in community events, or joining local organizations, can foster social connections and provide a sense of purpose and belonging.

• Professional support: Mental health professionals, such as therapists, counselors, or support groups led by professionals, offer specialized support and guidance tailored to specific mental health needs. They provide a safe and confidential space to explore emotions, develop coping strategies, and gain insights into our mental well-being.

• Online support: The digital age has opened up new avenues for social support. Online communities, forums, and social media platforms can connect individuals who may be geographically dispersed but share common interests or experiences. Online support can be a valuable resource, but it is important to ensure the reliability and safety of these platforms.

How to foster social support:

• Cultivate relationships: Nurturing and investing in meaningful relationships is essential for fostering social support. Reach out to friends and family, engage in shared activities, and make an effort to stay connected. Building relationships takes time and effort, but the rewards are invaluable.

• Communicate openly: Practice open and honest communication with your support network. Express your needs, concerns, and emotions. Share your experiences and actively listen to others. By fostering open dialogue, you can strengthen connections and deepen mutual understanding.

• Seek and offer help: Be willing to seek help when needed and accept support from others. Similarly, be ready to offer assistance and support when someone in your social network is going through a challenging time. Reciprocity fosters trust and strengthens relationships.

• Join support groups: Consider joining support groups or organizations that cater to your specific mental health concerns or life circumstances. These groups offer a safe space to share experiences, learn from others, and receive support from individuals who understand your unique challenges.

• Connect with your community: Engage with your local community by participating in activities, events, or volunteering opportunities. Building connections within your community can create a sense of belonging and expand your support network.

• Utilize technology: Explore online support groups, forums, and mental health apps that provide virtual support. Engaging with these platforms can offer access to a diverse range of experiences and perspectives, even when physical proximity is challenging.

• Set boundaries: While social support is essential, it is equally important to set healthy boundaries. Establish limits on the time and energy you invest in supporting others, and recognize when you need personal space and self-care.

The reciprocal nature of social support: Remember that social support is a two-way street. While receiving support is crucial, actively providing support to others can also enhance your own well-being. By being there for others, offering a listening ear, or providing assistance, you contribute to the strength and resilience of your social network.

Seeking professional help: While social support is invaluable, there may be times when professional help is necessary. Mental health professionals offer specialized knowledge and guidance to address specific mental health concerns. Seeking professional support does not diminish the importance of social support; rather, it complements and enhances the overall well-being.

So, social support plays a vital role in our mental health and well-being. By cultivating relationships, seeking, and offering support, joining support groups, connecting with our community, utilizing technology, and recognizing the reciprocal nature of social support, we can foster a robust network of support that positively impacts our mental health outcomes. Remember, no one is meant to navigate life's challenges alone, and by being part of a supportive social network, we can thrive and overcome obstacles together. Prioritize building and nurturing your social support system, and remember that reaching out for help is a sign of strength, not weakness. By fostering social connections, we create a foundation of support that can uplift us during difficult times, provide comfort, and contribute to our overall mental well-being. So, invest in your relationships, be open to giving and receiving support, and cherish the power of social connections in your journey toward improved mental health.

Chapter 65: The Link Between Childhood Adversity and Adult Mental Health

Childhood adversity refers to experiences of significant stress, trauma, or challenges during childhood. These experiences can range from physical, emotional, or sexual abuse, neglect, household dysfunction, parental separation, or divorce, to living in a household with substance abuse, mental illness, or domestic violence. Research has shown that childhood adversity can have lasting effects on mental health outcomes in adulthood. Let's explore this topic in more detail:

The impact of childhood adversity on mental health:

• Increased risk of mental health disorders: Childhood adversity has been linked to an increased risk of developing various mental health disorders, including depression, anxiety, post-traumatic stress disorder (PTSD), borderline personality disorder, and substance use disorders. The stress and trauma experienced during childhood can shape brain development and increase vulnerability to mental health challenges later in life.

• Altered stress response: Exposure to childhood adversity can dysregulate the body's stress response system, leading to an increased sensitivity to stress. This heightened stress response can make individuals more susceptible to experiencing chronic stress, which can have detrimental effects on mental health and overall well-being.

• Emotional and behavioral difficulties: Children who experience adversity may struggle with emotional regulation, exhibit behavioral problems, or face difficulties in forming healthy relationships. These challenges can persist into adulthood and impact various aspects of life, including work, relationships, and overall life satisfaction.

• Negative self-perception and low self-esteem: Childhood adversity can contribute to the development of negative self-perceptions and low self-esteem. Children who experience abuse, neglect, or other forms of adversity may internalize the belief that they are unworthy, unlovable, or responsible for the harm they endured. These negative self-perceptions can persist into adulthood and impact one's mental well-being.

• Interpersonal difficulties: Adverse childhood experiences can affect interpersonal relationships in adulthood. Individuals who have experienced childhood adversity may struggle with trust, intimacy, and forming secure attachments. These difficulties can lead to challenges in maintaining healthy relationships and may contribute to feelings of isolation or loneliness.

Healing from childhood adversity:

• Acknowledge and validate the experiences: Recognize and acknowledge the impact of childhood adversity on your life. It is essential to validate your experiences and understand that the challenges you faced were not your fault. Give yourself permission to explore and express your emotions related to the adversity you endured.

• Seek professional help: Consider seeking the support of mental health professionals who specialize in trauma-informed care. Therapists can provide a safe and supportive environment for you to process your experiences, develop coping strategies, and work towards healing and resilience. Therapeutic approaches such as cognitive-behavioral therapy (CBT), trauma-focused therapy, or EMDR (Eye Movement Desensitization and Reprocessing) can be effective in addressing the impact of childhood adversity.

• Build a support network: Surround yourself with a supportive network of friends, family, or support groups who can provide understanding, validation, and empathy. Connecting with others who have similar experiences can be particularly beneficial, as they can offer unique insights and support on the healing journey.

• Practice self-care: Engage in self-care activities that nurture your overall well-being. This can include exercise, mindfulness, or meditation, engaging in creative outlets, spending time in nature, or pursuing hobbies and interests that bring you joy. Self-care promotes resilience and supports mental and emotional healing.

• Develop healthy coping strategies: Explore healthy coping strategies to manage stress and emotional challenges. This can include journaling, deep breathing exercises, practicing relaxation techniques, or engaging in activities that promote self-expression and emotional release. Developing healthy coping skills empowers you to navigate the impact of childhood adversity and promote your mental well-being.

• Challenge negative beliefs: Work on challenging and reframing negative self-beliefs that may have developed as a result of childhood adversity. Engage in self-compassion and practice self-love by focusing on your strengths, accomplishments, and positive qualities. Replace self-blame with self-acceptance and understanding.

• Establish boundaries and prioritize self-care: Setting boundaries in relationships and prioritizing your own well-being is crucial. Recognize when certain situations or relationships may be triggering or detrimental to your mental health and take steps to protect yourself by establishing boundaries and seeking support when needed.

Breaking the cycle:

• Seek professional support when starting a family: If you are planning to start a family, consider seeking professional support to address any unresolved trauma or emotional wounds from your own childhood. This can help break the intergenerational cycle of adversity and create a nurturing and supportive environment for your future children.

• Parenting with compassion and awareness: If you have children, strive to provide them with a loving and supportive environment. Foster open communication, validate their emotions, and be mindful of the impact your actions and words may have on their well-being. Seek resources or parenting programs that can enhance your skills and understanding of positive parenting.

• Advocate for change: Promote awareness and advocate for policies that address childhood adversity, provide resources for prevention and intervention, and support those affected by adversity. By raising awareness and supporting initiatives focused on preventing and mitigating childhood adversity, you contribute to a healthier and more supportive society.

So, childhood adversity can have a profound impact on mental health outcomes in adulthood. However, healing and resilience are possible. By acknowledging your experiences, seeking professional help, building a support network, practicing self-care, developing healthy coping strategies, challenging negative beliefs, and breaking the cycle through compassionate parenting and advocacy, you can pave the path toward healing and create a brighter future for yourself and future generations. Remember, you are not defined by your childhood experiences, and with support and self-care, you can overcome the challenges and thrive in your journey toward mental well-being.

Chapter 66: Exploring the Influence of Cultural Beliefs on Mental Health Treatment

Culture plays a significant role in shaping our beliefs, values, and behaviors, including how we perceive and address mental health concerns. Cultural beliefs, norms, and practices can influence our understanding of mental illness, help-seeking behaviors, and the types of treatments we find acceptable and effective. It is crucial to recognize and respect the diverse cultural perspectives and experiences that shape our approach to mental health. Let's explore this topic in more detail:

Cultural perspectives on mental health:

• Cultural variations in defining mental health: Different cultures have diverse definitions and understandings of mental health. These definitions may encompass not only the absence of illness but also the presence of harmony, balance, and social well-being. Understanding and respecting these cultural variations are vital to providing culturally sensitive mental health care.

• Stigma and cultural attitudes: Cultural attitudes towards mental health can vary significantly, and stigma surrounding mental illness can be prevalent in some cultures. Stigma may arise from misconceptions, fear, or cultural beliefs that mental illness is a sign of weakness, personal failing, or divine punishment. These attitudes can prevent individuals from seeking help and accessing appropriate treatment.

• Cultural explanatory models: Cultural beliefs influence how individuals interpret and explain mental health issues. Some cultures may attribute mental health concerns to supernatural causes, while others may view them through a more biomedical or psychosocial lens. Understanding these explanatory models is essential for effective communication and treatment planning.

• Cultural identity and mental health: Cultural identity shapes our experiences and perceptions of mental health. Factors such as race, ethnicity, language, religion, and immigration experiences can influence how mental health is understood and addressed within specific cultural contexts. Recognizing and validating the influence of cultural identity is crucial in providing inclusive and effective mental health care.

Help-seeking behaviors and cultural barriers:

• Cultural influences on help-seeking: Cultural beliefs and norms significantly impact help-seeking behaviors. Some cultures prioritize community support, relying on family, friends, or spiritual leaders for assistance before considering professional help. Others may seek help primarily from traditional healers or alternative medicine practitioners. Understanding these cultural preferences is vital for engaging individuals in mental health treatment.

• Language and communication barriers: Language barriers can hinder effective communication between mental health providers and individuals from diverse cultural backgrounds. It is essential to provide interpretation services or access to multilingual mental health professionals to ensure accurate understanding and effective treatment.

• Lack of cultural representation in mental health care: Limited cultural representation within mental health care can create additional barriers for individuals from diverse backgrounds. Culturally responsive mental health services that embrace diversity and provide culturally competent care are essential in building trust and promoting effective treatment.

• Gender and cultural roles: Cultural norms and gender roles can influence help-seeking behaviors. In some cultures, seeking help for mental health concerns may be stigmatized for men due to expectations of strength and self-reliance. Understanding these cultural dynamics can inform the development of culturally sensitive approaches that address the unique needs and experiences of individuals.

The importance of cultural competency in mental health care:

• Cultural humility and self-reflection: Mental health professionals should engage in ongoing self-reflection and cultural humility. This involves recognizing and challenging personal biases, seeking to understand diverse cultural perspectives, and being open to learning from individuals with different backgrounds. Cultural humility promotes respectful and collaborative therapeutic relationships.

• Culturally sensitive assessment and treatment planning: Mental health assessments should consider cultural factors, including cultural beliefs, values, and experiences. Cultural formulation interviews and incorporating culturally appropriate assessment tools can provide a more comprehensive understanding of an individual's mental health needs and guide treatment planning.

• Collaboration and cultural adaptation: Collaborative partnerships between mental health professionals and individuals from diverse cultural backgrounds are essential. It is crucial to involve individuals in the treatment process, seeking their input and valuing their cultural perspectives. Adapting treatment approaches to align with cultural beliefs and practices can enhance treatment effectiveness.

• Training and education: Mental health professionals should receive training and education in cultural competence to enhance their understanding and skills in providing culturally sensitive care. This includes learning about diverse cultural beliefs, practices, and historical factors that influence mental health within different communities.

• Community engagement and advocacy: Engaging with community organizations and leaders can foster cultural understanding, promote mental health awareness, and reduce stigma surrounding mental illness within specific cultural contexts. Mental health professionals can collaborate with community members to develop culturally appropriate resources, programs, and outreach initiatives.

Supporting cultural diversity in mental health care:

• Diverse representation: Promote diverse representation within the mental health field to ensure that individuals from different cultural backgrounds can access care from professionals who understand their unique experiences and perspectives.

• Community-based collaborations: Collaborate with community organizations, faith-based groups, and cultural centers to provide mental health education, outreach, and support services that align with the cultural needs and preferences of the community.

• Language access and interpretation services: Ensure that mental health services are accessible to individuals with limited English proficiency by providing language access and interpretation services.

• Culturally tailored interventions: Develop and implement interventions that are culturally appropriate and sensitive to the needs and preferences of diverse populations. This can include incorporating traditional healing practices, addressing cultural stigma, and integrating cultural values and beliefs into treatment approaches.

So, cultural beliefs play a significant role in shaping our understanding of mental health and the ways in which we seek and engage in treatment. Recognizing the influence of cultural perspectives, addressing cultural barriers to help-seeking, promoting cultural competency in mental health care, and supporting diversity are essential steps toward providing inclusive and effective mental health services. By embracing cultural diversity, fostering understanding, and incorporating cultural beliefs and practices into treatment approaches, we can create a more inclusive and responsive mental health care system that respects and meets the diverse needs of individuals from all cultural backgrounds.

Chapter 67: Understanding Hoarding Disorder and Effective Interventions

Hoarding disorder is more than just having a cluttered home or being disorganized. It involves an intense emotional attachment to possessions, a fear of discarding them, and difficulty in making decisions about what to keep and what to let go. Hoarding behavior can lead to significant distress and impairment in various areas of life, including relationships, health, and safety. Let's explore this topic in more detail:

Understanding hoarding disorder:

• Diagnostic criteria: Hoarding disorder is recognized as a distinct mental health condition in the Diagnostic and Statistical Manual of Mental Disorders (DSM-5). To be diagnosed with hoarding disorder, individuals must meet specific criteria, including persistent difficulty discarding possessions, excessive accumulation of belongings, and significant distress or impairment as a result.

• Factors contributing to hoarding behavior: Hoarding behavior can arise from a combination of genetic, environmental, and psychological factors. It may be associated with underlying conditions such as obsessive-compulsive disorder (OCD), attention-deficit/hyperactivity disorder (ADHD), or depression. Traumatic life events, loss, or a history of deprivation can also contribute to the development of hoarding disorder.

• Emotional attachment and avoidance: Individuals with hoarding disorder often develop a strong emotional attachment to their possessions. They may assign deep personal value and meaning to items that others perceive as worthless. Discarding possessions can cause extreme distress, leading to avoidance of decluttering or organizing tasks.

• Cognitive distortions: Cognitive distortions, such as excessive sentimental attachment, perfectionism, or an inflated sense of responsibility for objects, can contribute to hoarding behavior. Individuals may have difficulty categorizing items, making decisions, or perceiving the potential consequences of their hoarding.

Impact on individuals' lives:

• Social isolation and strained relationships: Hoarding behavior can lead to social isolation and strained relationships with family, friends, and neighbors. The accumulation of possessions can create physical barriers and an unsanitary living environment, making it challenging for others to visit or engage with the individual.

• Health and safety risks: Hoarding can pose significant health and safety risks, including increased risk of falls, fire hazards, structural damage to the home, and poor sanitation. Cluttered living spaces can also impede emergency responders' ability to access the home during emergencies.

• Emotional distress and impaired well-being: Individuals with hoarding disorder often experience significant emotional distress, including anxiety, depression, shame, and guilt. The clutter and disorganization can negatively impact their overall well-being and quality of life.

• Functional impairment: Hoarding behavior can lead to functional impairment, making it challenging to perform daily activities such as cooking, cleaning, and personal hygiene. The cluttered environment can also interfere with work or school obligations, further exacerbating the individual's distress and isolation.

Effective interventions for hoarding disorder:

• Cognitive-behavioral therapy (CBT): CBT is a widely recognized and effective treatment approach for hoarding disorder. It involves identifying and challenging maladaptive beliefs and cognitive distortions related to hoarding, developing decision-making and organization skills, and gradually exposing individuals to discarding possessions in a structured and supportive manner.

• Motivational interviewing: Motivational interviewing techniques can help individuals explore their ambivalence about changing hoarding behavior and increase their motivation to engage in treatment. This collaborative approach focuses on enhancing intrinsic motivation and self-efficacy for change.

• Skills training: Skills training interventions, such as sorting and categorizing possessions, organizing strategies, and time management techniques, can be beneficial in building practical skills necessary for decluttering and maintaining an organized living environment.

• Supportive therapy: Providing a supportive and non-judgmental therapeutic environment is crucial in working with individuals with hoarding disorder. Addressing underlying emotional issues, fostering self-compassion, and building a trusting therapeutic relationship can facilitate the individual's willingness to explore and change their hoarding behaviors.

• Collaborative approach: Effective interventions for hoarding disorder often involve collaboration among mental health professionals, organizers, and other relevant professionals, such as occupational therapists or social workers. This multidisciplinary approach ensures a comprehensive assessment and addresses various aspects of the individual's needs.

• Harm reduction approach: In cases where individuals are not yet ready or able to engage in full-scale decluttering, a harm reduction approach can be utilized. This approach focuses on minimizing harm and improving safety by identifying and addressing immediate risks, implementing safety measures, and gradually working towards decluttering at a pace that feels manageable for the individual.

Building a supportive environment:

• Education and awareness: Educating family members, friends, and community members about hoarding disorder can help foster understanding and reduce stigma. Providing information about the nature of hoarding and its impact on individuals' lives can encourage empathy and support.

• Emotional support and empathy: Individuals with hoarding disorder often experience feelings of shame and isolation. Offering emotional support, empathy, and non-judgmental understanding can create a safe space for them to open up about their struggles and seek help.

• Collaborative decluttering: Engaging in decluttering efforts with the individual's consent and involvement can be more successful than imposing external decisions. Collaborative decluttering respects the individual's autonomy and helps build trust and a sense of ownership in the process.

- Maintenance and relapse prevention: Supporting individuals in maintaining an organized living environment after decluttering is essential. Developing strategies for ongoing organization and providing periodic check-ins or support can help prevent relapse and sustain the progress made.

So, hoarding disorder is a complex mental health condition that requires understanding, compassion, and effective interventions. By recognizing the impact of hoarding disorder on individuals' lives, providing appropriate treatment approaches, and building a supportive environment, we can empower individuals with hoarding disorder to embark on a journey of recovery and improved quality of life. Remember, recovery from hoarding disorder is possible, and with professional help, support, and a collaborative approach, individuals can gain control over their possessions, reduce distress, and cultivate a safe and healthy living environment.

Chapter 68: Examining Body-Focused Repetitive Behaviors and their Psychological Origins

Body-focused repetitive behaviors are a group of conditions characterized by repetitive self-grooming behaviors that result in damage to the body. These behaviors can serve as coping mechanisms for emotional distress, anxiety, or a way to regulate negative emotions. Let's explore this topic in more detail:

Understanding body-focused repetitive behaviors:

•   Types of BFRBs: Common BFRBs include hair pulling (trichotillomania), skin picking (excoriation disorder), and nail biting (onychophagia). These behaviors involve recurrent and compulsive actions that individuals find challenging to resist, leading to physical damage and emotional distress.

•   Prevalence and onset: BFRBs can occur across all age groups, genders, and cultural backgrounds. They often begin in childhood or adolescence and can persist into adulthood if left untreated. It is estimated that millions of people worldwide struggle with BFRBs, although many cases go undiagnosed and untreated.

•   Emotional regulation and coping: BFRBs are often associated with emotional regulation and coping difficulties. Individuals may engage in these behaviors as a way to relieve stress, anxiety, boredom, or to gain a sense of control. BFRBs can temporarily alleviate emotional discomfort, but they can also create a cycle of guilt, shame, and frustration.

•   Sensory and physiological factors: BFRBs can be associated with sensory experiences and physiological sensations. For example, hair pulling or skin picking may provide tactile sensations or a sense of relief when certain hairs or imperfections are removed. Understanding these sensory and physiological aspects is crucial in developing effective interventions.

Impact on individuals' lives:

•   Physical consequences: BFRBs can lead to physical damage, such as hair loss, skin lesions, infections, scarring, or dental issues (in the case of nail biting). These physical consequences can affect an individual's self-esteem, body image, and overall well-being.

• Psychological distress: BFRBs can cause significant psychological distress, including feelings of embarrassment, shame, guilt, and low self-esteem. Individuals may experience anxiety and depression related to their inability to control or stop the behaviors, leading to a diminished quality of life.

• Social and interpersonal challenges: BFRBs can impact individuals' social interactions and relationships. Embarrassment or fear of judgment may lead to social withdrawal, isolation, or difficulties engaging in activities that involve exposing the affected areas.

• Time and energy consumption: BFRBs can consume a significant amount of time and energy, as individuals may engage in the behaviors repeatedly throughout the day. This can interfere with daily functioning, productivity, and the pursuit of personal goals.

Psychological origins of BFRBs:

• Emotional regulation difficulties: BFRBs often arise as a means of regulating or managing emotional distress. Individuals may use these behaviors to cope with anxiety, stress, or other negative emotions. Understanding the underlying emotional triggers can guide treatment interventions.

• Perfectionism and self-criticism: BFRBs may be associated with perfectionism and a tendency towards self-criticism. The urge to remove perceived imperfections or irregularities can fuel the repetitive behaviors. Addressing underlying perfectionistic tendencies can be crucial in treatment.

• Trauma and past experiences: BFRBs can sometimes be linked to past traumatic experiences, such as childhood abuse, neglect, or other adverse events. Trauma-related triggers may contribute to the development or exacerbation of BFRBs. Trauma-informed approaches can be valuable in understanding and addressing these behaviors.

• Cognitive and behavioral patterns: Negative thought patterns, cognitive distortions, and specific behavioral patterns may contribute to the maintenance of BFRBs. These can include beliefs about the need for perfection, fear of losing control, or difficulties tolerating discomfort. Cognitive-behavioral interventions can target these patterns.

Effective interventions for BFRBs:

• Cognitive-behavioral therapy (CBT): CBT is the most commonly used and effective treatment approach for BFRBs. It involves identifying triggers, challenging negative thoughts and beliefs, developing alternative coping strategies, and gradually reducing and managing the behaviors.

• Habit reversal training (HRT): HRT is a specific technique within CBT that focuses on increasing awareness of the behaviors, identifying alternative responses, and implementing competing responses to replace the habitual behaviors. This can help interrupt the automatic cycle of BFRBs.

• Mindfulness-based techniques: Mindfulness can help individuals develop greater awareness of their urges, emotions, and triggers associated with BFRBs. Mindfulness practices can increase acceptance of discomfort and support the development of healthier coping mechanisms.

• Supportive therapy: Providing a supportive therapeutic environment that fosters understanding, empathy, and non-judgment is crucial in working with individuals struggling with BFRBs. Encouraging open communication, validating their experiences, and addressing underlying emotional distress can promote progress in treatment.

• Pharmacological interventions: In some cases, medication may be prescribed as an adjunct to therapy for BFRBs. Selective serotonin reuptake inhibitors (SSRIs) or other medications may be considered based on the individual's specific needs and in consultation with a psychiatrist.

Building a support network:

• Seek professional help: If you or someone you know is struggling with BFRBs, it is essential to seek professional help from mental health providers experienced in treating these conditions. They can provide an accurate diagnosis, create a tailored treatment plan, and offer guidance and support throughout the recovery process.

• Education and awareness: Raising awareness about BFRBs can help reduce stigma and promote understanding. Educate yourself and others about these conditions to foster empathy and support for individuals experiencing BFRBs.

•	Support groups and online communities: Connecting with others who share similar experiences can be beneficial. Support groups and online communities can provide a safe space for individuals to share their stories, exchange coping strategies, and receive support from those who understand their challenges.

•	Open communication: Encourage open communication with friends, family, and loved ones about BFRBs. Sharing your experiences and explaining the nature of these behaviors can help foster understanding and empathy within your support network.

•	Self-care and stress management: Engaging in self-care practices and stress management techniques can help individuals better cope with emotional distress, reduce the frequency of BFRBs, and promote overall well-being.

So, body-focused repetitive behaviors can have a significant impact on individuals' lives, causing physical damage and emotional distress. Understanding the psychological origins of these behaviors and implementing effective interventions are key to supporting individuals on their journey to recovery. By seeking professional help, building a supportive network, and exploring evidence-based interventions, individuals with BFRBs can gain control over their behaviors, reduce distress, and develop healthier ways of coping. Remember, recovery is possible, and with compassion, understanding, and the right resources, individuals can break free from the cycle of body-focused repetitive behaviors and regain a sense of well-being and self-empowerment.

Chapter 69: The Connection Between Loneliness and Mental Health

Loneliness is a universal human experience that can affect people of all ages and backgrounds. It is important to note that loneliness is not the same as being alone. Loneliness is the subjective feeling of being socially isolated or disconnected, even when surrounded by others. Let's explore this topic in more detail:

Understanding loneliness:

• Types of loneliness: Loneliness can be categorized into two types: situational loneliness and emotional loneliness. Situational loneliness occurs when individuals lack social contact or companionship, such as during a transition period or when physically isolated. Emotional loneliness, on the other hand, refers to the absence of deep and meaningful connections, even when surrounded by people.

• Causes of loneliness: Loneliness can arise from various factors, including changes in life circumstances, such as moving to a new location, the loss of a loved one, relationship difficulties, or social isolation due to physical or mental health conditions. Technology and the rise of social media can also contribute to feelings of loneliness when they are used as substitutes for real-life social interactions.

• Loneliness and social connection: Humans are social beings, and social connections are essential for our well-being. When we lack meaningful connections and a sense of belonging, we may experience feelings of loneliness. Loneliness can impact our mental health, leading to increased vulnerability to stress, anxiety, depression, and other mental health conditions.

Impact of loneliness on mental health:

• Emotional well-being: Loneliness can take a toll on our emotional well-being. Persistent feelings of loneliness can lead to increased levels of sadness, anxiety, and a diminished sense of self-worth. It can also contribute to the development or worsening of mental health conditions, such as depression and generalized anxiety disorder.

• Cognitive functioning: Loneliness has been linked to cognitive changes, including impaired attention, memory, and decision-making abilities. These cognitive changes may be related to the emotional distress and stress associated with chronic loneliness.

• Physical health: Loneliness is not just limited to its impact on mental health; it can also affect physical health. Chronic loneliness has been associated with increased risks of cardiovascular disease, weakened immune system function, sleep disturbances, and even premature mortality.

• Addiction and substance abuse: Loneliness can be a contributing factor to the development of addictive behaviors and substance abuse. Individuals may turn to substances as a way to cope with feelings of isolation and to temporarily alleviate emotional pain.

Addressing loneliness:

• Foster social connections: Building and maintaining social connections is crucial in combating loneliness. Actively seek opportunities to engage with others, such as joining clubs, community groups, or volunteering. Reach out to friends and family, schedule regular social activities, and make an effort to strengthen existing relationships.

• Seek support: If you are feeling lonely, don't hesitate to seek support from others. Talk to a trusted friend, family member, or mental health professional about your feelings. They can provide a listening ear, offer guidance, and help you explore strategies to overcome loneliness.

• Practice self-compassion: Loneliness can sometimes lead to self-blame or negative self-judgment. It is important to practice self-compassion and remind yourself that loneliness is a common human experience. Treat yourself with kindness and understanding, and challenge any negative self-talk that may contribute to feelings of loneliness.

• Engage in activities you enjoy: Pursue activities that bring you joy and fulfillment. Engaging in hobbies, creative pursuits, or physical activities not only provides opportunities for social interaction but also enhances your overall well-being and sense of purpose.

• Seek professional help: If feelings of loneliness persist and significantly impact your daily life, consider seeking professional help from a mental health professional. They can help you explore the underlying causes of loneliness, develop coping strategies, and provide support on your journey towards improved mental well-being.

Building a connected community:

• Community engagement: Engaging with your local community can foster a sense of belonging and reduce feelings of isolation. Participate in community events, support local organizations, and get involved in activities that align with your interests and values.

• Cultivate empathy and inclusivity: Foster a culture of empathy and inclusivity in your community. Reach out to individuals who may be experiencing loneliness or isolation, and create opportunities for social connection and support. Small acts of kindness can make a significant difference in someone's life.

• Utilize technology mindfully: While technology can contribute to feelings of loneliness, it can also be a valuable tool for connecting with others. Use technology mindfully to foster meaningful connections, such as video calls with loved ones or participating in online communities centered around your interests.

• Educate and raise awareness: Educate others about the impact of loneliness on mental health. Encourage open conversations about loneliness, challenge societal stigmas, and promote understanding and empathy towards those who may be experiencing loneliness.

So, loneliness can have a profound impact on our mental health and overall well-being. Understanding the causes and effects of loneliness allows us to develop strategies to address it effectively. By fostering social connections, seeking support, practicing self-compassion, and building connected communities, we can combat loneliness and promote mental well-being for ourselves and those around us. Remember, you are not alone, and there are resources and support available to help you navigate through feelings of loneliness and cultivate meaningful connections.

Chapter 70: Supporting Mental Health in the LGBTQ+ Youth Population

In this chapter, we will explore the unique challenges faced by LGBTQ+ youth, discuss the importance of creating inclusive and affirming environments, and provide insights on how to support their mental well-being.

Understanding the challenges faced by LGBTQ+ youth:

• Minority stress: LGBTQ+ youth often experience minority stress, which refers to the unique stressors and discrimination they face due to their sexual orientation or gender identity. This can include bullying, harassment, family rejection, and societal stigma. Minority stress can have a significant impact on their mental health and well-being.

• Identity exploration: LGBTQ+ youth go through a process of identity exploration, which can involve questioning their sexual orientation or gender identity. This journey can be accompanied by confusion, self-doubt, and a need for support and understanding.

• Lack of acceptance: Not all LGBTQ+ youth receive acceptance and support from their families, friends, or communities. This lack of acceptance can lead to feelings of isolation, shame, and rejection, which can greatly affect their mental health.

Creating inclusive and affirming environments:

• Education and awareness: It is essential to educate ourselves and others about LGBTQ+ identities and issues. Learning about diverse sexual orientations, gender identities, and the challenges faced by LGBTQ+ youth can help create a more inclusive and understanding environment.

• Respect and validation: Show respect for each individual's self-identified gender and sexual orientation. Use appropriate pronouns and terminology, and validate their experiences and feelings. Creating a safe space where LGBTQ+ youth feel seen, heard, and respected is crucial for their mental well-being.

• Supportive networks: Build supportive networks within families, schools, and communities to provide resources, guidance, and acceptance for LGBTQ+ youth. LGBTQ+ support groups, alliances, and community organizations can be valuable sources of support.

•   Anti-bullying policies: Advocate for and implement anti-bullying policies that explicitly address LGBTQ+ bullying and harassment in schools and other community settings. Creating a zero-tolerance environment for discrimination helps protect the mental health of LGBTQ+ youth.

Supporting mental well-being:

•   Cultivate open communication: Create an open and non-judgmental space where LGBTQ+ youth feel comfortable discussing their feelings, experiences, and challenges. Encourage open dialogue and active listening, allowing them to express themselves without fear of rejection.

•   Provide access to mental health resources: Ensure that LGBTQ+ youth have access to LGBTQ+-affirming mental health professionals who are knowledgeable about their unique experiences. These professionals can provide appropriate support and therapy that acknowledges and validates their identities.

•   Promote self-acceptance and self-care: Encourage LGBTQ+ youth to cultivate self-acceptance and self-care practices. This can include activities that promote self-expression, self-compassion, and self-discovery, such as journaling, art, meditation, or engaging in supportive online communities.

•   Foster social connections: Help LGBTQ+ youth build supportive friendships and connections within the LGBTQ+ community. This can be achieved through LGBTQ+ youth groups, LGBTQ+ community centers, or online platforms that provide spaces for connection and support.

•   Address family rejection: Family rejection can be particularly challenging for LGBTQ+ youth. Encourage family members to seek education and support to better understand and accept their LGBTQ+ child. Family therapy or support groups can help facilitate understanding, reconciliation, and improved mental well-being for both the youth and their families.

•   Advocate for inclusive policies: Advocate for inclusive policies and practices within schools, healthcare systems, and community organizations. This can include gender-neutral bathrooms, inclusive curricula, and policies that protect the rights and well-being of LGBTQ+ youth.

Resources and support:

•	LGBTQ+ organizations: Connect LGBTQ+ youth and their families with local LGBTQ+ organizations that provide support, education, and resources. These organizations often offer counseling services, helplines, support groups, and community events.

•	Online resources: Share reliable online resources that provide information and support for LGBTQ+ youth, such as LGBTQ+ youth websites, forums, and mental health websites with specialized LGBTQ+ sections.

•	LGBTQ+ literature and media: Recommend books, movies, and TV shows that feature LGBTQ+ characters and storylines. Representation in media can provide validation and a sense of belonging for LGBTQ+ youth.

•	Crisis intervention: Make sure LGBTQ+ youth are aware of helplines and crisis intervention services specifically designed for LGBTQ+ individuals. These services can offer immediate support in times of crisis or emotional distress.

Remember, supporting the mental health of LGBTQ+ youth requires empathy, education, and creating safe and inclusive environments. By actively listening, providing resources, fostering acceptance, and advocating for change, we can contribute to the well-being and happiness of LGBTQ+ youth. Together, we can create a world where every young person, regardless of their sexual orientation or gender identity, can thrive and be proud of who they are.

Chapter 71: The Role of Trauma-Informed Yoga in Healing from PTSD

In this chapter, we will delve into the profound impact of trauma on mental health, discuss the principles of trauma-informed yoga, and provide insights on how this practice can support individuals in their healing journey.

Understanding PTSD and the impact of trauma:
• Post-Traumatic Stress Disorder (PTSD): PTSD is a mental health condition that can develop after experiencing or witnessing a traumatic event. Symptoms may include flashbacks, nightmares, hypervigilance, avoidance of triggers, and emotional distress. It is important to recognize that trauma can affect individuals differently, and healing is a unique and individualized process.

• The mind-body connection: Trauma affects both the mind and the body. It can disrupt the nervous system, leading to dysregulation of stress responses and a heightened state of arousal. This dysregulation can manifest as physical symptoms, emotional distress, and challenges in interpersonal relationships.

Introducing trauma-informed yoga:
• What is trauma-informed yoga? Trauma-informed yoga is an approach that recognizes and addresses the specific needs and vulnerabilities of individuals who have experienced trauma. It emphasizes creating a safe and supportive environment, informed consent, choice, and empowerment.

• The principles of trauma-informed yoga: Trauma-informed yoga is guided by several principles, including safety, trustworthiness, choice, collaboration, and empowerment. These principles ensure that the practice respects individuals' boundaries and supports their healing process.

Benefits of trauma-informed yoga for healing from PTSD:
• Regulation of the nervous system: Trauma-informed yoga incorporates breathing exercises, gentle movements, and mindfulness practices that can help regulate the nervous system. These practices

support individuals in developing a sense of safety and grounding, allowing them to reconnect with their bodies and release tension.

•	Body awareness and empowerment: Trauma can disconnect individuals from their bodies, leading to a sense of detachment or disownership. Trauma-informed yoga encourages body awareness, promoting a sense of empowerment and agency over one's body. This can help individuals rebuild a positive relationship with their physical selves.

•	Mindfulness and emotional regulation: Trauma-informed yoga incorporates mindfulness practices that cultivate present-moment awareness and non-judgmental observation. These practices can enhance emotional regulation skills, helping individuals develop the ability to tolerate and manage challenging emotions that may arise during their healing journey.

•	Self-compassion and self-care: Trauma-informed yoga fosters a compassionate and non-judgmental attitude towards oneself. It encourages self-care practices, such as gentle movement, relaxation techniques, and nurturing self-talk, which can support individuals in developing self-compassion and a greater sense of well-being.

Incorporating trauma-informed yoga into healing:

•	Finding a qualified instructor: When exploring trauma-informed yoga, it is essential to find an instructor who has received specialized training in trauma sensitivity. Look for instructors who prioritize safety, consent, and inclusivity, and who have experience working with individuals who have experienced trauma.

•	Creating a safe space: Whether practicing yoga individually or in a group setting, it is crucial to create a safe space where individuals feel supported and comfortable. This may include dimming the lights, using grounding props, providing options for modifications, and allowing participants to make choices that feel right for them.

•	Integrating mindfulness practices: Mindfulness is an integral part of trauma-informed yoga. Encourage the cultivation of mindfulness off the mat as well, by inviting individuals to incorporate mindfulness into their daily lives. This can include simple practices such as mindful breathing, body scans, or moment-to-moment awareness.

•	Honoring individual experiences: Recognize that each individual's healing journey is unique. Some individuals may find trauma-informed yoga to be a valuable tool in their healing process, while others may prefer or require additional therapeutic approaches. It is important to honor and respect each person's choices and preferences.

•	Collaboration with mental health professionals: Trauma-informed yoga is not a substitute for professional mental health treatment. Encourage individuals to collaborate with mental health professionals who can provide comprehensive support tailored to their specific needs. This collaboration ensures an integrated approach to healing and promotes the individual's overall well-being.

Exploring other resources:

•	Trauma-sensitive meditation and mindfulness: In addition to trauma-informed yoga, individuals may find benefit in exploring trauma-sensitive meditation and mindfulness practices. These practices can further support the regulation of the nervous system, cultivate self-awareness, and enhance emotional well-being.

•	Peer support and group therapy: Connecting with others who have experienced trauma can provide a sense of validation and support. Peer support groups and group therapy sessions specifically designed for trauma survivors can create a safe space for sharing experiences, receiving empathy, and learning from others' journeys.

•	Individualized trauma therapies: Trauma-informed yoga can be a complementary component of a comprehensive treatment plan. Individualized trauma therapies, such as Eye Movement Desensitization and Reprocessing (EMDR), Cognitive-Behavioral Therapy (CBT), or Dialectical Behavior Therapy (DBT), may also be beneficial for individuals with PTSD.

So, trauma-informed yoga can be a valuable tool in the healing journey of individuals with PTSD. By integrating the principles of safety, trust, choice, collaboration, and empowerment, trauma-informed yoga offers a supportive environment for individuals to reconnect with their bodies, regulate their nervous systems, and cultivate self-compassion. Remember, healing is a unique and personal process, and it is important to honor and respect each individual's choices and needs on their journey toward healing and well-being.

Chapter 72: Exploring the Connection Between Seasonal Affective Disorder (SAD) and Mental Health

In this chapter, we will delve into the nature of SAD, discuss its impact on mental well-being, and provide insights on understanding and managing this condition.

Understanding Seasonal Affective Disorder (SAD):

•	What is SAD? SAD is a type of depression that follows a seasonal pattern, typically occurring during the fall and winter months when daylight is limited. It is believed to be linked to changes in exposure to natural light and affects individuals in varying degrees of severity.

•	Common symptoms: Symptoms of SAD often include low mood, fatigue, loss of interest in activities, changes in appetite, weight fluctuations, difficulty concentrating, and increased need for sleep. These symptoms tend to dissipate as the seasons change, and individuals with SAD may experience relief during the spring and summer months.

•	Factors contributing to SAD: The exact cause of SAD is not fully understood, but several factors may contribute to its development. Reduced exposure to sunlight and disruptions in circadian rhythms, which regulate sleep-wake cycles, are thought to play a role. Other factors may include changes in serotonin and melatonin levels, as well as genetic and environmental factors.

Impact of SAD on mental well-being:

•	Emotional well-being: SAD can significantly impact an individual's emotional well-being. Feelings of sadness, hopelessness, and irritability are common during episodes of SAD. These emotional changes can affect relationships, work or school performance, and overall quality of life.

•	Disruption of daily functioning: The symptoms of SAD can interfere with daily functioning, making it challenging to carry out regular activities and meet responsibilities. Reduced energy levels and difficulty concentrating may contribute to decreased productivity and engagement in personal and professional pursuits.

•	Relationship with other mental health conditions: SAD is often linked to other mental health conditions, such as major depressive disorder and generalized anxiety disorder. Individuals with a history of these conditions may be more susceptible to experiencing SAD symptoms during specific seasons.

Managing and coping with SAD:

•	Light therapy: Light therapy, or phototherapy, is a common treatment for SAD. It involves exposure to bright artificial light, typically using a lightbox or special lamps that mimic natural sunlight. Light therapy has shown to be effective in reducing SAD symptoms by helping to regulate circadian rhythms and elevate mood.

•	Spending time outdoors: Increasing exposure to natural light can be beneficial for individuals with SAD. Making an effort to spend time outdoors during daylight hours, even on cloudy days, can help improve mood and provide a boost of energy. Taking walks in nature or engaging in outdoor activities can be particularly beneficial.

•	Maintaining a consistent routine: Establishing a consistent daily routine, including regular sleep patterns, meal times, and exercise, can help regulate circadian rhythms and stabilize mood. Structuring your day with activities you enjoy and finding ways to stay engaged and connected can also contribute to improved mental well-being.

•	Exercise and physical activity: Engaging in regular exercise and physical activity has been shown to have positive effects on mental health. Exercise releases endorphins, which are natural mood boosters, and can help reduce symptoms of depression and anxiety associated with SAD. Finding activities that you enjoy, such as walking, swimming, or dancing, can make exercise more enjoyable and sustainable.

•	Healthy lifestyle choices: Paying attention to your overall health can help alleviate symptoms of SAD. Eating a balanced diet, getting sufficient sleep, and managing stress through techniques like meditation or relaxation exercises can support your mental well-being. Avoiding excessive .... consumption and reducing caffeine intake can also be helpful.

• Seeking professional support: If SAD symptoms persist or significantly impact your daily life, seeking professional support is important. Mental health professionals, such as therapists or psychiatrists, can provide guidance, develop personalized treatment plans, and explore other treatment options, such as medication, if necessary.

Creating a supportive environment:

• Communication and support: Openly communicate with friends, family, and loved ones about your experience with SAD. Share your feelings and needs, allowing them to understand and support you better. Encourage open conversations about mental health and seek their understanding and empathy.

• Social connections: Maintaining social connections is crucial for mental well-being. Engage in activities with friends and loved ones, even if you may feel less motivated during periods of SAD. Seek out support groups or online communities where you can connect with others who understand and share similar experiences.

• Self-care practices: Prioritize self-care activities that bring you joy and relaxation. Engage in activities that you find soothing or uplifting, such as practicing mindfulness, taking warm baths, reading, or engaging in creative pursuits. Nurturing your emotional and physical well-being is important for managing SAD symptoms.

• Mindfulness and stress reduction: Incorporate mindfulness and stress reduction techniques into your daily life. This can include practices like meditation, deep breathing exercises, or yoga. These techniques can help reduce anxiety, promote relaxation, and enhance your overall sense of well-being.

• Embracing the seasons: Finding ways to appreciate and embrace the unique qualities of each season can also contribute to a more positive outlook. Engage in seasonal activities, such as enjoying the colors of autumn or participating in winter sports. By focusing on the positive aspects of each season, you can shift your perspective and cultivate a sense of gratitude and enjoyment.

Seeking professional help:

• If your symptoms of SAD are severe or persist despite self-care efforts, it is essential to seek professional help. A mental health professional can conduct a thorough assessment, diagnose SAD, and develop an appropriate treatment plan tailored to your needs. They may recommend psychotherapy, medication, or a combination of both.

•	Psychotherapy: Cognitive-Behavioral Therapy (CBT) and other evidence-based therapeutic approaches can be effective in managing SAD symptoms. These therapies help individuals identify and challenge negative thought patterns, develop coping strategies, and learn skills to manage their mood and behavior.

•	Medication: In some cases, medication may be prescribed to manage symptoms of SAD. Selective Serotonin Reuptake Inhibitors (SSRIs) and other antidepressant medications may be prescribed to help alleviate symptoms. It is important to consult with a healthcare professional to determine the most appropriate medication and dosage for your specific situation.

Remember, you are not alone in your experience with Seasonal Affective Disorder. Reach out to friends, family, and mental health professionals for support and guidance. By implementing self-care practices, seeking professional help when needed, and creating a supportive environment, you can effectively manage SAD and maintain your mental well-being throughout the seasons.

Chapter 73: Understanding Antisocial Personality Disorder and Sociopathy

In this chapter, we will explore the characteristics, causes, and challenges associated with ASPD and sociopathy, aiming to provide an overview of these complex conditions.

Defining Antisocial Personality Disorder and Sociopathy:

• Antisocial Personality Disorder (ASPD): ASPD is a mental health condition characterized by a pervasive pattern of disregard for the rights and feelings of others, as well as a lack of empathy, remorse, and regard for societal norms. Individuals with ASPD often engage in impulsive, manipulative, and antisocial behaviors.

• Sociopathy: Sociopathy is a term often used interchangeably with ASPD. It refers to a subset of individuals with ASPD who exhibit particularly severe antisocial traits and behaviors, including a lack of remorse, shallow emotions, and a propensity for manipulation and deceit.

Key characteristics and behaviors:

• Lack of empathy and remorse: Individuals with ASPD and sociopathy often exhibit a profound lack of empathy and remorse for their actions, making it difficult for them to understand or care about the impact of their behaviors on others. They may exploit and manipulate others without guilt or remorse.

• Impulsivity and irresponsibility: Impulsive and reckless behavior is a common trait among individuals with ASPD and sociopathy. They may engage in substance abuse, disregard legal and social boundaries, and show little regard for their own safety or the safety of others. They often have difficulty maintaining stable employment or fulfilling responsibilities.

• Deception and manipulation: Those with ASPD and sociopathy are adept at deceiving and manipulating others for personal gain. They may lie, charm, and manipulate to exploit the trust and vulnerabilities of those around them. Their manipulation skills can be instrumental in achieving their goals or avoiding consequences.

• Violation of societal norms: Individuals with ASPD and sociopathy frequently exhibit a disregard for societal rules and norms. They may engage in criminal behavior, engage in aggression or violence, and show a pattern of impulsive and irresponsible actions that repeatedly put themselves and others at risk.

Causes and risk factors:

• Biological factors: Research suggests that both genetic and neurological factors play a role in the development of ASPD and sociopathy. Genetic predispositions, abnormalities in brain structure and function, and alterations in neurotransmitter systems are thought to contribute to the manifestation of these conditions.

• Environmental factors: Adverse childhood experiences, such as abuse, neglect, or inconsistent parenting, may increase the risk of developing ASPD and sociopathy. Growing up in an environment that lacks empathy, warmth, and positive role models can contribute to the development of antisocial traits.

• Interaction of nature and nurture: It is important to recognize that the development of ASPD and sociopathy is complex and influenced by both genetic and environmental factors. The interplay between genetic predispositions and adverse experiences can shape the expression of antisocial behaviors.

Challenges and implications:

• Impact on relationships: Individuals with ASPD and sociopathy often struggle to form and maintain healthy relationships. Their lack of empathy, manipulative tendencies, and disregard for others' emotions can lead to broken trust and emotional harm to those around them.

• Legal and societal consequences: The impulsive and antisocial behaviors exhibited by individuals with ASPD and sociopathy can result in legal and societal consequences. Their disregard for rules and norms may lead to criminal behavior, legal involvement, and difficulties reintegrating into society.

• Treatment challenges: Treating ASPD and sociopathy can be challenging due to the inherent difficulties in fostering empathy, remorse, and willingness to change. These conditions often coexist with other mental health issues, such as substance abuse or mood disorders, which further complicate treatment approaches.

Support and management strategies:

•	Professional help: Individuals with ASPD and sociopathy can benefit from therapy, although treatment approaches may vary depending on the individual's motivation and level of insight. Therapies such as Cognitive-Behavioral Therapy (CBT), Dialectical Behavior Therapy (DBT), and group therapy can help individuals develop pro-social skills and address underlying issues.

•	Emphasis on personal responsibility: Encouraging individuals with ASPD and sociopathy to take responsibility for their actions and their impact on others can be an important step in their healing process. Recognizing the consequences of their behavior and fostering a sense of accountability can contribute to personal growth.

•	Support for affected individuals: Supporting family members, partners, or friends of individuals with ASPD and sociopathy is essential. These individuals may experience emotional distress, trauma, and confusion. Providing a safe and supportive environment and helping them access appropriate resources can assist in their own healing process.

•	Boundaries and self-care: Establishing and maintaining personal boundaries is crucial when interacting with individuals with ASPD and sociopathy. Setting limits on behavior and prioritizing self-care can help protect one's well-being when engaging with individuals who may exhibit manipulative or harmful tendencies.

•	Community awareness and education: Raising awareness about ASPD and sociopathy can help reduce stigma and promote understanding. By fostering empathy and compassion, society can work toward creating supportive environments that encourage rehabilitation, prevention, and effective management of these conditions.

It is important to approach the topic of ASPD and sociopathy with sensitivity and empathy, recognizing the challenges faced by both individuals with these conditions and those impacted by their behaviors. By fostering awareness, promoting support, and advocating for effective interventions, we can contribute to a more compassionate and inclusive society.

Chapter 74: Exploring the Link Between Childhood Abuse and Borderline Personality Disorder

In this chapter, we will delve into the nature of BPD, discuss the impact of childhood abuse on its development, and provide an understanding of this complex relationship.

Understanding Borderline Personality Disorder (BPD):

• What is BPD? BPD is a mental health disorder characterized by unstable emotions, self-image, and relationships. Individuals with BPD often experience intense and fluctuating emotions, have a fear of abandonment, engage in impulsive behaviors, and struggle with maintaining stable relationships.

• Common symptoms: Symptoms of BPD can vary but may include chronic feelings of emptiness, intense fear of abandonment, self-destructive behaviors, mood swings, difficulty regulating emotions, unstable self-image, and a pattern of unstable and intense relationships.

• The complex nature of BPD: BPD is a complex condition that arises from a combination of genetic, neurobiological, and environmental factors. While the exact cause is unknown, research suggests that a history of childhood abuse or neglect may play a significant role in its development.

The Impact of Childhood Abuse on BPD:

• Understanding childhood abuse: Childhood abuse refers to any form of physical, emotional, or sexual mistreatment experienced during childhood. It can also include neglect, where a child's basic needs for love, care, and protection are not met. Childhood abuse can have long-lasting effects on an individual's mental and emotional well-being.

• Relationship between childhood abuse and BPD: Research suggests a strong association between childhood abuse and the development of BPD. Many individuals diagnosed with BPD report a history of childhood abuse, with studies indicating that a significant percentage of BPD cases involve a background of abuse or neglect.

•	Impact on emotional regulation: Childhood abuse can disrupt the development of healthy emotion regulation skills. Individuals who have experienced abuse may struggle to effectively manage and regulate their emotions, leading to the emotional instability characteristic of BPD.

•	Attachment difficulties: Childhood abuse can negatively impact attachment styles, which are crucial for developing secure and healthy relationships. Individuals who have experienced abuse may have difficulties trusting others, fear of abandonment, and difficulties forming stable and secure relationships.

•	Distorted self-image: Childhood abuse can contribute to a distorted self-image. Individuals who have experienced abuse may internalize negative messages and beliefs about themselves, leading to feelings of worthlessness, shame, and a fragile self-identity, which are often seen in individuals with BPD.

Healing and Treatment:

•	Seeking therapy: Therapy, particularly dialectical behavior therapy (DBT), is a widely recognized and effective treatment for individuals with BPD. DBT focuses on developing skills for emotional regulation, distress tolerance, interpersonal effectiveness, and mindfulness. Therapy can provide a safe and supportive space to explore past experiences and develop healthier coping mechanisms.

•	Trauma-focused therapy: For individuals with BPD who have experienced childhood abuse, trauma-focused therapy can be beneficial. Therapeutic approaches such as Eye Movement Desensitization and Reprocessing (EMDR) or Cognitive Processing Therapy (CPT) can help individuals process and heal from traumatic experiences.

•	Building healthy relationships: Developing healthy relationships is an important aspect of healing for individuals with BPD. Engaging in therapy and participating in support groups can provide opportunities to learn and practice healthy communication, boundaries, and trust-building skills.

•	Self-care and self-compassion: Engaging in self-care practices and cultivating self-compassion are essential for individuals with BPD. This can involve activities such as practicing mindfulness, engaging in hobbies, setting boundaries, seeking support from loved ones, and prioritizing one's physical and emotional well-being.

•	Support networks: Building a supportive network of friends, family, and mental health professionals is crucial for individuals with BPD. Having a strong support system can provide validation, understanding, and a sense of belonging, which are essential for the healing process.

•	Advocacy and awareness: It is important to raise awareness about the impact of childhood abuse on BPD and advocate for better prevention and support systems. By promoting education and understanding, we can help reduce stigma, enhance access to resources, and support individuals on their journey to recovery.

Chapter 75: Mental Health Challenges in the Workplace: Burnout and Stress

In this chapter, we will delve into the nature of burnout and stress, discuss their impact on mental well-being, and provide an understanding of these challenges that many individuals face in their work lives.

Understanding Burnout:
• Defining burnout: Burnout is a state of physical, emotional, and mental exhaustion that results from chronic work-related stress. It is characterized by feelings of depletion, cynicism, and a reduced sense of accomplishment. Burnout can affect various aspects of a person's life, including their work performance, relationships, and overall well-being.
• Recognizing the signs: The signs of burnout can vary, but common indicators include chronic fatigue, decreased motivation, irritability, feelings of cynicism or detachment, reduced productivity, and increased physical symptoms such as headaches or stomachaches.
• Causes of burnout: Burnout can arise from various factors, including high work demands, lack of control over work tasks, insufficient support from colleagues or supervisors, a mismatch between an individual's values and their work environment, and a poor work-life balance.

Understanding Workplace Stress:
• Defining workplace stress: Workplace stress refers to the physical and emotional responses that individuals experience when they perceive their work demands to exceed their ability to cope effectively. Stress can arise from various sources, including high workloads, time pressures, conflicts with colleagues, and organizational changes.
• Impact on mental well-being: Prolonged or chronic workplace stress can have a significant impact on mental well-being. It can contribute to feelings of anxiety, irritability, and overwhelm, as well as physical symptoms such as headaches, muscle tension, and sleep disturbances.
• The role of work environment: The work environment plays a crucial role in contributing to or alleviating workplace stress. Factors such as excessive workload, lack of support, poor communication, and

a negative organizational culture can significantly contribute to stress levels.

Addressing Burnout and Workplace Stress:

• Self-care practices: Practicing self-care is essential for managing burnout and workplace stress. Engage in activities that promote relaxation, such as exercise, mindfulness, hobbies, and spending quality time with loved ones. Taking breaks throughout the workday and establishing healthy boundaries between work and personal life can also help prevent burnout.

• Seeking support: Reach out to colleagues, supervisors, or mental health professionals for support. Sharing your feelings and experiences with trusted individuals can provide a sense of validation and help identify potential solutions or coping strategies.

• Building resilience: Developing resilience can help individuals better navigate workplace challenges. Resilience involves cultivating skills such as problem-solving, adaptability, and self-compassion. Seeking opportunities for growth and learning, practicing positive self-talk, and maintaining a support network can contribute to resilience.

• Communicating needs: Effective communication is key in addressing workplace stress and burnout. Clearly express your needs and concerns to supervisors or colleagues, advocating for changes that may improve your work environment. Collaborative problem-solving and open dialogue can lead to meaningful improvements.

• Work-life balance: Striving for a healthy work-life balance is crucial for managing stress and preventing burnout. Prioritize activities and relationships outside of work that bring you joy and fulfillment. Set boundaries around work hours and responsibilities to create a more sustainable and fulfilling lifestyle.

• Organizational interventions: Employers play a vital role in creating a mentally healthy work environment. Organizations can implement strategies such as promoting work-life balance, providing employee assistance programs (EAPs), offering stress management workshops, and fostering a culture that values employee well-being.

Cultivating a Supportive Work Environment:

- Encouraging open communication: Establishing an environment where employees feel comfortable discussing their stress levels and burnout experiences is crucial. Encourage open communication, active listening, and regular check-ins to ensure employees feel supported and heard.
- Providing resources and support: Employers should provide resources to help employees manage stress and prevent burnout. This can include access to mental health services, stress management programs, and flexible work arrangements that promote work-life balance.
- Promoting work-life balance: Encourage employees to prioritize self-care and maintain a healthy work-life balance. Recognize the importance of rest, leisure, and time spent with loved ones in fostering overall well-being.
- Employee recognition and appreciation: Recognize and appreciate employees' hard work and achievements. Regularly acknowledging their efforts and contributions can boost morale, motivation, and job satisfaction.
- Training and education: Offer training and education on stress management, resilience-building, and mental health awareness. Equip employees with the skills and knowledge needed to navigate workplace challenges effectively and support their mental well-being.

By understanding the nature of burnout and workplace stress, practicing self-care, seeking support, and cultivating a supportive work environment, individuals and organizations can work together to promote mental well-being in the workplace. Remember, your mental health matters, and taking proactive steps to manage stress and prevent burnout is essential for a fulfilling and sustainable work life.

Chapter 76: The Influence of Social Determinants on Mental Health Disparities

In this chapter, we will delve into the concept of social determinants, discuss their impact on mental health, and provide an understanding of how these factors contribute to disparities in mental well-being among different populations.

Understanding Social Determinants:

• Defining social determinants: Social determinants are the conditions in which people are born, grow, live, work, and age, including factors such as socioeconomic status, education, employment, social support networks, access to healthcare, and exposure to discrimination and systemic inequalities.

• Impact on mental health: Social determinants can significantly influence mental health outcomes. These factors shape the environments and resources available to individuals, influencing their ability to cope with stress, access support, and maintain optimal mental well-being.

Socioeconomic Status and Mental Health Disparities:

• Income and mental health: Socioeconomic status, including income level and educational attainment, plays a significant role in mental health disparities. Individuals with lower income levels may face increased stressors, limited access to mental healthcare, and higher rates of adverse life events, leading to higher rates of mental health challenges.

• Education and mental health: Education level is closely linked to mental health outcomes. Higher levels of education are associated with better mental health outcomes due to increased access to resources, opportunities, and knowledge that support resilience and coping skills.

• Employment and mental health: Employment status and job quality can impact mental health. Unemployment, job insecurity, and stressful work environments can contribute to increased levels of stress, anxiety, and depression. Access to fair wages, job benefits, and supportive work environments are crucial for promoting mental well-being.

Social Support Networks and Mental Health:
- Impact of social support: Social support networks, including family, friends, and community connections, play a vital role in mental health. Strong social support systems provide emotional support, a sense of belonging, and practical assistance during challenging times, reducing the risk of mental health difficulties.
- Social isolation and loneliness: Social isolation and loneliness can have negative effects on mental health. Lack of social connections and support can contribute to increased rates of depression, anxiety, and overall poorer mental well-being. Efforts to promote social inclusion and combat loneliness are essential for addressing mental health disparities.

Discrimination and Systemic Inequalities:
- Effects of discrimination: Discrimination, including racism, sexism, homophobia, and other forms of oppression, can have profound effects on mental health. Experiencing discrimination increases the risk of mental health challenges, including depression, anxiety, post-traumatic stress disorder (PTSD), and decreased overall well-being.
- Intersectionality and multiple oppressions: Intersectionality recognizes that individuals may experience multiple forms of oppression simultaneously. The compounding effects of intersecting identities, such as race, gender, sexuality, and socioeconomic status, can further increase the risk of mental health disparities.
- Trauma and systemic inequalities: Systemic inequalities, such as unequal access to resources and opportunities, can contribute to trauma and chronic stress. Individuals from marginalized communities may experience higher rates of trauma and have limited access to mental health services, perpetuating mental health disparities.

Addressing Mental Health Disparities:
- Equitable access to healthcare: Ensuring equitable access to quality mental healthcare is crucial for addressing mental health disparities. This involves reducing barriers to accessing mental health services, increasing culturally competent care, and integrating mental health into primary healthcare settings.

• Social and economic policies: Implementing social and economic policies that address poverty, inequality, and discrimination is essential for promoting mental health equity. Policies such as affordable housing, livable wages, and anti-discrimination laws can help create supportive environments for mental well-being.

• Community interventions: Community-based interventions that address social determinants, promote social connections, and provide resources for vulnerable populations are effective in reducing mental health disparities. These interventions may include community outreach programs, support groups, and initiatives that foster social inclusion.

• Education and awareness: Increasing education and awareness about the impact of social determinants on mental health disparities is crucial. This involves promoting understanding and empathy, challenging stereotypes, and stigma, and advocating for social justice and equality.

• Collaboration and advocacy: Collaboration between policymakers, healthcare professionals, community organizations, and individuals with lived experiences is key to addressing mental health disparities. By working together, we can advocate for change, raise awareness, and implement strategies that promote mental health equity. It is important to recognize that mental health disparities are complex and influenced by multiple interconnected factors. By addressing social determinants, advocating for equitable policies, fostering social support networks, and challenging systemic inequalities, we can work towards creating a society where mental well-being is accessible to all.

Chapter 77: Promoting Mental Health in Marginalized Communities

In this chapter, we will delve into the unique challenges faced by marginalized populations, discuss the importance of cultural competence, and provide an understanding of how to promote mental well-being in these communities.

Understanding Marginalized Communities:

• Defining marginalized communities: Marginalized communities are groups of individuals who experience social, economic, and political disadvantages due to various factors such as race, ethnicity, gender identity, sexual orientation, socioeconomic status, disability, or immigration status. These communities often face systemic discrimination and inequalities that can impact mental health outcomes.

• Intersectionality: It is crucial to recognize the intersectionality of identities within marginalized communities. Individuals may face multiple forms of discrimination and oppression, and their mental health experiences are influenced by the complex interplay of these intersecting identities.

Culturally Competent Approaches:

• Importance of cultural competence: Cultural competence is essential in promoting mental health in marginalized communities. It involves understanding and respecting the cultural backgrounds, values, beliefs, and experiences of individuals within these communities. Culturally competent approaches foster trust, enhance communication, and ensure that mental health services are tailored to meet the specific needs of each community.

• Collaborative partnerships: Building collaborative partnerships with community organizations, leaders, and members is crucial. By involving individuals from marginalized communities in the planning and implementation of mental health initiatives, we can ensure that interventions are culturally sensitive, relevant, and effective.

• Language accessibility: Language accessibility is vital in providing mental health support. Ensuring that mental health resources, information, and services are available in multiple languages helps overcome barriers and ensures that individuals from diverse linguistic backgrounds can access the help they need.

• Addressing cultural stigma: Many marginalized communities face cultural stigma surrounding mental health. It is important to engage in community education and awareness campaigns to challenge stigma, promote understanding, and foster supportive attitudes towards mental health.

Community Empowerment and Support:

• Community-based interventions: Community-based interventions can play a significant role in promoting mental health. These initiatives can include support groups, peer-led programs, and community centers that provide a safe and inclusive space for individuals to access mental health resources, seek support, and engage in activities that promote well-being.

• Community leadership: Empowering community leaders within marginalized populations can facilitate mental health promotion. Supporting the development of grassroots leaders who understand the unique challenges and strengths of their communities can help drive change, advocate for resources, and reduce barriers to mental health services.

• Providing resources and services: Ensuring that mental health resources and services are accessible to marginalized communities is crucial. This includes offering culturally competent therapy and counseling, affordable or free mental health services, and targeted programs that address specific mental health concerns within these communities.

• Nurturing social connections: Building strong social connections within marginalized communities is essential for promoting mental well-being. Encouraging community engagement, facilitating social support networks, and creating spaces for collective healing and resilience can help combat isolation and foster a sense of belonging.

Advocacy and Policy Change:

• Systemic change: Addressing mental health disparities in marginalized communities requires advocacy for systemic change. This involves challenging discriminatory policies, promoting equity in healthcare, and advocating for policies that prioritize mental health resources and services for marginalized populations.

•	Intersectional approaches: Recognizing the intersectional nature of marginalization is vital in advocacy efforts. By addressing the interconnected systems of oppression that affect individuals within marginalized communities, we can work towards creating comprehensive solutions that address the unique needs and challenges faced by these populations.

•	Amplifying diverse voices: Ensuring that the voices of individuals from marginalized communities are heard and amplified is essential. Centering their experiences and perspectives in mental health conversations, research, and policymaking can lead to more inclusive and effective strategies for promoting mental well-being.

•	Collaborative networks: Building collaborative networks between mental health professionals, community organizations, policymakers, and individuals within marginalized communities can drive change and create a collective voice for mental health advocacy.

By embracing cultural competence, empowering communities, providing accessible resources, and advocating for systemic change, we can promote mental health and well-being in marginalized communities. Remember, every individual deserves the opportunity to thrive, and by working together, we can create a more inclusive and supportive society for all.

Chapter 78: Cognitive-Behavioral Therapy (CBT) and its Applications in Mental Health

In this chapter, we will delve into the principles of CBT, discuss its effectiveness in treating various mental health conditions, and provide an understanding of how this therapy can help individuals improve their well-being.

Understanding Cognitive-Behavioral Therapy (CBT):

• What is CBT: Cognitive-Behavioral Therapy is a form of psychotherapy that focuses on the connection between thoughts, feelings, and behaviors. It recognizes that our thoughts (cognition) and actions (behavior) influence our emotions and overall well-being. By identifying and modifying negative or unhelpful patterns of thinking and behavior, CBT aims to alleviate mental health symptoms and promote positive change.

• Collaborative approach: CBT is a collaborative approach between the therapist and the individual seeking treatment. The therapist works with the individual to identify problematic thoughts and behaviors and develop strategies to replace them with healthier alternatives. The emphasis is on active participation, learning new skills, and applying them in real-life situations.

• Time-limited and structured: CBT is typically a time-limited therapy, with a specific number of sessions agreed upon between the therapist and the individual. It follows a structured format, focusing on specific goals and utilizing various techniques to address specific issues.

Applications of CBT in Mental Health:

• Anxiety disorders: CBT has been shown to be highly effective in treating anxiety disorders such as generalized anxiety disorder, panic disorder, social anxiety disorder, and specific phobias. It helps individuals identify and challenge anxious thoughts, gradually face feared situations, and develop coping strategies to manage anxiety symptoms.

• Depression: CBT is an evidence-based treatment for depression. It helps individuals identify negative thinking patterns and replace them with more balanced and realistic thoughts. It also focuses on behavioral activation, encouraging individuals to engage in pleasurable and fulfilling activities to improve mood and motivation.

• Eating disorders: CBT is often used in the treatment of eating disorders such as anorexia nervosa, bulimia nervosa, and binge-eating disorder. It addresses distorted thoughts and beliefs about body image, food, and weight, as well as behavioral patterns related to disordered eating. CBT also helps individuals develop healthier relationships with food and their bodies.

• Substance use disorders: CBT is effective in treating substance use disorders by addressing the cognitive and behavioral factors that contribute to addiction. It helps individuals identify triggers, develop coping skills to resist cravings, and replace substance use with healthier behaviors. CBT can also address underlying emotional issues that contribute to substance abuse.

• Post-Traumatic Stress Disorder (PTSD): CBT, particularly Cognitive Processing Therapy (CPT) and Prolonged Exposure Therapy (PE), is effective in treating PTSD. These approaches focus on processing traumatic memories, challenging distorted thoughts related to the trauma, and developing skills to cope with distressing symptoms.

• Insomnia: CBT for insomnia, also known as CBT-I, is a structured program that addresses sleep-related difficulties. It involves techniques such as sleep hygiene education, stimulus control, and cognitive restructuring to improve sleep quality and quantity.

Key Components and Techniques of CBT:

• Cognitive restructuring: This technique involves identifying and challenging negative or irrational thoughts, known as cognitive distortions, and replacing them with more realistic and adaptive thoughts. By changing the way we think, we can influence our emotions and behaviors.

• Behavioral activation: This technique focuses on increasing engagement in pleasurable and meaningful activities to improve mood and motivation. By scheduling and participating in activities that align with personal values and interests, individuals can counteract feelings of depression or anxiety.

• Exposure and response prevention: This technique is commonly used in treating anxiety disorders and OCD. It involves gradually and systematically exposing individuals to feared situations or triggers while refraining from engaging in the associated avoidance or ritualistic behaviors. Over time, this helps individuals build tolerance and reduce anxiety.

• Skills training: CBT often involves teaching individuals specific skills to cope with challenging situations. This may include stress management techniques, problem-solving skills, communication skills, relaxation exercises, and assertiveness training.

• Homework assignments: CBT typically includes homework assignments between sessions to practice and reinforce the skills learned in therapy. These assignments encourage individuals to apply new strategies in their daily lives and provide opportunities for further learning and growth.

Benefits and Effectiveness of CBT:

• Evidence-based approach: CBT is supported by a substantial body of research and has been shown to be effective in treating various mental health conditions. It is recommended as a first-line treatment for many disorders by organizations such as the American Psychological Association and the National Institute for Health and Care Excellence (NICE).

• Collaborative and empowering: CBT empowers individuals by providing them with practical tools and strategies to manage their symptoms. It emphasizes active participation, allowing individuals to take an active role in their treatment and develop long-lasting skills for maintaining mental well-being.

• Long-term impact: CBT equips individuals with valuable skills that can be applied beyond the therapy setting. The techniques learned in CBT can be utilized in everyday life to address future challenges, promote resilience, and prevent relapse.

• Personalized approach: CBT is flexible and tailored to each individual's unique needs and goals. Therapists work collaboratively with individuals, taking into account their specific circumstances, cultural background, and preferences.

So, Cognitive-Behavioral Therapy (CBT) is a widely used and effective approach in the field of mental health. By targeting negative thoughts and behaviors and replacing them with more adaptive ones, CBT helps individuals overcome a range of mental health challenges. With its evidence-based foundation, collaborative nature, and focus on skill-building, CBT provides individuals with the tools to improve their mental well-being and lead more fulfilling lives. Whether you're dealing with anxiety, depression, an eating disorder, substance use, or other mental health concerns, CBT offers a practical and empowering approach to help you overcome your challenges.

Remember, CBT is a collaborative process between you and your therapist. Together, you will identify negative thought patterns, explore their underlying beliefs, and challenge them with evidence-based reasoning. You'll also work on replacing unhelpful behaviors with healthier alternatives, practicing new coping skills, and gradually facing feared situations or triggers.

One of the key components of CBT is cognitive restructuring, which involves examining and reframing your thoughts. This process helps you identify cognitive distortions, such as all-or-nothing thinking or catastrophizing, and replace them with more balanced and realistic thoughts. By changing the way you think, you can influence your emotions and behaviors in a positive way.

Behavioral activation is another important technique in CBT. It focuses on increasing your engagement in activities that bring you joy and fulfillment. By scheduling and participating in pleasurable and meaningful activities, even when you don't feel like it, you can boost your mood, motivation, and overall well-being.

Exposure and response prevention is commonly used in treating anxiety disorders and obsessive-compulsive disorder (OCD). It involves gradually exposing yourself to feared situations or triggers while refraining from engaging in associated avoidance or ritualistic behaviors. Over time, this helps you build tolerance and reduce anxiety or distress.

CBT also incorporates skills training, where you learn specific techniques to cope with challenging situations. These skills may include stress management techniques, problem-solving strategies, effective communication skills, relaxation exercises, and assertiveness training. Your therapist will guide you in practicing these skills and incorporating them into your daily life.

Outside of therapy sessions, homework assignments play an essential role in CBT. These assignments provide opportunities for you to practice and reinforce the skills learned in therapy. They may involve keeping thought records, practicing relaxation exercises, implementing problem-solving strategies, or gradually confronting feared situations. By actively engaging in these assignments, you enhance the effectiveness and long-term impact of CBT.

Research consistently supports the effectiveness of CBT for a wide range of mental health conditions. It is considered an evidence-based approach and is recommended as a first-line treatment by leading professional organizations. The collaborative and empowering nature of CBT, coupled with its personalized approach, makes it an invaluable tool for promoting mental well-being and helping individuals achieve lasting change.

So, CBT offers practical and effective strategies for managing mental health challenges. By addressing the connection between thoughts, feelings, and behaviors, CBT empowers you to take an active role in improving your mental well-being. Through cognitive restructuring, behavioral activation, exposure and response prevention, skills training, and homework assignments, you can develop the tools and skills necessary to overcome your challenges and thrive in your daily life.

Remember, seeking support from a qualified therapist or mental health professional is crucial when engaging in CBT. They will guide you through the process, provide you with valuable insights and techniques, and support you on your journey to better mental health. With CBT, you have the opportunity to take control of your thoughts, behaviors, and emotions, and create positive and lasting change in your life.

Chapter 79: Dialectical Behavior Therapy (DBT):

Effective Strategies for Emotional Regulation

In this chapter, we will delve into the principles of DBT, discuss its applications in mental health, and provide an understanding of how this therapy can help individuals develop healthier ways to manage their emotions.

Understanding Dialectical Behavior Therapy (DBT):

• What is DBT: Dialectical Behavior Therapy is a comprehensive and evidence-based form of therapy originally developed to treat individuals with borderline personality disorder (BPD). It has since been expanded to help individuals struggling with various mental health concerns, particularly those involving emotional dysregulation.

• Dialectics: The term "dialectics" in DBT refers to the integration of opposing perspectives. It recognizes that individuals often experience conflicting emotions and that change happens through finding a balance between acceptance and change. DBT emphasizes validating and accepting individuals' experiences while also encouraging them to develop new skills and behaviors.

• Four modules of DBT: DBT consists of four main modules: mindfulness, distress tolerance, emotion regulation, and interpersonal effectiveness. These modules work together to address different aspects of emotional regulation and promote healthier ways of managing distressing emotions.

Core Components and Strategies of DBT:

• Mindfulness: Mindfulness is a key component of DBT and serves as the foundation for the other modules. It involves developing present-moment awareness, non-judgmental observation of thoughts and emotions, and acceptance of one's experiences. Mindfulness practices, such as meditation and breathing exercises, help individuals cultivate self-awareness and regulate their emotions more effectively.

• Distress tolerance: Distress tolerance skills help individuals cope with intense emotions and distressing situations when they cannot be immediately changed. Strategies such as self-soothing, distraction techniques, and radical acceptance enable individuals to navigate through difficult moments without resorting to destructive or impulsive behaviors.

• Emotion regulation: Emotion regulation skills focus on identifying and understanding emotions, as well as learning to modulate their intensity and duration. Techniques include emotion labeling, opposite action, problem-solving, and building positive emotional experiences. By developing these skills, individuals gain greater control over their emotional responses and reduce impulsive or harmful behaviors.

• Interpersonal effectiveness: Interpersonal effectiveness skills assist individuals in navigating relationships and effectively expressing their needs, boundaries, and emotions. These skills encompass assertiveness training, effective communication, and conflict resolution strategies. By improving interpersonal skills, individuals can build healthier and more fulfilling relationships while reducing the impact of interpersonal conflicts on their emotional well-being.

Applications of DBT in Mental Health:

• Borderline personality disorder (BPD): DBT was initially developed to treat individuals with BPD. It has been extensively studied and shown to be effective in reducing self-harm behaviors, suicide attempts, and improving overall functioning and quality of life for individuals with BPD.

• Substance use disorders: DBT has been adapted for individuals struggling with substance use disorders. By addressing emotional dysregulation and enhancing distress tolerance skills, DBT helps individuals manage cravings, cope with triggers, and develop healthier ways of managing distress without turning to substance use.

• Eating disorders: DBT has also been integrated into the treatment of eating disorders, such as binge eating disorder and bulimia nervosa. By targeting emotional dysregulation, distress tolerance, and interpersonal effectiveness, DBT helps individuals develop alternative coping strategies to replace disordered eating behaviors.

• Mood disorders: DBT has shown promise in treating mood disorders, such as depression and bipolar disorder. The emotion regulation and distress tolerance skills taught in DBT can help individuals manage mood swings, prevent depressive relapses, and improve overall emotional well-being.

• Trauma-related disorders: DBT has been adapted to address the needs of individuals with post-traumatic stress disorder (PTSD) and other trauma-related disorders. By focusing on emotion regulation and distress tolerance, DBT helps individuals develop strategies to manage trauma-related symptoms and promote healing.

Benefits and Effectiveness of DBT:

• Evidence-based approach: DBT is supported by a substantial body of research and has demonstrated effectiveness in treating a range of mental health concerns. It is considered an evidence-based treatment and is recommended by professional organizations for specific conditions.

• Holistic approach: DBT takes a holistic approach to mental health by addressing emotional dysregulation, interpersonal difficulties, and distress tolerance. By targeting multiple aspects of an individual's life, DBT offers a comprehensive framework for change and growth.

• Supportive and validating: DBT provides a supportive and validating therapeutic environment. It recognizes the unique challenges individuals face and aims to help them feel understood and accepted. This validation can foster a sense of safety and trust, which is essential for individuals to engage fully in the therapy process.

• Skill-building for long-term change: DBT equips individuals with practical skills that can be applied beyond therapy sessions. By learning and practicing these skills, individuals develop a foundation for long-term emotional well-being and improved interpersonal relationships.

• Individualized treatment: DBT is tailored to the individual's specific needs and goals. Therapists work collaboratively with individuals to create treatment plans that address their unique challenges and provide them with the tools to overcome them.

So, Dialectical Behavior Therapy (DBT) offers effective strategies for emotional regulation and has been successfully applied to various mental health concerns. By incorporating mindfulness, distress tolerance, emotion regulation, and interpersonal effectiveness, DBT provides individuals with a comprehensive toolkit for managing intense emotions, developing healthier coping mechanisms, and improving their overall well-being. With its evidence-based foundation, holistic approach, and focus on skill-building, DBT offers individuals the opportunity to cultivate greater emotional stability, resilience, and interpersonal effectiveness.

Chapter 80: Acceptance and Commitment Therapy (ACT) for Mental Health and Well-being

In this chapter, we will delve into the principles of ACT, discuss its unique approach to psychological flexibility, and provide an understanding of how this therapy can help individuals overcome challenges and live a meaningful life.

Understanding Acceptance and Commitment Therapy (ACT):

• What is ACT: Acceptance and Commitment Therapy is a form of therapy that focuses on developing psychological flexibility. It is based on the idea that suffering is a normal part of the human experience and that individuals can live fulfilling lives by accepting what is out of their control and committing to actions aligned with their values.

• Psychological flexibility: ACT places a strong emphasis on psychological flexibility, which involves being present in the moment, choosing actions based on personal values, and being open to experiencing all emotions. It is about learning to accept uncomfortable thoughts and feelings while still taking steps toward a rich and meaningful life.

• The six core processes of ACT: ACT incorporates six core processes: acceptance, cognitive defusion, being present, self-as-context, values, and committed action. These processes work together to help individuals develop psychological flexibility and move toward a more fulfilling and purposeful life.

Core Components and Strategies of ACT:

• Acceptance: Acceptance involves embracing all thoughts, emotions, and sensations without trying to change or control them. It is about allowing these experiences to come and go, recognizing that they are temporary and do not define one's identity or dictate one's actions.

• Cognitive defusion: Cognitive defusion aims to help individuals step back from their thoughts and observe them without getting caught up or fused with them. It involves recognizing that thoughts are just mental events and not necessarily accurate or objective representations of reality.

• Being present: Being present, also known as mindfulness, involves cultivating awareness of the present moment without judgment. It is about fully engaging in the here and now, rather than getting caught up in worries about the past or future.

• Self-as-context: Self-as-context refers to the ability to observe oneself from a broader perspective. It involves recognizing that thoughts, emotions, and experiences are constantly changing and that one's true self is not defined solely by these fleeting aspects.

• Values: Values represent what is truly important and meaningful to an individual. ACT helps individuals clarify their values and connect their actions and choices to those values. This process allows individuals to live in alignment with what matters most to them, even in the face of challenges.

• Committed action: Committed action involves taking purposeful steps toward one's values, even in the presence of discomfort or difficulties. It is about making choices and engaging in behaviors that align with one's values and move them toward a more fulfilling life.

Applications of ACT in Mental Health:

• Anxiety disorders: ACT has been shown to be effective in treating various anxiety disorders, such as generalized anxiety disorder, social anxiety disorder, and panic disorder. By promoting acceptance of anxious thoughts and sensations and helping individuals engage in value-driven actions, ACT reduces the impact of anxiety on daily life.

• Depression: ACT can be beneficial in treating depression by helping individuals create distance from depressive thoughts and develop a greater sense of purpose and meaning in life. By focusing on values and committed action, individuals can experience a shift in their relationship with depression and take steps toward a more fulfilling life.

• Chronic pain: ACT has been found to be helpful in managing chronic pain by teaching individuals to accept pain sensations while focusing on living a meaningful life despite pain. By shifting the focus from pain avoidance to valued living, individuals can reduce the impact of pain on their overall well-being.

• Eating disorders: ACT is also utilized in the treatment of eating disorders, such as anorexia nervosa, bulimia nervosa, and binge eating disorder. By helping individuals develop a more accepting and compassionate relationship with their bodies and thoughts related to food, ACT supports long-term recovery and improved body image.

• Substance use disorders: ACT can be integrated into the treatment of substance use disorders by promoting acceptance of cravings and uncomfortable emotions while encouraging individuals to make value-based choices that support sobriety and overall well-being.

Benefits and Effectiveness of ACT:

• Embracing the human experience: ACT offers a compassionate and accepting approach to the human experience. It acknowledges that difficulties, pain, and discomfort are a natural part of life and aims to help individuals navigate these challenges in a way that aligns with their values.

• Enhanced psychological flexibility: The focus on psychological flexibility in ACT allows individuals to respond adaptively to internal experiences and external circumstances. By developing the skills of acceptance, defusion, mindfulness, and value-based action, individuals can build resilience and adaptability.

• Promoting values-driven living: ACT helps individuals clarify their values and take purposeful actions that align with those values. By connecting actions to values, individuals experience a sense of meaning and fulfillment, even in the presence of difficulties.

• Sustainable change: ACT fosters sustainable change by emphasizing long-term behavior change based on personal values, rather than relying on short-lived motivation or external rewards. By cultivating intrinsic motivation and commitment, individuals are more likely to maintain progress and continue growing.

• Empowering individuals: ACT empowers individuals to take control of their own lives and make choices that align with their values, even in the face of challenging thoughts, emotions, or circumstances. It encourages autonomy, self-compassion, and personal growth.

So, Acceptance and Commitment Therapy (ACT) offers a unique approach to promoting mental health and well-being. By focusing on psychological flexibility, acceptance, present-moment awareness, values, and committed action, ACT provides individuals with a framework to navigate challenges, develop resilience, and live a meaningful life. Whether you are struggling with anxiety, depression, chronic pain, or other mental health concerns, ACT offers strategies and tools to help you embrace the full range of human experience and move toward a more fulfilling and values-driven life.

Chapter 81: The Role of Trauma-Focused Therapy in Healing from Traumatic Events

In this chapter, we will delve into the principles of Trauma-Focused Therapy, discuss its unique approach to addressing trauma-related symptoms, and provide an understanding of how this therapy can support individuals on their journey toward healing and recovery.

Understanding Trauma-Focused Therapy:

• What is Trauma-Focused Therapy: Trauma-Focused Therapy is an evidence-based approach designed to help individuals recover from the effects of traumatic experiences. It is specifically tailored to address the emotional, cognitive, and behavioral consequences of trauma, promoting healing and resilience.

• Key features of Trauma-Focused Therapy: Trauma-Focused Therapy provides a safe and supportive environment where individuals can process traumatic memories, reduce distressing symptoms, and develop healthier coping strategies. It is characterized by a collaborative and empowering therapeutic relationship between the client and the therapist.

Core Components and Strategies of Trauma-Focused Therapy:

• Psychoeducation: Psychoeducation is an essential component of Trauma-Focused Therapy. It involves providing individuals with information about the effects of trauma on the mind and body, helping them understand their symptoms and normalizing their experiences. Psychoeducation creates a foundation for individuals to develop insight and empowers them to actively participate in their healing process.

• Trauma-focused cognitive restructuring: Trauma-focused cognitive restructuring focuses on challenging and modifying unhelpful thoughts and beliefs that have developed as a result of the trauma. By identifying and addressing cognitive distortions, individuals can gain a more accurate and balanced perspective, reducing self-blame and negative self-perceptions.

• Exposure therapy: Exposure therapy is often utilized in Trauma-Focused Therapy to help individuals gradually and safely confront traumatic memories and reminders. Through controlled and structured exposure, individuals can reduce avoidance behaviors and learn that they can tolerate distressing emotions associated with the trauma.

•	Cognitive processing therapy: Cognitive processing therapy aims to help individuals make sense of their traumatic experiences and integrate them into their broader understanding of themselves and the world. By addressing the thoughts and beliefs related to the trauma, individuals can challenge and modify any distorted perceptions, leading to a more adaptive and accurate cognitive framework.

•	Skill-building: Trauma-Focused Therapy incorporates skill-building components to help individuals develop coping strategies for managing distressing emotions and improving interpersonal functioning. Skills such as emotion regulation, stress management, and communication techniques are taught to enhance resilience and promote adaptive responses to triggers or stressors.

Applications of Trauma-Focused Therapy:

•	Post-Traumatic Stress Disorder (PTSD): Trauma-Focused Therapy is highly effective in treating individuals with PTSD. It can help individuals process traumatic memories, manage hyperarousal symptoms, challenge avoidance behaviors, and reduce the impact of intrusive thoughts and flashbacks on daily functioning.

•	Childhood trauma: Trauma-Focused Therapy is particularly well-suited for addressing childhood trauma, including physical, sexual, and emotional abuse, neglect, and witnessing violence. It offers age-appropriate interventions and recognizes the unique needs and vulnerabilities of children and adolescents who have experienced trauma.

•	Complex trauma: Trauma-Focused Therapy can be beneficial for individuals who have experienced repeated or prolonged trauma, such as those with a history of ongoing abuse or neglect. It addresses the complex impact of trauma on various areas of functioning, including relationships, self-esteem, and emotional regulation.

•	Dissociative disorders: Trauma-Focused Therapy can be adapted to address dissociative symptoms and disorders that often result from severe or prolonged trauma. It helps individuals develop a sense of safety and stability while working through traumatic memories and improving co-consciousness and integration.

Benefits and Effectiveness of Trauma-Focused Therapy:

• Empowerment and agency: Trauma-Focused Therapy promotes empowerment and agency by providing individuals with tools and strategies to actively participate in their healing process. It allows individuals to regain a sense of control over their lives and move toward post-traumatic growth.

• Integration of traumatic experiences: Trauma-Focused Therapy helps individuals integrate their traumatic experiences into their life narrative, reducing the fragmentation and intrusiveness of traumatic memories. It supports individuals in making meaning out of their experiences and fostering a sense of coherence and resilience.

• Symptom reduction: Trauma-Focused Therapy aims to reduce trauma-related symptoms, such as intrusive thoughts, nightmares, flashbacks, and avoidance behaviors. By addressing the underlying causes of these symptoms, individuals can experience relief and an improved quality of life.

• Improved interpersonal functioning: Trauma-Focused Therapy recognizes the impact of trauma on interpersonal relationships and provides individuals with skills to enhance their communication, establish healthy boundaries, and develop trusting connections with others.

• Enhanced resilience and post-traumatic growth: Through Trauma-Focused Therapy, individuals can develop increased resilience, post-traumatic growth, and a greater sense of self-compassion. By working through trauma-related challenges, individuals have the opportunity to transform their experiences and build a more hopeful future.

So, Trauma-Focused Therapy offers a comprehensive and evidence-based approach to healing from traumatic events. By incorporating psychoeducation, cognitive restructuring, exposure therapy, cognitive processing therapy, and skill-building, this therapy empowers individuals to address the impact of trauma on their lives, reduce distressing symptoms, and develop healthier coping strategies. Whether you are struggling with PTSD, childhood trauma, or complex trauma,

Trauma-Focused Therapy provides a supportive and effective framework for healing and moving forward on the path to recovery.

Chapter 82: Integrating Mindfulness-Based Stress Reduction (MBSR) into Mental Health Care

In this chapter, we will delve into the principles of MBSR, discuss its unique approach to stress reduction and emotional well-being, and provide an understanding of how this practice can enhance mental health and overall quality of life.

Understanding Mindfulness-Based Stress Reduction (MBSR):

• What is MBSR: Mindfulness-Based Stress Reduction is a program developed by Dr. Jon Kabat-Zinn in the late 1970s. It combines mindfulness meditation, body awareness, and yoga to help individuals manage stress, improve self-awareness, and cultivate a sense of calm and presence.

• Core principles of MBSR: MBSR is based on the principles of mindfulness, which involve paying attention to the present moment with a non-judgmental and accepting attitude. It encourages individuals to cultivate a curious and compassionate stance toward their experiences, including thoughts, emotions, and physical sensations.

• The role of mindfulness in stress reduction: Mindfulness has been found to reduce stress by promoting greater awareness of stress triggers and allowing individuals to respond rather than react. It helps individuals develop the capacity to observe their thoughts and emotions without getting entangled in them, leading to a greater sense of calm and resilience.

Components and Techniques of MBSR:

• Mindfulness meditation: Mindfulness meditation is a foundational practice in MBSR. It involves sitting in a comfortable position, focusing on the breath or a chosen anchor, and gently redirecting attention back to the present moment whenever the mind wanders. This practice cultivates attentional stability and enhances awareness.

• Body scan: The body scan is a technique used in MBSR to bring attention to different parts of the body, systematically observing physical sensations and promoting body awareness. It helps individuals develop a deeper connection with their bodies and increases their ability to recognize and release tension or discomfort.

• Mindful movement: Mindful movement practices, such as gentle yoga or walking meditation, are integral to MBSR. These practices combine movement and awareness, allowing individuals to connect with their bodies and cultivate a sense of presence and embodiment.

• Informal mindfulness: Informal mindfulness involves bringing mindfulness into everyday activities, such as eating, walking, or engaging in conversations. It encourages individuals to be fully present and attentive to their experiences, enhancing the integration of mindfulness into daily life.

Applications of MBSR in Mental Health Care:

• Stress reduction: MBSR has been widely used to alleviate stress in various populations, including individuals with anxiety, depression, chronic pain, and work-related stress. By cultivating mindfulness and developing a different relationship with stressors, individuals can experience a greater sense of calm and well-being.

• Anxiety and depression: MBSR has shown promising results in reducing symptoms of anxiety and depression. By practicing mindfulness, individuals can develop a greater capacity to observe and relate to their thoughts and emotions, reducing rumination and increasing self-compassion.

• Chronic pain management: MBSR has been effective in helping individuals manage chronic pain. By increasing awareness of bodily sensations and practicing non-judgmental acceptance, individuals can develop a new relationship with pain and reduce the suffering associated with it.

• Addiction recovery: MBSR can be beneficial in addiction recovery by increasing individuals' awareness of triggers, cravings, and underlying emotional states. By practicing mindfulness, individuals can develop greater self-regulation and make more conscious choices in their recovery journey.

• Workplace well-being: MBSR has been introduced in workplace settings to promote employee well-being and reduce stress. By incorporating mindfulness practices into the workday, individuals can improve focus, reduce burnout, and enhance resilience in the face of work-related challenges.

Benefits and Effectiveness of MBSR:

•   Stress reduction and resilience: MBSR helps individuals develop resilience by cultivating greater self-awareness and equipping them with tools to respond skillfully to stress. Regular practice can lead to a reduced perception of stressors and an increased ability to bounce back from difficulties.

•   Emotional well-being: MBSR promotes emotional well-being by providing individuals with a space to observe and accept their emotions without judgment. By developing emotional regulation skills and increasing self-compassion, individuals can experience greater emotional balance and satisfaction in life.

•   Improved cognitive functioning: MBSR has been found to enhance cognitive functions, such as attention, working memory, and decision-making. By training the mind to focus and be present, individuals can improve cognitive flexibility and problem-solving abilities.

•   Enhanced relationships: MBSR fosters qualities such as empathy, active listening, and non-reactivity, which can improve interpersonal relationships. By practicing mindfulness, individuals can be fully present with others, fostering deeper connections and more effective communication.

•   Overall well-being: Regular practice of MBSR has been associated with increased overall well-being and a greater sense of life satisfaction. By cultivating mindfulness, individuals can savor the present moment, enhance their appreciation for life, and find meaning and purpose.

So, Mindfulness-Based Stress Reduction (MBSR) offers a transformative approach to stress reduction and emotional well-being. By incorporating mindfulness meditation, body awareness, and mindful movement, individuals can develop greater self-awareness, reduce stress, and enhance overall quality of life. Whether you are seeking stress reduction, improved mental health, or a greater sense of well-being, MBSR provides a practical and accessible pathway to cultivating mindfulness and finding inner peace amidst life's challenges.

Chapter 83: Eye Movement Desensitization and Reprocessing (EMDR) for Trauma Recovery

In this chapter, we will delve into the principles of EMDR, discuss its unique approach to processing traumatic memories, and provide an understanding of how this therapy can support individuals in their journey toward healing and recovery from trauma.

Understanding Eye Movement Desensitization and Reprocessing (EMDR):

• What is EMDR: Eye Movement Desensitization and Reprocessing is a psychotherapy approach developed by Dr. Francine Shapiro in the late 1980s. It is based on the understanding that traumatic experiences can overwhelm the brain's natural coping mechanisms, leading to the development of persistent distressing symptoms. EMDR aims to facilitate the processing of traumatic memories and help individuals integrate them into a healthier and more adaptive narrative.

• Core principles of EMDR: EMDR is grounded in the belief that individuals have inherent resources for healing and recovery. It emphasizes the role of bilateral stimulation, such as eye movements, in facilitating the brain's natural capacity to process and resolve traumatic memories. EMDR also recognizes the importance of creating a safe and trusting therapeutic environment.

The Phases of EMDR Therapy:

• Assessment and preparation: The therapist begins by conducting a comprehensive assessment of the client's trauma history, current symptoms, and resources. This phase also involves building a therapeutic alliance and providing psychoeducation about EMDR to ensure that the client is informed and prepared for the process.

• Resource development: The therapist helps the client identify and strengthen internal and external resources that can support them during the processing of traumatic memories. This may involve teaching relaxation techniques, developing coping skills, and fostering a sense of safety and stabilization.

• Desensitization and reprocessing: In this phase, the client focuses on specific traumatic memories while simultaneously engaging in bilateral stimulation, such as following the therapist's fingers with their eyes. This process allows for the reprocessing of the traumatic memories, facilitating the integration of thoughts, emotions, and physical sensations.

• Installation: The therapist helps the client strengthen positive beliefs and adaptive responses related to the traumatic memories. This phase involves guiding the client to replace negative self-perceptions with more positive and empowering beliefs.

• Body scan and closure: The therapist guides the client through a body scan to ensure that any residual physical sensations or emotional distress associated with the traumatic memories have been addressed. The session concludes with a sense of closure and grounding.

Applications of EMDR Therapy:

• Post-Traumatic Stress Disorder (PTSD): EMDR is particularly effective in treating individuals with PTSD. It can help alleviate symptoms such as intrusive thoughts, nightmares, flashbacks, and hyperarousal. EMDR aims to reduce the emotional intensity and vividness of traumatic memories, allowing individuals to regain a sense of control over their thoughts and emotions.

• Complex trauma and developmental trauma: EMDR can be adapted to address complex trauma and the cumulative effects of prolonged or repeated trauma, including childhood abuse, neglect, or interpersonal violence. It focuses on processing the various components of traumatic experiences and fostering integration and healing.

• Other anxiety disorders: EMDR has shown promising results in treating other anxiety disorders, such as panic disorder, phobias, and generalized anxiety disorder. By targeting underlying traumatic memories and related beliefs, EMDR can help alleviate anxiety symptoms and improve overall well-being.

• Performance enhancement: EMDR has been used to enhance performance in various domains, including sports, academics, and public speaking. By addressing past negative experiences or performance-related traumas, individuals can overcome barriers and tap into their full potential.

Benefits and Effectiveness of EMDR:

• Rapid symptom reduction: EMDR has been found to lead to rapid symptom reduction, with many individuals experiencing significant improvements in a relatively short period. By reprocessing traumatic memories, EMDR helps individuals release emotional distress and replace negative beliefs with more adaptive ones.

• Long-lasting effects: EMDR therapy has demonstrated long-lasting effects, with individuals reporting sustained improvements even after therapy has ended. The processing of traumatic memories and the integration of new beliefs can lead to lasting changes in emotional well-being and overall functioning.

• Safety and non-invasiveness: EMDR provides a safe and non-invasive approach to trauma therapy. Unlike traditional exposure therapies, EMDR does not require individuals to extensively recount or relive traumatic events in detail. The focus is on processing and integrating traumatic memories in a controlled and supportive environment.

• Holistic approach: EMDR acknowledges the interconnectedness of thoughts, emotions, and physical sensations in trauma recovery. By targeting all these aspects, EMDR promotes holistic healing and facilitates the integration of traumatic experiences into the individual's narrative, fostering a sense of coherence and self-compassion.

• Wide-ranging applicability: EMDR can be adapted to various populations and settings, making it a versatile therapy. It has been successfully used with children, adolescents, adults, and older adults, as well as in individual, group, and online therapy formats.

So, Eye Movement Desensitization and Reprocessing (EMDR) offers a unique and effective approach to trauma recovery. By facilitating the processing and integration of traumatic memories, EMDR helps individuals alleviate distressing symptoms, replace negative beliefs, and foster resilience and well-being. Whether you are seeking treatment for PTSD, complex trauma, or other anxiety disorders, EMDR provides a supportive and transformative therapeutic journey toward healing and recovery from trauma.

Chapter 84: Exploring Psychodynamic Therapy and Unconscious Processes in Mental Health

In this chapter, we will delve into the principles of psychodynamic therapy, discuss its unique approach to understanding the unconscious mind, and provide an understanding of how this therapy can support individuals in their journey toward self-discovery and emotional healing.

Understanding Psychodynamic Therapy:

• What is psychodynamic therapy: Psychodynamic therapy is a form of talk therapy that focuses on exploring the unconscious processes and unresolved conflicts that may contribute to emotional distress and psychological difficulties. It is rooted in the belief that our thoughts, emotions, and behaviors are influenced by unconscious motives and past experiences.

• Core principles of psychodynamic therapy: Psychodynamic therapy is guided by several core principles, including the belief that early childhood experiences shape our personality and the way we relate to others. It emphasizes the importance of the therapeutic relationship, transference and countertransference dynamics, and the exploration of unconscious thoughts and feelings.

The Role of the Unconscious Mind:

• The unconscious mind: According to psychodynamic theory, the unconscious mind contains thoughts, feelings, and memories that are outside of our conscious awareness. It is believed to influence our thoughts, emotions, and behaviors, even though we may not be fully aware of it. Psychodynamic therapy aims to bring these unconscious processes to light for exploration and healing.

• Unresolved conflicts: Psychodynamic therapy suggests that unresolved conflicts from childhood or past experiences can continue to affect our lives and contribute to emotional difficulties. By exploring these unconscious conflicts, individuals can gain insight into their patterns of thinking, feeling, and behaving and work towards resolution and healing.

• Defense mechanisms: The unconscious mind employs defense mechanisms to protect us from experiencing overwhelming emotions or thoughts. These defense mechanisms, such as repression, denial, or projection, can be explored in therapy to uncover underlying issues and promote self-awareness.

Techniques and Approaches in Psychodynamic Therapy:

• Free association: Free association is a technique used in psychodynamic therapy where individuals are encouraged to express their thoughts, feelings, and associations without censorship. By allowing thoughts to flow freely, individuals can tap into their unconscious mind and reveal underlying emotions and conflicts.

• Dream analysis: Dreams are seen as expressions of unconscious processes in psychodynamic therapy. Therapists may explore the content and symbolism of dreams to gain insight into unconscious thoughts, desires, and conflicts.

• Transference and countertransference: Transference occurs when individuals project feelings and reactions from past relationships onto the therapist. Countertransference refers to the therapist's emotional reactions to the client. Both transference and countertransference dynamics can provide valuable information about unconscious processes and relationship patterns.

• Interpretation: Therapists in psychodynamic therapy may offer interpretations to help individuals gain insight into unconscious thoughts and emotions. Interpretations are aimed at helping individuals make connections between past experiences and current patterns of behavior or emotional distress.

Applications of Psychodynamic Therapy:

• Resolving childhood trauma: Psychodynamic therapy can be particularly helpful in addressing unresolved childhood trauma. By exploring the impact of early experiences and the associated emotions, individuals can work towards healing and developing healthier coping mechanisms.

• Relationship difficulties: Psychodynamic therapy focuses on understanding how past relationship dynamics influence present relationships. It can help individuals gain insight into patterns of interaction, attachment styles, and the role of unconscious processes in relationship difficulties.

• Emotional regulation: By exploring unconscious emotions and defenses, psychodynamic therapy can help individuals develop greater emotional awareness and regulation. This can lead to a deeper understanding of one's emotional experiences and the ability to respond to them in more adaptive ways.

• Self-exploration and personal growth: Psychodynamic therapy offers individuals an opportunity for self-exploration and personal growth. By gaining insight into unconscious processes, individuals can develop a deeper understanding of themselves, their motivations, and their goals, leading to enhanced self-esteem and a greater sense of meaning and purpose.

Benefits and Effectiveness of Psychodynamic Therapy:

• Insight and self-awareness: Psychodynamic therapy helps individuals gain insight into their thoughts, feelings, and behaviors. By uncovering unconscious processes, individuals can develop a deeper understanding of themselves and their experiences, leading to greater self-awareness and personal growth.

• Emotional healing: Through the exploration of unconscious conflicts and unresolved issues, psychodynamic therapy can promote emotional healing. By understanding the underlying causes of emotional distress, individuals can develop healthier ways of coping and experience relief from symptoms.

• Relationship improvement: Psychodynamic therapy can improve interpersonal relationships by addressing patterns of relating that stem from unconscious processes. By gaining insight into relationship dynamics and unresolved conflicts, individuals can develop healthier ways of relating and enhance their communication skills.

• Long-lasting effects: Psychodynamic therapy has shown to have long-lasting effects even after therapy has ended. The insights gained and the emotional healing experienced in therapy can continue to positively impact individuals' lives and relationships.

So, psychodynamic therapy offers a unique and valuable approach to understanding the unconscious mind and addressing unresolved conflicts that may contribute to mental health challenges. By exploring unconscious processes, individuals can gain insight, promote emotional healing, and enhance self-awareness. Whether you are seeking to resolve past trauma, improve relationships, or embark on a journey of self-exploration, psychodynamic therapy provides a supportive and transformative path toward emotional well-being and personal growth.

Chapter 85: The Benefits of Group Therapy in Promoting Mental Health

In this chapter, we will delve into the principles of group therapy, discuss its unique advantages and effectiveness, and provide an understanding of how this therapeutic approach can support individuals in their journey toward healing and personal growth.

Understanding Group Therapy:

• What is group therapy: Group therapy is a form of psychotherapy where a small group of individuals, typically led by one or more trained therapists, come together to support each other, share experiences, and work on common mental health concerns. It provides a safe and confidential space for individuals to explore their thoughts, emotions, and behaviors while receiving support and feedback from both the therapists and the other group members.

• Core principles of group therapy: Group therapy is based on several core principles, including the belief that individuals can benefit from the support and insights gained through interactions with others who are experiencing similar challenges. It emphasizes the importance of trust, confidentiality, and mutual respect within the group setting.

The Advantages of Group Therapy:

• Universality: Group therapy creates a sense of universality, as individuals realize that they are not alone in their struggles. Sharing experiences, hearing others' stories, and witnessing the progress of fellow group members can provide a powerful sense of validation, reducing feelings of isolation and fostering a sense of belonging.

• Support and empathy: Group therapy offers a unique opportunity for individuals to receive support and empathy from others who are going through similar experiences. Group members can offer understanding, encouragement, and a sense of camaraderie, creating a supportive network that extends beyond the therapy sessions.

• Feedback and perspective: Group therapy provides a diverse range of perspectives and feedback from both the therapists and the group members. This can offer valuable insights and alternative viewpoints, helping individuals gain a deeper understanding of their challenges and explore new approaches to problem-solving.

• Skill-building and modeling: Group therapy allows individuals to observe and learn from the experiences and coping strategies of others. Positive role modeling within the group can inspire individuals to develop new skills, adopt healthier behaviors, and overcome challenges.

• Social skills and interpersonal growth: Group therapy offers a unique opportunity to practice and improve social skills within a supportive environment. By engaging in interpersonal interactions, individuals can develop greater self-awareness, enhance communication skills, and improve their ability to form and maintain healthy relationships.

Types of Group Therapy:

• Psychoeducation groups: These groups focus on providing education and information about specific mental health conditions or topics. They aim to enhance individuals' understanding of their challenges and equip them with knowledge and skills for managing their symptoms effectively.

• Process-oriented groups: These groups emphasize exploring and processing individuals' thoughts, emotions, and behaviors within a therapeutic context. They provide a space for individuals to share their experiences, gain insights, and receive support and feedback from the group members and therapists.

• Support groups: Support groups focus on creating a supportive community for individuals facing similar challenges, such as grief, addiction recovery, or specific health conditions. They offer a safe space for individuals to share their experiences, receive validation, and gain emotional support from others who can relate to their struggles.

• Skills-based groups: These groups are designed to teach specific skills or strategies for managing mental health concerns. They may focus on topics such as stress management, emotion regulation, assertiveness, or mindfulness. Participants learn and practice these skills together, supporting each other in their growth and progress.

Effectiveness of Group Therapy:

• Shared experiences and normalization: Group therapy has been found to be effective in reducing feelings of isolation and promoting a sense of normalization. Through the sharing of experiences, individuals realize that their struggles are not unique and that others are facing similar challenges. This normalization can reduce shame, increase self-acceptance, and foster a sense of hope.

• Improved self-awareness and insight: Group therapy provides a reflective and supportive environment where individuals can gain insight into their thoughts, emotions, and patterns of behavior. By listening to others' perspectives and receiving feedback from the group, individuals can develop a deeper understanding of themselves, their strengths, and areas for growth.

• Enhanced interpersonal skills: The interactive nature of group therapy offers opportunities for individuals to practice and refine their interpersonal skills. Through giving and receiving support, expressing emotions, and navigating group dynamics, individuals can develop greater self-confidence, assertiveness, and empathy.

• Real-life application: Group therapy allows individuals to apply the insights and skills gained in therapy to real-life situations. The supportive and collaborative nature of the group can provide a bridge between the therapeutic environment and the challenges individuals face outside of therapy.

• Long-term benefits: Group therapy has been shown to have long-term benefits, with individuals reporting sustained improvements even after the therapy has ended. The skills learned, relationships formed, and self-awareness gained in group therapy can continue to support individuals' mental health and well-being.

So, group therapy offers a valuable and effective approach to promoting mental health and well-being. Through shared experiences, support, and feedback, individuals can gain insight, develop interpersonal skills, and experience a sense of belonging. Whether you are seeking support for specific challenges or looking to enhance your personal growth, group therapy provides a safe and transformative space for healing, learning, and connection with others on a similar journey.

Chapter 86: Online Therapy and Telehealth: Expanding Access to Mental Health Services

In this chapter, we will delve into the principles of online therapy, discuss its unique advantages and considerations, and provide an understanding of how this form of therapy is revolutionizing the field and making mental health care more accessible to individuals worldwide.

Understanding Online Therapy:

• What is online therapy: Online therapy, also known as teletherapy or telehealth, is a form of therapy that takes place over the internet, using video conferencing platforms, phone calls, or messaging apps. It allows individuals to receive mental health support and treatment from the comfort of their own homes, removing geographical barriers and expanding access to care.

• Core principles of online therapy: Online therapy follows the same core principles as traditional therapy, with a focus on providing a safe, confidential, and supportive environment for individuals to explore their thoughts, emotions, and behaviors. It adheres to ethical and professional guidelines to ensure the delivery of effective and ethical mental health care.

Advantages of Online Therapy:

• Accessibility and convenience: Online therapy eliminates geographical barriers and allows individuals to access mental health services from anywhere with an internet connection. It is particularly beneficial for individuals who live in remote areas, have limited mobility, or face transportation challenges.

• Flexible scheduling: Online therapy offers greater flexibility in scheduling appointments, as individuals can choose times that best fit their busy lives. It can be particularly beneficial for those with demanding work schedules, childcare responsibilities, or other commitments that make attending in-person therapy difficult.

• Privacy and comfort: Online therapy provides individuals with a sense of privacy and comfort as they engage in therapy from the familiar and safe environment of their own homes. This can reduce feelings of self-consciousness and create a space where individuals feel more at ease discussing sensitive or personal topics.

• Continuity of care: Online therapy ensures continuity of care for individuals who may need to travel or relocate. They can continue working with the same therapist, maintaining the therapeutic relationship, and avoiding disruptions in their progress.

• Expanded therapist options: Online therapy allows individuals to access a wider pool of therapists, including those who specialize in specific areas or have expertise in certain modalities. This expands the options and increases the likelihood of finding a therapist who is the right fit for their unique needs.

Considerations and Adaptations:

• Technology requirements: Engaging in online therapy requires access to a reliable internet connection and a device (such as a computer, smartphone, or tablet) with video and audio capabilities. It is important for individuals to ensure they have the necessary technology and a private space for their therapy sessions.

• Confidentiality and privacy: Online therapists follow strict confidentiality protocols to protect the privacy of individuals. It is essential for individuals to choose a secure and encrypted platform for their therapy sessions and ensure that they are in a private and confidential setting during their sessions.

• Therapeutic rapport: Building a strong therapeutic rapport is crucial in online therapy. Therapists may need to adapt their approaches to create a sense of connection and trust through a digital medium. Video conferencing can provide visual cues and nonverbal communication, enhancing the therapeutic relationship.

• Emergency procedures: Online therapists have protocols in place to address emergency situations. They establish clear procedures for addressing crisis situations, including contacting emergency services or local resources when necessary.

Effectiveness of Online Therapy:

• Research evidence: Numerous studies have shown the effectiveness of online therapy in treating a wide range of mental health concerns, including anxiety, depression, post-traumatic stress disorder, and more. Online therapy has been found to be as effective as traditional in-person therapy in many cases.

• Client satisfaction: Many individuals report high levels of satisfaction with online therapy. They appreciate the convenience, flexibility, and accessibility it offers. Online therapy allows individuals to engage in therapy at their own pace and in a way that best suits their preferences and needs.

• Positive outcomes: Online therapy has demonstrated positive outcomes in reducing symptoms, improving well-being, and enhancing overall functioning. Individuals who engage in online therapy often experience improvements in their mental health, gain insight into their challenges, and develop coping strategies for managing their symptoms.

• Continued growth and development: The field of online therapy continues to evolve and improve. Therapists are continually adapting their approaches to optimize the online therapeutic experience and address the unique needs of their clients. This ongoing development ensures that online therapy remains effective and relevant in meeting individuals' mental health needs.

So, online therapy and telehealth have transformed the mental health care landscape, expanding access to services, and making therapy more convenient and flexible. With its advantages of accessibility, flexibility, and privacy, online therapy offers individuals the opportunity to receive quality mental health care from the comfort of their own homes. By leveraging technology, mental health professionals can provide effective treatment, support, and guidance to individuals across geographical distances, breaking down barriers and fostering healing and personal growth. Whether you are seeking therapy for yourself or considering it as a mental health professional, online therapy represents an innovative and valuable approach to supporting mental well-being in today's digital age.

Chapter 87: Exploring the Role of Peer Specialists in Mental Health Recovery

In this chapter, we will delve into the concept of peer support, discuss the unique contributions of peer specialists, and provide an understanding of how peer specialists play a vital role in supporting individuals on their journey to mental health recovery.

Understanding Peer Support:

•	What is peer support: Peer support is a form of support provided by individuals who have lived experience with mental health challenges. These individuals, known as peer specialists, have personal insights and knowledge gained from their own recovery journeys, which they use to provide understanding, empathy, and encouragement to others facing similar struggles.

•	Core principles of peer support: Peer support is rooted in the principles of mutual respect, shared understanding, and the belief in the potential for recovery. It emphasizes the importance of peer specialists drawing on their own experiences to offer hope, guidance, and practical assistance to individuals navigating their own recovery paths.

The Role of Peer Specialists:

•	Sharing lived experiences: Peer specialists play a crucial role in connecting with individuals by sharing their own lived experiences of mental health challenges. By openly discussing their own journeys, they create a sense of validation and hope, showing that recovery is possible and that individuals are not alone in their struggles.

•	Providing emotional support: Peer specialists offer empathetic and non-judgmental support to individuals, acknowledging their emotions and providing a safe space for them to express their feelings. Through active listening and understanding, peer specialists help individuals process their experiences and cope with the emotional challenges they may face.

•	Offering practical assistance: Peer specialists provide practical guidance and assistance in navigating the mental health system, accessing resources, and developing coping strategies. They can offer insights into various treatment options, share information about community support services, and help individuals develop self-advocacy skills.

• Encouraging self-empowerment: Peer specialists empower individuals to take an active role in their recovery journey. They foster a sense of self-determination and self-empowerment by encouraging individuals to set goals, make informed decisions, and take steps towards positive change in their lives.

• Advocacy and reducing stigma: Peer specialists advocate for the rights and needs of individuals with lived experience of mental health challenges. They work to reduce stigma and discrimination by sharing their stories, challenging stereotypes, and promoting understanding and acceptance in the community.

Training and Certification:

• Peer specialist training: Peer specialists typically undergo specialized training programs that provide them with the necessary skills and knowledge to effectively support others in their recovery. Training programs cover topics such as active listening, communication skills, boundaries, ethics, and self-care.

• Certification and credentialing: In some regions, peer specialists can obtain certification or credentials to demonstrate their expertise and commitment to providing quality peer support. Certification processes vary but often involve a combination of training, supervised experience, and adherence to ethical guidelines.

Benefits of Peer Support:

• Shared understanding and validation: Peer support creates a unique sense of shared understanding and validation that can be particularly impactful in the recovery process. Individuals receiving support from peer specialists often find comfort in knowing that someone who has walked a similar path genuinely understands their experiences and challenges.

• Hope and inspiration: Peer support offers hope and inspiration to individuals who may feel overwhelmed or discouraged by their mental health challenges. Seeing the recovery and success of peer specialists can instill a sense of optimism and belief in one's own ability to overcome obstacles.

• Empowerment and self-confidence: Through peer support, individuals gain a sense of empowerment and increased self-confidence. Peer specialists encourage individuals to recognize their strengths, set realistic goals, and take steps towards achieving them. This empowerment fosters a sense of agency and ownership over one's recovery journey.

• Sense of belonging and community: Peer support provides a sense of belonging and community for individuals who may feel isolated or disconnected due to their mental health challenges. By connecting with others who have faced similar struggles, individuals can build meaningful relationships and create a support network that extends beyond formal therapy settings.

• Enhanced treatment outcomes: Research suggests that peer support can lead to improved treatment outcomes, including increased engagement in treatment, reduced hospitalizations, and enhanced overall well-being. The unique perspective and support offered by peer specialists complement traditional mental health services, leading to more comprehensive and holistic care.

So, peer specialists play a valuable and integral role in mental health recovery. Through their lived experiences, empathy, and support, they offer unique insights, understanding, and hope to individuals navigating their own recovery journeys. Peer support contributes to a sense of community, empowerment, and self-confidence, enhancing treatment outcomes and promoting overall well-being. By acknowledging the significance of peer specialists and integrating their expertise into mental health care systems, we can create a more inclusive, person-centered, and supportive environment for individuals seeking to reclaim their lives and thrive in their mental health recovery.

Chapter 88: The Impact of COVID-19 on Mental Health: Challenges and Resilience

In this chapter, we will delve into the challenges posed by the pandemic, discuss the unique stressors individuals have faced, and provide an understanding of the ways people have demonstrated resilience in the face of adversity.

Understanding the Mental Health Impact of COVID-19:

•	Increased stress and anxiety: The uncertainty and rapid changes brought about by the pandemic have led to heightened levels of stress and anxiety. Concerns about personal health, the health of loved ones, financial insecurity, and social isolation have taken a toll on individuals' mental well-being.

•	Social and emotional impact: Social distancing measures, lockdowns, and restrictions on social gatherings have resulted in feelings of loneliness, isolation, and disconnection. The inability to engage in typical social activities and the loss of face-to-face interactions have affected individuals' emotional well-being.

•	Grief and loss: Many individuals have experienced the loss of loved ones, jobs, and familiar routines due to the pandemic. The grief associated with these losses, compounded by the challenges of physical distancing and limited opportunities for mourning, has had a significant impact on mental health.

•	Impact on vulnerable populations: COVID-19 has disproportionately affected vulnerable populations, including those with pre-existing mental health conditions, frontline workers, and individuals from marginalized communities. These groups may face additional stressors and barriers to accessing necessary mental health support.

Challenges Faced During the Pandemic:

•	Uncertainty and fear: The ever-changing nature of the pandemic has fueled uncertainty and fear. Concerns about contracting the virus, the effectiveness of public health measures, and the long-term consequences of the pandemic have contributed to heightened anxiety and stress.

•	Disruption of routines and stability: The disruption of daily routines and the loss of stability have had a significant impact on mental health. Remote work, remote learning, and the blurring of boundaries between work and personal life have created additional stressors and challenges.

•	Digital overload and information overload: The increased reliance on technology for work, education, and social connections has led to digital overload. The constant exposure to news and information related to the pandemic has contributed to feelings of overwhelm and anxiety.

•	Limited access to support: The closure of mental health facilities, limited in-person therapy sessions, and reduced social support networks have made it challenging for individuals to access the support they need. This has led to increased feelings of isolation and vulnerability.

Resilience and Coping Strategies:

•	Adapting to change: Individuals have demonstrated resilience by adapting to the changes brought about by the pandemic. They have found creative ways to maintain social connections, establish new routines, and adapt to remote work and learning environments.

•	Seeking social support: Despite physical distancing, individuals have sought out social support through virtual platforms, phone calls, and other means of communication. Connecting with others and sharing experiences has provided a sense of belonging and comfort.

•	Prioritizing self-care: Many individuals have recognized the importance of self-care during the pandemic. Engaging in activities such as exercise, mindfulness, hobbies, and self-reflection has helped to alleviate stress and promote mental well-being.

•	Seeking professional help: Recognizing the need for professional support, individuals have sought teletherapy and online counseling services. Mental health professionals have adapted to the challenges of the pandemic by offering remote services to ensure individuals can access the care they require.

•	Finding meaning and purpose: Amidst the difficulties, individuals have searched for meaning and purpose in their experiences.

Engaging in activities that promote personal growth, contributing to community efforts, and developing resilience narratives have fostered a sense of hope and strength.

Building a Resilient Future:

•	Fostering mental health awareness: The pandemic has shed light on the importance of mental health and the need for accessible and inclusive mental health services. By fostering mental health awareness, reducing stigma, and advocating for resources, individuals and communities can work towards a more resilient future.

•	Investing in mental health support: Governments, organizations, and communities can invest in mental health support services and resources to ensure individuals have access to timely and effective care. This includes increased funding for mental health initiatives and programs.

•	Strengthening social support networks: Building and strengthening social support networks can play a crucial role in promoting mental well-being. Individuals, communities, and organizations can work together to create inclusive spaces where individuals feel supported and connected.

•	Cultivating resilience skills: Promoting resilience skills such as problem-solving, emotion regulation, and positive coping strategies can equip individuals to navigate future challenges. This can be achieved through educational initiatives, support groups, and workshops focused on building resilience.

•	Advocating for systemic change: The pandemic has exposed existing systemic inequalities and gaps in mental health care. By advocating for systemic change, individuals and organizations can work towards creating a more equitable and accessible mental health care system that addresses the diverse needs of all individuals.

So, the COVID-19 pandemic has posed significant challenges to mental health, but it has also highlighted the resilience and strength of individuals and communities. By acknowledging the impact of the pandemic on mental well-being, implementing coping strategies, and advocating for systemic change, we can foster resilience and support mental health recovery. Through collective efforts and a commitment to promoting mental well-being, we can build a more resilient future that prioritizes the mental health needs of individuals and communities alike.

Chapter 89: Promoting Mental Health in the Aging Population

In this chapter, we will explore the unique challenges faced by older adults, discuss the importance of mental well-being in later life, and provide an understanding of strategies to promote and support mental health in the aging population.

Understanding the Challenges:

• Social isolation and loneliness: As individuals age, they may face increased social isolation and loneliness due to factors such as retirement, the loss of loved ones, and physical limitations. These feelings of isolation can have a significant impact on mental health and well-being.

• Physical health conditions: Older adults often experience age-related physical health conditions, such as chronic pain, mobility issues, and cognitive decline. These conditions can contribute to mental health challenges and may require additional support and management.

• Life transitions and losses: Aging is accompanied by various life transitions and losses, including retirement, changes in living arrangements, and the loss of independence. These transitions can be emotionally challenging and may lead to feelings of grief, loss, and uncertainty.

The Importance of Mental Well-being in Later Life:

• Quality of life: Mental well-being is crucial for maintaining a high quality of life in later years. It contributes to overall satisfaction, happiness, and fulfillment, allowing individuals to engage in activities they enjoy and maintain meaningful relationships.

• Cognitive functioning: Mental health plays a vital role in cognitive functioning and the preservation of cognitive abilities. By prioritizing mental well-being, older adults can enhance their cognitive resilience and reduce the risk of cognitive decline.

• Physical health outcomes: There is a strong connection between mental and physical health. Promoting mental well-being can have a positive impact on physical health outcomes, such as reducing the risk of chronic conditions and enhancing overall longevity.

Strategies to Promote Mental Health:

• Social engagement: Encouraging older adults to maintain social connections and engage in social activities can combat feelings of isolation and loneliness. This can involve participating in community programs, joining social groups, or staying connected with family and friends.

• Physical activity: Regular physical activity has numerous benefits for mental health. Encouraging older adults to engage in exercise routines tailored to their abilities can enhance mood, reduce stress, and improve overall well-being.

• Cognitive stimulation: Engaging in activities that provide cognitive stimulation, such as puzzles, reading, and learning new skills, can help maintain mental sharpness and contribute to a sense of purpose and fulfillment.

• Emotional support: Providing emotional support to older adults is crucial for their mental well-being. This may involve actively listening to their concerns, validating their feelings, and offering empathy and understanding.

• Accessible mental health services: Ensuring that mental health services are accessible and tailored to the needs of older adults is essential. This can include specialized geriatric mental health programs, counseling services, and support groups that address the unique challenges faced by this population.

• Healthy lifestyle habits: Encouraging healthy lifestyle habits, such as a balanced diet, sufficient sleep, and stress management techniques, can have a positive impact on mental well-being in later life.

Creating Age-Friendly Environments:

• Age-friendly communities: Creating age-friendly communities involves designing physical environments that support older adults' needs and fostering a sense of inclusion and belonging. This can include accessible infrastructure, community centers, and social activities specifically tailored for older adults.

• Intergenerational connections: Encouraging intergenerational connections can foster mutual understanding, support, and learning. Bringing older adults together with younger generations can create opportunities for social interaction and the exchange of knowledge and experiences.

•	Caregiver support: Recognizing the crucial role of caregivers in supporting older adults' mental health is essential. Providing resources, respite care, and support services for caregivers can help alleviate their burden and enhance the well-being of both caregivers and older adults.

•	Age-positive attitudes: Challenging ageism and promoting age-positive attitudes is essential for fostering mental health in the aging population. This involves recognizing the value and contributions of older adults and combating stereotypes and prejudices associated with aging.

So, promoting mental health in the aging population is crucial for enhancing overall well-being and quality of life. By understanding the unique challenges faced by older adults, prioritizing mental well-being, and implementing strategies to promote and support mental health, we can create environments that enable older adults to thrive and age with dignity. Through community support, accessible mental health services, and age-friendly initiatives, we can ensure that older adults receive the care, understanding, and opportunities they deserve to maintain optimal mental well-being in their later years.

Chapter 90: The Link Between Traumatic Experiences and Dissociative Identity Disorder

In this chapter, we will delve into the nature of DID, discuss the impact of traumatic experiences on its development, and provide an understanding of the complexities surrounding this disorder.

Understanding Dissociative Identity Disorder (DID): Dissociative Identity Disorder, previously known as Multiple Personality Disorder, is a complex and rare dissociative disorder characterized by the presence of two or more distinct identities or personality states within an individual. These identities, also referred to as alters, may have unique behaviors, memories, and perceptions, and may even manifest distinct physical characteristics. Individuals with DID often experience significant gaps in memory and a sense of detachment from their identity or personal history. The disorder is typically rooted in severe and repeated childhood trauma, particularly in the form of abuse, neglect, or other traumatic experiences that occurred during critical developmental stages.

The Impact of Traumatic Experiences: Traumatic experiences play a significant role in the development of Dissociative Identity Disorder. Here are some key factors to consider:

• Severe and chronic trauma: Traumatic experiences that occur during childhood, such as physical, sexual, or emotional abuse, can overwhelm a child's capacity to cope. The repeated exposure to traumatic events disrupts the normal development of a cohesive sense of self, leading to the fragmentation of identity seen in DID.

• Disruption of attachment and safety: Trauma often disrupts secure attachment relationships and a sense of safety. The absence of reliable caregivers and a lack of a safe environment can contribute to the development of dissociation as a coping mechanism.

• Age and developmental stage: The age at which trauma occurs and the developmental stage of the individual play a role in shaping the manifestation of DID. Trauma experienced during early childhood, when identity development is still evolving, can have a profound impact on identity fragmentation.

Dissociation as a Coping Mechanism: Dissociation is a natural defense mechanism that the mind employs in response to overwhelming or traumatic experiences. It involves a detachment from one's thoughts, feelings, memories, or sense of identity. For individuals with DID, dissociation becomes a pervasive and adaptive coping mechanism that allows them to separate themselves from the distressing and traumatic events they have experienced. Dissociation can take various forms, ranging from mild detachment to full-blown dissociative episodes where individuals may lose awareness of their actions and experiences. These dissociative episodes contribute to the formation of distinct alters or personality states within the individual.

Treatment and Recovery: Treatment for DID typically involves a comprehensive and individualized approach. Here are some important aspects to consider:

• Psychotherapy: Therapy is a cornerstone of treatment for DID. Therapists with expertise in trauma and dissociation work collaboratively with individuals to help them understand and integrate their experiences. Approaches such as Trauma-Focused Therapy, Cognitive Behavioral Therapy, and Eye Movement Desensitization and Reprocessing (EMDR) may be utilized to address traumatic memories and promote healing.

• Safety and stabilization: Establishing a sense of safety and stabilization is crucial before delving into traumatic memories. Therapists work with individuals to develop coping strategies, self-soothing techniques, and grounding exercises to manage distress and build a solid foundation for further therapy.

• Integration and co-consciousness: The ultimate goal of therapy is to achieve integration, where the different identities or personality states within an individual merge into a cohesive sense of self. Along this journey, individuals learn to develop co-consciousness, enabling them to have better communication and cooperation between alters.

• Support and self-care: A strong support system and self-care practices are vital for individuals with DID. Engaging in activities that promote relaxation, self-expression, and self-compassion can help individuals manage symptoms and maintain their overall well-being.

Building Awareness and Reducing Stigma: Increasing awareness and reducing stigma surrounding Dissociative Identity Disorder is essential. Education and open conversations about the disorder can help dispel misconceptions and foster empathy and understanding. By creating a supportive and inclusive environment, individuals with DID can feel empowered to seek help, access appropriate treatment, and find acceptance in society.

So, the development of Dissociative Identity Disorder is intricately linked to traumatic experiences, particularly those endured during childhood. Understanding the impact of trauma and the adaptive nature of dissociation can shed light on the complexities of this disorder. Through comprehensive treatment, support, and compassion, individuals with DID can embark on a healing journey towards integration and a more cohesive sense of self. By promoting awareness and reducing stigma, we can create a society that supports and embraces those living with Dissociative Identity Disorder on their path to recovery.

Chapter 91: Exploring Spirituality-Based Interventions for Mental Health

In this chapter, we will delve into the connection between spirituality and mental well-being, discuss various approaches to incorporating spirituality in mental health care, and provide an understanding of the potential benefits and considerations of these interventions.

Understanding the Connection between Spirituality and Mental Well-being: Spirituality is a deeply personal and subjective aspect of human experience that involves a sense of meaning, purpose, and connection to something greater than oneself. While spirituality is often associated with religious beliefs and practices, it can also encompass broader beliefs about life, values, and the search for meaning. Research has shown a positive correlation between spirituality and mental well-being. Engaging in spiritual practices and beliefs can provide individuals with a sense of hope, comfort, and resilience, which can contribute to improved mental health outcomes.

Incorporating Spirituality in Mental Health Care: It is important to note that spirituality-based interventions should be approached with respect for individual beliefs and preferences. Here are some approaches commonly used in mental health care:

• Mindfulness and meditation: Mindfulness, rooted in various spiritual traditions, involves cultivating present-moment awareness and acceptance. Mindfulness-based interventions, such as Mindfulness-Based Stress Reduction (MBSR) and Mindfulness-Based Cognitive Therapy (MBCT), have shown promising results in reducing stress, anxiety, and depression.

• Prayer and spiritual practices: For individuals who find solace in prayer or engage in specific religious or spiritual practices, integrating these practices into therapy can provide a sense of comfort, connection, and support.

• Existential therapy: This approach focuses on exploring existential questions related to meaning, purpose, and the nature of existence. It can help individuals examine their values, beliefs, and life goals, ultimately contributing to a sense of purpose and well-being.

•	Transpersonal psychology: Transpersonal psychology recognizes the spiritual dimension of human experience and explores the integration of spirituality and psychology. It emphasizes the exploration of higher states of consciousness, mystical experiences, and the interconnectedness of all beings.

Potential Benefits of Spirituality-Based Interventions:

•	Enhanced resilience: Spirituality-based interventions can foster a sense of resilience by providing individuals with a framework for coping with life's challenges and finding meaning in difficult experiences.

•	Increased self-awareness: Engaging in spiritual practices can facilitate self-reflection and introspection, leading to a deeper understanding of oneself, one's values, and one's purpose in life.

•	Source of comfort and support: For many individuals, spirituality offers a source of comfort, solace, and support during times of distress. Spiritual beliefs and practices can provide a sense of hope, connection, and guidance.

•	Alleviation of stress and anxiety: Mindfulness-based spiritual practices, such as meditation and breathing exercises, have been shown to reduce stress, anxiety, and symptoms of depression, promoting overall mental well-being.

•	Cultivation of compassion and gratitude: Spiritual practices often emphasize qualities such as compassion, forgiveness, and gratitude. Engaging in these practices can promote positive emotions, improve relationships, and enhance overall psychological well-being.

Considerations and Ethical Guidelines: It is essential to approach spirituality-based interventions with sensitivity, respect, and ethical considerations. Some important points to consider include:

•	Cultural and religious diversity: Recognize and respect the diversity of spiritual and religious beliefs among individuals. Avoid imposing specific beliefs or practices and tailor interventions to each person's unique needs and preferences.

•	Collaboration and consent: Engage in open and collaborative discussions with clients regarding their spiritual beliefs, values, and the potential integration of spirituality in their treatment plan. Obtain informed consent and ensure ongoing communication throughout the therapeutic process.

•	Integration with evidence-based approaches: Spirituality-based interventions can be integrated with evidence-based therapeutic approaches to create a comprehensive treatment plan that addresses both psychological and spiritual dimensions of well-being.

•	Professional competence and self-awareness: Mental health professionals should maintain self-awareness of their own beliefs and biases and continuously educate themselves about different spiritual traditions. Seek consultation or supervision when working with clients whose spiritual needs may differ from your own.

The Role of Spirituality in Self-care: In addition to its application in therapy, spirituality can play a significant role in self-care and personal well-being. Engaging in spiritual practices, such as meditation, prayer, or journaling, can foster self-reflection, promote relaxation, and enhance overall mental and emotional balance.

So, spirituality-based interventions can be valuable in promoting mental well-being by addressing the spiritual aspects of human experience. By incorporating mindfulness, prayer, existential exploration, or transpersonal approaches, mental health professionals can create a therapeutic space that respects and integrates spirituality into the healing process. However, it is crucial to approach spirituality-based interventions with sensitivity, cultural competence, and ethical considerations to ensure that clients' beliefs and values are respected. By recognizing the potential benefits of spirituality and incorporating these approaches ethically, mental health professionals can provide a comprehensive and holistic approach to promoting mental health and well-being.

Chapter 92: The Role of Trauma-Informed Care in Mental Health Organizations

In this chapter, we will delve into the concept of trauma-informed care, discuss its importance in providing effective and compassionate mental health services, and provide an understanding of its implementation and impact.

Understanding Trauma-Informed Care: Trauma-informed care is an approach that recognizes and responds to the pervasive impact of trauma on individuals' lives. It is a framework that shifts the focus from "What is wrong with you?" to "What happened to you?" It acknowledges that many individuals seeking mental health services have experienced trauma and that trauma can profoundly shape their thoughts, feelings, behaviors, and overall well-being. The core principles of trauma-informed care include safety, trustworthiness, choice, collaboration, and empowerment. This approach emphasizes creating an environment that is sensitive to trauma triggers, prioritizes physical and emotional safety, and fosters a sense of control and autonomy for individuals in their healing journey.

Implementing Trauma-Informed Care: Implementing trauma-informed care requires a systemic approach that encompasses the entire organization. Here are some key elements to consider:

•	Education and training: Mental health professionals and staff members should receive comprehensive education and training on trauma, its impact, and trauma-informed practices. This includes understanding the prevalence of trauma, recognizing trauma symptoms, and developing skills to respond empathetically and compassionately.

•	Creating a safe environment: A trauma-informed organization prioritizes physical and emotional safety for both clients and staff. This may involve implementing trauma-sensitive policies, such as ensuring private and comfortable spaces, minimizing triggers, and practicing active listening and non-judgmental communication.

•	Building trust and collaboration: Establishing trusting relationships with clients is crucial. Mental health professionals should create a collaborative and empowering environment where individuals' voices are heard, choices are respected, and shared decision-making is encouraged. Building trust takes time and requires consistent support and validation.

• Screening and assessment: Implementing trauma-informed screening and assessment tools can help identify individuals who have experienced trauma and tailor treatment plans accordingly. This involves using trauma-informed assessment measures and conducting comprehensive trauma histories to inform appropriate interventions.

• Trauma-specific interventions: Offering evidence-based trauma-specific interventions, such as Eye Movement Desensitization and Reprocessing (EMDR), Cognitive Processing Therapy (CPT), or Trauma-Focused Cognitive Behavioral Therapy (TF-CBT), can significantly support individuals in their healing process. These interventions address trauma-related symptoms and help individuals develop healthy coping strategies.

• Self-care for staff: Providing ongoing support and self-care opportunities for mental health professionals is essential in maintaining their well-being and preventing burnout. Organizations can offer regular supervision, peer support, and training on self-care practices to ensure staff members have the resources to effectively support their clients.

The Impact of Trauma-Informed Care: Implementing trauma-informed care has numerous positive impacts on individuals, mental health organizations, and the wider community:

• Improved client outcomes: Trauma-informed care enhances treatment effectiveness by addressing the root causes of individuals' distress and providing a safe and supportive environment. It can lead to decreased symptoms, improved emotional regulation, and increased engagement in treatment.

• Increased client satisfaction and engagement: When individuals feel understood, respected, and empowered, they are more likely to engage actively in their treatment process. Trauma-informed care fosters a collaborative therapeutic relationship, which promotes trust, openness, and willingness to participate.

• Reduced re-traumatization: Trauma-informed care minimizes the risk of re-traumatization by avoiding practices that may trigger trauma responses. This includes respecting boundaries, offering choices, and using trauma-sensitive language and interventions.

•   Enhanced staff well-being: A trauma-informed organization supports the well-being of its staff by acknowledging the emotional demands of their work, providing ongoing training and support, and fostering a culture of self-care. This, in turn, reduces burnout rates and increases staff satisfaction and retention.

•   Positive community impact: By implementing trauma-informed care, mental health organizations contribute to creating a community that recognizes the prevalence and impact of trauma. This can lead to broader awareness, reduced stigma, and increased access to trauma-informed services across various sectors.

Overcoming Challenges and Moving Forward: Implementing trauma-informed care may present challenges such as limited resources, resistance to change, and the need for organizational buy-in. However, by adopting a phased and collaborative approach, organizations can overcome these challenges. Engaging in ongoing evaluation and feedback from clients and staff, seeking consultation from trauma experts, and creating a culture of continuous learning and improvement are essential in sustaining trauma-informed practices. Moreover, collaborations between mental health organizations, community agencies, and policymakers can facilitate the integration of trauma-informed care into a broader systemic framework. This can lead to policy changes, increased funding, and the development of trauma-informed practices across various service sectors.

So, trauma-informed care is a vital approach in mental health organizations that acknowledges the impact of trauma and promotes healing, safety, and empowerment for individuals seeking support. By implementing trauma-informed principles and practices, organizations can create a compassionate and effective environment that supports the recovery and well-being of clients. Through education, training, collaboration, and ongoing evaluation, mental health organizations can make a significant difference in the lives of those who have experienced trauma, while also fostering a more trauma-informed community.

Chapter 93: Supporting Mental Health in First Responders: Addressing PTSD and Burnout

In this chapter, we will delve into the unique challenges faced by first responders, discuss the prevalence of post-traumatic stress disorder (PTSD) and burnout within this population, and provide an understanding of the strategies and resources available to support their mental well-being.

The Challenges Faced by First Responders: First responders, including paramedics, firefighters, police officers, and emergency medical technicians, play a vital role in ensuring public safety. However, their work often exposes them to highly stressful and traumatic events on a regular basis. The nature of their duties, such as witnessing accidents, disasters, violence, and loss of life, can have a significant impact on their mental health and well-being. First responders are often required to remain composed and make split-second decisions in high-pressure situations, which can result in emotional and psychological strain. The cumulative exposure to trauma, long working hours, shift work, and the challenging nature of the job can contribute to increased risk for mental health issues, including PTSD and burnout.

Post-Traumatic Stress Disorder (PTSD) in First Responders: PTSD is a mental health condition that can develop after a person has experienced or witnessed a traumatic event. It is particularly prevalent among first responders due to the nature of their work. Symptoms of PTSD may include intrusive memories, flashbacks, nightmares, hyperarousal, avoidance of reminders, and negative changes in mood and cognition. It is essential to recognize the signs and symptoms of PTSD in first responders and ensure that they have access to appropriate support and treatment. Early intervention and comprehensive mental health care can help manage symptoms, reduce distress, and promote recovery.

Burnout and Compassion Fatigue: Burnout is another significant concern in the first responder community. It is a state of emotional, mental, and physical exhaustion caused by prolonged exposure to stressors. The demanding nature of their work, combined with a constant need to be alert and respond quickly, can lead to feelings of depletion, cynicism, and detachment. Additionally, first responders may experience compassion fatigue, which is a specific type of burnout that arises from providing care and support to others who are suffering. Witnessing and empathizing with the pain and trauma of others can take a toll on their own mental well-being.

Strategies for Supporting Mental Health in First Responders: Recognizing the importance of mental health support for first responders, several strategies can be implemented to address PTSD and burnout:

• Comprehensive mental health programs: Organizations should prioritize the implementation of comprehensive mental health programs that include education, training, and ongoing support for first responders. These programs can focus on building resilience, stress management, trauma-informed care, and self-care techniques.

• Cultivating a supportive culture: Fostering a supportive and understanding work culture is crucial in creating an environment where first responders feel safe to discuss their mental health concerns without fear of stigma or judgment. Open communication, peer support networks, and access to confidential mental health resources can contribute to a culture of support.

• Mental health training and awareness: Providing specialized training on mental health, trauma, and stress management equips first responders with the knowledge and skills to recognize and address their own mental health needs and those of their colleagues. This training can also help reduce the stigma associated with seeking mental health support.

• Access to mental health resources: Ensuring easy access to mental health resources is vital. This includes providing confidential counseling services, mental health screenings, and resources for self-care, such as mindfulness practices, exercise programs, and support groups. Organizations should actively promote the availability of these resources and encourage their utilization.

• Regular debriefing and peer support: Establishing a system of regular debriefing sessions after critical incidents can provide an opportunity for first responders to process their emotions and experiences. Peer support programs, where individuals can share their challenges and receive support from colleagues who understand their unique experiences, can also play a crucial role in promoting mental well-being.

• Work-life balance and self-care: Encouraging work-life balance and self-care practices is essential for preventing burnout and maintaining mental well-being. Organizations can implement policies that promote regular breaks, adequate rest, and time off. Additionally, providing resources and education on self-care practices, such as stress reduction techniques, healthy coping strategies, and access to mental health professionals, can support first responders in maintaining their mental well-being.

The Importance of Seeking Professional Help: It is crucial to emphasize that seeking professional help is a sign of strength, not weakness, for first responders experiencing mental health challenges. Mental health professionals who specialize in trauma and understand the unique needs of first responders can provide the necessary support and evidence-based treatments for PTSD and burnout. Early intervention and timely access to mental health care can significantly improve outcomes and enhance overall well-being.

So, supporting the mental health of first responders is of utmost importance to ensure their well-being and the effectiveness of their vital work. Addressing PTSD and burnout requires a comprehensive approach that includes education, training, supportive organizational cultures, access to mental health resources, and a focus on self-care. By implementing these strategies, we can create a supportive environment that acknowledges the challenges faced by first responders and provides the necessary support to promote their mental well-being. Remember, taking care of those who take care of us is essential for the overall health and resilience of our communities.

Chapter 94: Exploring the Connection Between Adverse Childhood Experiences and Mental Health

In this chapter, we will delve into the definition of ACEs, discuss their prevalence, and impact on mental health, and provide an understanding of the long-lasting effects of ACEs and strategies to promote resilience and healing.

Understanding Adverse Childhood Experiences (ACEs): Adverse childhood experiences refer to stressful or traumatic events that occur during childhood. These experiences can range from physical, emotional, or sexual abuse to household dysfunction such as parental substance abuse, domestic violence, or the presence of mental illness. ACEs are often chronic and can have a profound impact on a child's development and well-being. ACEs can disrupt the healthy development of a child's brain, emotional regulation, and social skills. They can also shape their beliefs about themselves and the world around them. The effects of ACEs are not limited to childhood but can extend into adulthood, impacting mental health, physical health, and overall quality of life.

The Prevalence and Impact of ACEs on Mental Health: ACEs are unfortunately more common than we may realize. Numerous studies have shown a high prevalence of ACEs across different populations. The cumulative effect of multiple ACEs increases the risk of mental health problems such as depression, anxiety, post-traumatic stress disorder (PTSD), substance abuse, self-harm, and even suicidal ideation.

ACEs can disrupt the development of healthy coping mechanisms, leading to difficulties in regulating emotions and managing stress. They can also affect the formation of secure attachments, which are crucial for building healthy relationships later in life. The toxic stress caused by ACEs can alter the structure and function of the brain, increasing vulnerability to mental health disorders.

Promoting Resilience and Healing: Despite the challenges posed by ACEs, it is important to remember that resilience is possible. There are strategies and interventions that can help individuals overcome the negative effects of ACEs and promote healing:

• Building supportive relationships: Nurturing supportive relationships, whether with family, friends, or professionals, can provide a safe space for individuals to express their emotions, seek support, and develop healthy coping strategies. Positive relationships can help buffer the negative impact of ACEs and foster resilience.

• Seeking professional help: Engaging with mental health professionals who specialize in trauma can provide valuable guidance and support. Therapies such as Trauma-Focused Cognitive Behavioral Therapy (TF-CBT), Eye Movement Desensitization and Reprocessing (EMDR), or Dialectical Behavior Therapy (DBT) can help individuals process their traumatic experiences, develop coping skills, and improve overall well-being.

• Strengthening protective factors: Identifying and strengthening protective factors can enhance resilience. These may include fostering a sense of belonging, cultivating self-esteem and self-worth, developing problem-solving and emotion regulation skills, and engaging in activities that promote self-care and stress reduction.

• Building community support: Creating community-wide awareness about ACEs and their impact is essential. Establishing trauma-informed communities that prioritize prevention, early intervention, and support can help break the cycle of ACEs and promote resilience in individuals and families.

• Education and prevention: Educating individuals, families, and communities about ACEs, their impact, and the importance of early intervention is crucial for prevention. Providing resources and support to parents, caregivers, and educators can help create nurturing environments that protect children from ACEs and foster healthy development.

The Importance of Trauma-Informed Care: Trauma-informed care is an approach that recognizes the impact of trauma and promotes sensitivity and compassion in service delivery. Mental health professionals, educators, healthcare providers, and community

organizations can benefit from adopting trauma-informed practices. This involves creating safe and supportive environments, implementing trauma-sensitive policies and procedures, and incorporating trauma-informed screening and assessment tools. Trauma-informed care emphasizes empowerment, collaboration, and choice. It recognizes the resilience and strengths of individuals who have experienced ACEs and aims to provide them with the support they need to heal and thrive.
So, adverse childhood experiences can have a significant impact on mental health throughout the lifespan. However, by understanding the connection between ACEs and mental health, promoting resilience, and implementing trauma-informed practices, we can work towards mitigating the effects of ACEs and supporting individuals in their healing journey. Together, we can create a more compassionate and nurturing society that prioritizes the well-being and mental health of all individuals, regardless of their past experiences.

Chapter 95: Mental Health Challenges in College Students: Academic Pressure and Beyond

In this chapter, we will delve into the unique stressors and pressures experienced by college students, discuss the impact of academic demands on mental well-being, and provide an understanding of the broader factors that contribute to mental health challenges in this population.

The Pressures of College Life: College is a time of transition and self-discovery, but it also comes with its own set of challenges. For many students, it is their first taste of independence and the start of adulthood. Alongside newfound freedom, college brings academic demands, social pressures, financial responsibilities, and the need to navigate new relationships and environments. These multiple stressors can significantly impact a student's mental health. The pressure to excel academically, maintain a social life, and make important life decisions can create a sense of overwhelm and contribute to mental health challenges.

The Impact of Academic Pressure: Academic pressure is one of the primary stressors for college students. The expectation to perform well academically, meet deadlines, and balance coursework can lead to feelings of anxiety, self-doubt, and burnout. The competitive nature of college, especially in high-demand fields, can intensify the pressure students feel to succeed. The fear of failure and the constant need to prove oneself can take a toll on mental well-being and contribute to the development of mental health disorders such as anxiety and depression.

Broader Factors Influencing Mental Health Challenges: While academic pressure plays a significant role in the mental health challenges faced by college students, it is important to recognize that other factors contribute to their well-being:

• Social challenges: College is a time of building new relationships and social networks. However, feelings of loneliness, social anxiety, and the pressure to fit in can affect a student's mental health.

Balancing social life with academic responsibilities can be challenging and may lead to feelings of isolation and exclusion.

•   Financial stress: Many students face financial challenges during their college years. The need to cover tuition fees, living expenses, and other financial obligations can be overwhelming. Financial stress adds an additional layer of pressure and can impact a student's mental well-being.

•   Transition and identity exploration: College is a period of self-discovery and identity formation. Students may grapple with questions about their future, career goals, and personal values. Exploring one's identity and making important life decisions can be stressful and contribute to mental health challenges.

•   Lack of support systems: The transition to college often involves leaving behind familiar support systems such as family and close friends. Limited access to emotional support, coupled with a new environment, can make it more challenging for students to cope with stress and seek help when needed.

Strategies for Promoting Mental Well-being in College Students: It is crucial to prioritize mental health and well-being in college settings. Here are some strategies to support college students' mental health:

•   Mental health education and awareness: Providing information and education about mental health, stress management, and coping strategies can empower students to take care of their well-being. Workshops, seminars, and campus-wide campaigns can help reduce stigma and encourage help-seeking behaviors.

•   Accessible mental health services: Colleges should provide accessible and comprehensive mental health services. Counseling centers, therapy services, and support groups can offer a safe space for students to seek help, receive guidance, and develop coping skills.

•   Campus-wide support systems: Creating a supportive campus environment is crucial. This can include the establishment of peer support groups, mentorship programs, and student organizations that focus on mental health and well-being. Engaging faculty and staff in promoting a culture of support and understanding can also make a significant difference.

• Promoting work-life balance: Encouraging a healthy work-life balance is essential. This involves advocating for reasonable workload expectations, promoting breaks, and emphasizing the importance of self-care activities such as exercise, relaxation techniques, and pursuing hobbies.

• Building resilience skills: Equipping students with resilience skills can help them navigate the challenges of college life. This can include teaching stress management techniques, fostering healthy coping strategies, and promoting self-reflection and self-compassion.

• Peer support networks: Encouraging students to connect with peers and develop support networks is vital. Peer support groups and mentorship programs can provide a sense of belonging and help students navigate the challenges of college life together.

Destigmatizing Mental Health: It is essential to destigmatize mental health issues and create an environment where students feel comfortable seeking help. Encouraging open conversations about mental health, challenging stereotypes, and normalizing help-seeking behavior can reduce the barriers that prevent students from accessing the support they need.

So, the mental health challenges faced by college students are complex and multifaceted. While academic pressure is a significant factor, it is essential to recognize the broader context in which these challenges arise. By implementing strategies to promote mental well-being, colleges can create an environment that supports students' mental health, fosters resilience, and enables them to thrive during their college years and beyond. Remember, mental health matters, and supporting college students' well-being is an investment in their future success and happiness.

Chapter 96: The Intersection of Substance Use Disorders and Mental Health

In this chapter, we will delve into the complex relationship between these two conditions, discuss the impact they have on individuals' lives, and provide an understanding of the challenges and strategies for support and recovery.

Understanding Substance Use Disorders (SUDs) and Mental Health: Substance use disorders involve the recurrent use of substances such as ...., drugs, or prescription medications in a way that leads to significant impairment or distress. Mental health disorders, on the other hand, refer to conditions that affect a person's thoughts, emotions, and behaviors, such as depression, anxiety, or bipolar disorder. It is important to recognize that SUDs and mental health disorders often coexist and can influence each other. Individuals with mental health disorders may turn to substances as a way to cope with their symptoms or self-medicate, leading to the development of a substance use disorder. Conversely, substance abuse can worsen mental health symptoms or even trigger the onset of a mental health disorder in individuals who were previously unaffected.

The Impact of Co-occurring SUDs and Mental Health Disorders: The co-occurrence of SUDs and mental health disorders can complicate diagnosis, treatment, and recovery. These individuals often experience more severe symptoms, higher rates of relapse, and a decreased quality of life compared to those with either condition alone.

Substance abuse can exacerbate mental health symptoms and impair an individual's ability to engage in treatment effectively. Likewise, untreated mental health disorders can undermine recovery efforts and increase the risk of relapse. The intertwined nature of these conditions underscores the importance of addressing them simultaneously for comprehensive and effective treatment.

Integrated Treatment Approaches: Integrated treatment approaches are designed to address both SUDs and mental health disorders concurrently. These approaches recognize the interconnected nature of these conditions and emphasize the need for a holistic and personalized treatment plan. Integrated treatment often involves a combination of therapy modalities, such as cognitive-behavioral therapy (CBT), dialectical behavior therapy (DBT), or motivational interviewing. These approaches help individuals develop coping skills, manage cravings, address underlying emotional issues, and improve overall well-being. Medication-assisted treatment (MAT) can also be a valuable component of integrated care for certain substance use disorders. Medications, when combined with therapy and support, can help individuals reduce cravings, manage withdrawal symptoms, and stabilize their mental health.

Dual Diagnosis and Coordinated Care: Dual diagnosis refers to the co-occurrence of a substance use disorder and a mental health disorder. Individuals with dual diagnosis require specialized care that addresses both conditions simultaneously. Coordinated care, involving collaboration between mental health providers and addiction specialists, is essential for effective treatment. This collaboration ensures that both conditions are recognized, assessed, and treated in a coordinated manner. Additionally, ongoing monitoring and support are crucial to manage the complexities of dual diagnosis.

Recovery and Support: Recovery from co-occurring SUDs and mental health disorders is a lifelong journey that requires ongoing support and self-care. Here are some key strategies for recovery and support:

• Building a strong support network: Surrounding oneself with a supportive network of family, friends, and professionals can provide encouragement, guidance, and accountability throughout the recovery process.

• Engaging in therapy and counseling: Regular therapy sessions, both individual and group, can provide a safe space to address underlying issues, develop coping strategies, and receive support from peers who have experienced similar challenges.

• Implementing self-care practices: Prioritizing self-care activities such as exercise, mindfulness, healthy eating, and sufficient sleep can improve overall well-being and support recovery efforts.

•	Developing healthy coping mechanisms: Learning and practicing healthy coping mechanisms, such as stress management techniques, communication skills, and problem-solving strategies, can replace reliance on substances and enhance emotional well-being.

•	Seeking community support: Engaging with community support groups and organizations, such as 12-step programs, can provide a sense of belonging, shared experiences, and ongoing support during recovery.

Breaking the Stigma: It is essential to break the stigma surrounding SUDs and mental health disorders. By fostering an environment of empathy, understanding, and compassion, we can encourage individuals to seek help without fear of judgment or shame. Education and awareness campaigns can play a significant role in challenging stigmatizing beliefs and promoting a more inclusive and supportive society.

So, the intersection of substance use disorders and mental health represents a complex challenge that requires comprehensive and integrated care. By recognizing the co-occurrence of these conditions, providing integrated treatment approaches, and offering ongoing support, individuals can achieve recovery, improve their overall well-being, and lead fulfilling lives. Remember, there is hope, help, and support available for those navigating the complexities of co-occurring SUDs and mental health disorders.

Chapter 97: Understanding the Impact of Grief and Loss on Mental Health

In this chapter, we will delve into the complexities of grief, discuss the emotional and psychological effects it can have on individuals, and provide an understanding of the grieving process and strategies for supporting mental well-being during times of loss.

The Experience of Grief: Grief is a natural and universal response to loss. It is a complex and multifaceted emotional journey that individuals go through when they experience the death of a loved one, the end of a significant relationship, or other significant life changes. It is important to recognize that grief is a unique and deeply personal experience. It can manifest in various ways, including intense sadness, anger, guilt, confusion, numbness, or a combination of these emotions. Each person's grief journey is shaped by their relationship with the person or thing lost, their personal history, and their cultural and social context.

The Impact on Mental Health: The experience of grief can have a significant impact on an individual's mental health. It can affect various aspects of their well-being, including their emotions, thoughts, behaviors, and physical health. Emotionally, grief can lead to feelings of sadness, loneliness, anxiety, anger, and despair. Individuals may experience a sense of emptiness or a profound longing for what has been lost. These emotions can fluctuate and intensify over time, making it challenging to navigate daily life and maintain mental well-being. Grief can also affect an individual's cognitive functioning. They may have difficulty concentrating, making decisions, or remembering things. They may experience intrusive thoughts or memories related to the loss, which can contribute to feelings of distress and emotional overwhelm.

In terms of behavior, grief can disrupt sleep patterns, appetite, and energy levels. Some individuals may withdraw from social activities or have difficulty engaging in their usual routines. The process of grieving can be exhausting and leave individuals feeling physically and mentally drained.

The Grieving Process: The grieving process is not linear, and it does not have a predetermined timeline. It is a unique and individual journey that unfolds at its own pace. However, there are common stages and patterns that many individuals experience during the grieving process. These include:

•	Denial and disbelief: Initially, individuals may struggle to accept the reality of the loss. They may feel a sense of numbness or disbelief, finding it difficult to comprehend that their loved one or a significant aspect of their life is no longer present.

•	Anger and bargaining: As the reality of the loss sinks in, individuals may experience anger, directed towards themselves, others, or even the person who has passed away. They may also engage in bargaining, seeking to find a way to reverse or change what has happened.

•	Depression and sadness: Feelings of deep sadness and depression are common during grief. Individuals may experience a profound sense of loss and longing. They may withdraw from social activities and struggle with a lack of motivation and interest in previously enjoyed activities.

•	Acceptance and meaning making: Over time, individuals may begin to find a sense of acceptance and start to rebuild their lives. This does not mean forgetting or moving on from the loss but rather finding ways to honor the memory of what has been lost and integrate it into their new reality.

Strategies for Supporting Mental Well-being during Grief: Supporting mental well-being during grief is essential for individuals to navigate the grieving process in a healthy and adaptive way. Here are some strategies that can be helpful:

•	Acknowledge and express emotions: Allowing oneself to feel and express a wide range of emotions is important. Encouraging open and honest communication about feelings can provide a sense of validation and support.

•	Seek support: It is crucial to reach out to trusted friends, family members, or mental health professionals for support. Talking about the loss and sharing memories can provide comfort and a sense of connection during difficult times.

•	Practice self-care: Engaging in self-care activities that promote physical and emotional well-being can be beneficial. This can include activities such as exercise, journaling, mindfulness, spending time in nature, or seeking professional therapy or counseling.

•	Join support groups: Connecting with others who have experienced similar losses can provide a sense of understanding and community. Support groups or grief counseling can offer a safe space for sharing experiences, gaining insight, and finding support from those who can relate.

•	Be patient with yourself: Recognize that grief takes time, and that healing is a gradual process. It is important to be patient and kind to yourself as you navigate the ups and downs of the grieving journey.

•	Create rituals and memorialize the loss: Finding ways to honor the memory of what has been lost can be healing. This can involve creating rituals or engaging in activities that hold personal significance, such as writing letters, creating memory boxes, or participating in memorial events.

Cultivating Resilience and Growth: While grief can be incredibly challenging, it can also be an opportunity for personal growth and resilience. The process of navigating grief can teach individuals valuable lessons about their own strength and resilience, as well as deepen their appreciation for life and the connections they have with others. Finding meaning in the midst of grief is a deeply personal journey. Some individuals may find solace in engaging in activities that honor the memory of their loved one, such as volunteering, starting a foundation, or participating in advocacy work. Others may find comfort in seeking spiritual or philosophical perspectives that provide a broader context for their loss. It is important to remember that the journey of grief is unique to each individual, and there is no right or wrong way to grieve. Everyone copes with loss in their own way and at their own pace. What matters most is allowing oneself the time and space to grieve, seeking support when needed, and embracing the healing process with kindness and compassion.

So, the impact of grief and loss on mental health is profound and complex. Understanding the emotional and psychological effects of grief and adopting strategies to support mental well-being during the grieving process are essential. By acknowledging and expressing emotions, seeking support, practicing self-care, joining support groups, and being patient with oneself, individuals can navigate the journey of grief with resilience and find ways to honor the memory of what has been lost. Remember, healing takes time, and with support and self-compassion, it is possible to find meaning and growth amidst the pain of loss.

Chapter 98: Exploring the Role of Exercise in Improving Mental Health Outcomes

In this chapter, we will dive into the numerous benefits of exercise for mental well-being, discuss the science behind this connection, and provide practical tips for incorporating exercise into your daily routine.

The Mind-Body Connection: It's no secret that physical activity is beneficial for our physical health, but did you know that exercise also plays a crucial role in promoting mental well-being? The mind and body are interconnected, and what affects one has an impact on the other. Engaging in regular exercise can have a profound positive effect on our mental health.

The Benefits of Exercise for Mental Health: Exercise has been shown to have a wide range of benefits for mental health. Here are just a few:

• Improved mood: Exercise has a direct impact on our brain chemistry, increasing the production of endorphins, which are natural mood enhancers. Regular physical activity can help reduce feelings of anxiety, stress, and depression, while boosting feelings of happiness and well-being.

• Stress reduction: Exercise acts as a natural stress reliever. It helps to lower cortisol levels, the hormone associated with stress, and triggers the release of feel-good neurotransmitters like serotonin and dopamine. Engaging in physical activity can provide a healthy outlet for managing and reducing stress.

• Enhanced cognitive function: Exercise has been linked to improved cognitive function, including better memory, concentration, and focus. It promotes neuroplasticity, which is the brain's ability to adapt and form new connections. Regular exercise can enhance brain health and reduce the risk of cognitive decline.

• Increased self-esteem and body image: Engaging in exercise can boost self-esteem and body image. Achieving fitness goals, improving physical strength, and feeling more confident in our bodies can have a positive impact on our overall self-perception and self-worth.

• Better sleep: Regular exercise can help regulate sleep patterns and improve sleep quality. It promotes a more restful sleep, which in turn contributes to better mental health and overall well-being.

The Science behind Exercise and Mental Health: The positive impact of exercise on mental health is supported by scientific research. When we exercise, our brain releases endorphins, which are natural painkillers and mood boosters. Exercise also increases the production of brain-derived neurotrophic factor (BDNF), a protein that plays a crucial role in neuroplasticity and the growth of new neurons. Additionally, exercise has been shown to reduce inflammation in the body, which is linked to various mental health disorders. It can also increase the release of neurotransmitters like serotonin, which regulates mood, and reduce the activity of stress hormones like cortisol.

Incorporating Exercise into Your Routine: Now that we understand the benefits of exercise for mental health, let's discuss how to incorporate it into our daily lives:

• Find activities you enjoy: Choose activities that you find enjoyable and that fit your preferences and lifestyle. Whether it's walking, running, dancing, swimming, or playing a sport, engaging in activities you genuinely enjoy will increase your motivation to stick with them.

• Start small and build gradually: It's important to start at a level that is comfortable for you and gradually increase the intensity and duration of your workouts. This will help you avoid injuries and prevent burnout. Remember, every small step counts.

• Make it a habit: Consistency is key when it comes to reaping the mental health benefits of exercise. Set specific goals and establish a routine that works for you. Schedule exercise sessions in your calendar and make them non-negotiable.

• Mix it up: Variety is not only enjoyable but also beneficial for your overall fitness and mental health. Incorporate different types of exercises and activities to keep things interesting and challenge your body and mind in different ways.

• Get social: Exercise doesn't have to be a solitary activity. Consider joining a group fitness class, participating in team sports, or finding a workout buddy. Exercising with others can provide a sense of community and motivation.

• Practice mindfulness during exercise: Use your exercise time as an opportunity to practice mindfulness. Focus on your body's sensations, your breathing, and the present moment. This can help enhance the mental and emotional benefits of exercise.

Overcoming Barriers to Exercise: It's common to encounter barriers that may hinder our motivation to exercise. Here are some strategies to overcome them:

• Prioritize self-care: Remember that exercise is an essential part of self-care and mental well-being. Make it a priority in your life and allocate time for it.

• Find creative solutions: If time is an issue, break up your exercise routine into shorter sessions throughout the day. Explore different options, such as exercising at home, utilizing workout videos, or incorporating physical activity into your daily routine, such as taking the stairs instead of the elevator.

• Seek support: If motivation is lacking, reach out to friends, family, or a supportive community for accountability and encouragement. Consider working with a personal trainer or joining fitness groups that align with your goals.

• Modify and adapt: Be flexible and adapt your exercise routine to fit your current circumstances. If you're facing physical limitations or health conditions, consult with a healthcare professional to find suitable activities or modifications.

Listening to Your Body: It's important to listen to your body and find a balance between challenging yourself and respecting your limits. Pushing too hard or overexerting yourself can lead to burnout or injuries. Always honor your body's cues and adjust your exercise intensity accordingly.

Celebrating Progress: Celebrate your progress along the way, no matter how small. Remember that exercise is a journey, and each step you take contributes to your overall well-being. Notice and appreciate the positive changes in your mental health, energy levels, and overall outlook on life.

So, exercise is not just about physical fitness; it is a powerful tool for promoting mental well-being. The benefits of exercise for mental health are vast, including improved mood, stress reduction, enhanced cognitive function, increased self-esteem, and better sleep. By incorporating exercise into our daily routines, finding activities we enjoy, and being consistent, we can harness the transformative power of exercise to support our mental health and overall well-being. Remember, it's not about perfection or performance—it's about taking care of ourselves and finding joy in the process.

Chapter 99: Integrating Technology and Innovation in Mental Health Treatment

In this chapter, we will delve into how advancements in technology have revolutionized the field of mental health, providing new tools and approaches for diagnosis, treatment, and support. We will discuss the benefits, challenges, and ethical considerations of integrating technology into mental health care.

The Digital Transformation of Mental Health Care: Over the past decade, technology has transformed almost every aspect of our lives, and mental health care is no exception. With the widespread use of smartphones, wearables, and digital platforms, accessing mental health resources and support has become more convenient and accessible than ever before.

Benefits of Technology in Mental Health Treatment: Technology offers several benefits in the realm of mental health treatment:

• Increased access to care: Technology has expanded access to mental health services, particularly for individuals in remote areas or with limited mobility. Teletherapy and virtual counseling sessions provide a convenient and confidential way to connect with mental health professionals.

• Personalized interventions: Digital tools and apps can offer personalized interventions based on an individual's specific needs and preferences. These interventions can range from self-help resources to guided therapeutic exercises, empowering individuals to take an active role in their mental well-being.

• Improved monitoring and assessment: Technology allows for real-time monitoring and assessment of mental health symptoms. Wearable devices and smartphone apps can track vital signs, sleep patterns, and mood fluctuations, providing valuable data for clinicians to tailor treatment plans accordingly.

• Enhanced self-care and self-management: Digital platforms and apps provide individuals with resources for self-care and self-management. They offer educational materials, relaxation techniques, mindfulness exercises, and reminders for medication adherence, empowering individuals to take control of their mental health.

Innovative Technological Approaches in Mental Health Treatment: Let's explore some of the innovative technological approaches that are transforming mental health treatment:

• Virtual Reality (VR) therapy: VR technology immerses individuals in simulated environments, allowing them to confront and overcome fears, manage anxiety, and practice coping skills in a controlled and supportive environment.

• Artificial Intelligence (AI): AI-powered chatbots and virtual assistants can provide immediate support and resources, offering personalized recommendations based on an individual's needs and symptoms. AI algorithms can also assist in diagnosing mental health conditions and predicting treatment outcomes.

• Digital therapeutics: These are evidence-based digital interventions that aim to prevent, manage, or treat mental health conditions. They often consist of interactive programs, cognitive training exercises, and guided interventions that can be accessed through smartphones or computers.

• Online support communities: Online platforms and forums provide a space for individuals to connect with others who are going through similar challenges. These communities foster peer support, sharing of experiences, and the exchange of coping strategies, reducing feelings of isolation, and providing a sense of belonging.

Ethical Considerations and Challenges: While the integration of technology in mental health care holds great promise, it is essential to consider the ethical implications and address potential challenges:

• Privacy and data security: Safeguarding individuals' personal information and maintaining confidentiality are paramount. Mental health technology must adhere to strict privacy regulations and employ robust data security measures to protect sensitive information.

• Equity and accessibility: Ensuring equitable access to technology-based interventions is crucial. It is important to consider the digital divide, affordability, and individuals' varying levels of technological literacy when developing and implementing these tools.

• Human connection: While technology can enhance mental health care, it should not replace the importance of human connection and the therapeutic relationship. The human element in mental health treatment is essential for empathy, understanding, and providing tailored support.

Collaborative Approach to Technology and Mental Health: The most effective approach to integrating technology in mental health treatment is a collaborative one, where clinicians, researchers, and technology developers work together. By combining clinical expertise with technological advancements, we can create evidence-based interventions and tools that truly address the needs of individuals.

Maximizing the Potential of Technology in Mental Health: To maximize the potential of technology in mental health care, it is important to:

• Continuously evaluate and refine technological interventions: Research and clinical trials should be conducted to assess the effectiveness and safety of digital interventions. Feedback from users should be collected to inform improvements and address any limitations.

• Promote digital literacy: Educating individuals about mental health technology, its benefits, and potential risks is crucial. Promoting digital literacy empowers individuals to make informed decisions and effectively utilize available resources.

• Foster collaboration and interdisciplinary research: Collaboration between mental health professionals, technologists, researchers, and policymakers is key to driving innovation in mental health technology. Sharing knowledge, expertise, and best practices can lead to more effective and user-friendly solutions.

So, technology has revolutionized the field of mental health care, offering new possibilities for diagnosis, treatment, and support. From virtual reality therapy to AI-powered interventions, the integration of technology holds immense potential for improving access, personalization, and effectiveness of mental health services. However, it is important to navigate the ethical considerations, prioritize human connection, and ensure equitable access for all. By embracing technology as a tool in a collaborative and evidence-based approach, we can harness its power to enhance mental health care and support individuals on their journey towards improved well-being.

So,

As we come to the end of this book, we reflect upon the profound insights, strategies, and stories that have unfolded within its pages. We have traversed a vast landscape of mental health, exploring topics ranging from the mind-body connection to the impact of technology, trauma, culture, and relationships. Through this exploration, we have gained a deeper understanding of the complexities of mental health and the various factors that influence our well-being.

Throughout these chapters, we have emphasized the importance of holistic approaches to mental health, recognizing that our emotional well-being is intricately connected to our physical, social, and spiritual dimensions. We have witnessed the power of therapies such as cognitive-behavioral therapy, dialectical behavior therapy, and trauma-focused therapy in guiding individuals towards healing and resilience. We have explored the potential of mindfulness, art, music, and animal-assisted therapies as innovative and effective tools in mental health care. The integration of technology and the digital transformation of mental health care have emerged as game-changers, offering greater access, personalization, and support. We have discussed the benefits and ethical considerations surrounding technology in mental health, highlighting the need to balance innovation with the preservation of human connection and the assurance of privacy and security.

Moreover, this book has stressed the significance of addressing mental health disparities, promoting cultural competence, and creating inclusive spaces for marginalized communities. We have recognized the unique challenges faced by different populations, such as veterans, LGBTQ+ individuals, older adults, and individuals with chronic illnesses. By addressing these challenges and fostering a sense of belonging and support, we pave the way for greater well-being and resilience.

So, we want to remind you that your mental health matters. It is not a sign of weakness to seek help or support; in fact, it is a courageous act of self-care. Remember that you are not alone on this journey. Reach out to trusted friends, family members, or professionals who can provide guidance and support.

In closing, we invite you to embrace the knowledge and strategies shared in this book and apply them in your own life or in your work supporting others. Remember that mental health is a lifelong journey, and it requires continuous effort, self-compassion, and resilience. The road may not always be smooth, but with knowledge, support, and the right tools, you have the power to navigate the challenges and cultivate your own well-being.

May this book serve as a source of inspiration, empowerment, and hope—a reminder that mental health is a universal concern that deserves our attention, compassion, and action. Together, let us continue to break down barriers, reduce stigma, and foster a world that values and prioritizes mental health for all.

Thank you for accompanying us on this transformative journey. May you find strength, healing, and a renewed sense of purpose as you embark on your own path towards mental well-being. Remember, you are resilient, and you have the capacity to thrive.

*__Thanks__ for going through all of the book chapters until the end!
Your review is **__Valuable__** to us as publishers.*

Please consider leaving your <u>honest feedback</u> on this book and help others benefit from it.

Made with the help of: chat.openai.com